Princes of Wales

DAVID LOADES

Princes of Wales

Royal Heirs in Waiting

First published in 2008 by
The National Archives
Kew, Richmond
Surrey TW9 4DU
United Kingdom

www.nationalarchives.gov.uk

The National Archives brings together
the Public Record Office,
Historical Manuscripts Commission,
Office of Public Sector Information
and Her Majesty's Stationery Office.

A catalogue card for this book is available
from the British Library.

ISBN 978 1 905615 27 8

Jacket, typographic design and typesetting
Ken Wilson | point918

Printed in Great Britain by
TJ International Ltd, Padstow, Cornwall

COVER ILLUSTRATION
Portrait of the Prince Regent by Sir Thomas
Lawrence, 1816. Bridgeman Art Library

Contents

Preface and Acknowledgements

This book sets out to examine one of the great continuities of English, and more recently British, history. Just below the level of the monarch there has usually lurked, and occasionally spluttered, the Prince of Wales. The creation of such Princes is, and always has been, entirely at the discretion of the monarch, and the rank is reserved to the monarch's immediate heir. It has never to date been held by a woman, even when the heir has been female. Neither Mary I, nor Elizabeth I, nor Anne, nor Victoria, nor Elizabeth II, each of whom was acknowledged as heir for several years before their respective accessions, has been created Princess of Wales. When such a Prince has existed, he has been the highest ranking nobleman in the land, which was originally a matter of great political significance, but has since the nineteenth century been a question of formal precedence only. Until the sixteenth century an adult Prince was expected to assume a formal responsibility for the government of Wales, and in the eighteenth century to be a leader of political opposition, but for the last 150 years the role has been harder to define. Both Edward VII and Edward VIII were, in their different ways, social leaders as Princes of Wales, while the present Prince has adopted a role of cultural and environmental creativity indicative of the changing nature of the context within which he is operating. As Britain has evolved and changed, so has the Principate, but it is still with us, as challenging and fascinating as ever.

My chief debt of gratitude in the production of this book is to the scholars and other writers who have examined the lives and circumstances of individual Princes, and whose work has been of inestimable value to me in the compiling of this overview. Secondly, I am grateful to my wife, Judith, who, as an historian in her own right, has not only done her best to keep me on track, but also has contributed immensely to the whole of the work. Any errors or infelicities that remain are entirely my own responsibility. Thirdly, I am grateful to the National Archives, and particularly to Catherine Bradley, for originating this project, and for nursing it through to a conclusion with many helpful contributions.

DAVID LOADES

Introduction

In 1301, in a parliament held at Lincoln, Edward I conferred upon his son—Edward of Caernarfon—the Earldom of Chester and the entire royal lands in Wales. A few months later, bearing the title 'Prince of Wales', the young man was sent to spend five weeks receiving the homage of his tenants there. He did not visit his birthplace at Caernarfon because the castle was still incomplete and the building work temporarily suspended.[1] In fact he never went back to the place where he had spent the first few weeks of his life, and his relationship with Wales was governed entirely by his father. Although Edward I's tomb in Westminster Abbey describes him as 'the hammer of the Scots', the King was more remarkable for his total subjugation of Wales—a feat symbolized by the position that he created for his son.

There had been a Prince of Wales before young Edward. Llewellyn ap Gruffudd assumed the title in 1258 after conquering a disparate band of fellow warlords; his title was formally recognized in a treaty signed by the King in 1267.[2] This treaty granted the Prince most of north and mid-Wales, leaving the south in the hands of the Anglo-Norman Marcher Lords.[3] Llewellyn was to perform homage and fealty in return, but the settlement did not last, and the Prince was killed in his second rebellion in 1282. Edward I was left to reorganize Wales as he chose, which he did in the so-called Statute of Wales (or Rhuddlan)—not a 'statute' in the sense of an enactment by parliament, but rather a royal decree. The King, who had succeeded his father Henry III in 1272, established a Principality of the later counties of Anglesey, Caernarfon and Merioneth in the north, Carmarthen and Cardigan in the south.[4] The rest of Wales, that is the future counties of Denbigh, Montgomery, Radnor, Brecknock, Monmouth, Glamorgan and Pembroke, was formally recognized as consisting of Marcher Lordships, the majority of which were held by private lords.[5]

Edward by the Grace of God, King of England, Lord of Ireland and Duke of Aquitaine, to all his faithful of his land of Snowdon, and all other of his lands in Wales, greeting. Divine providence … has now of its grace wholly and entirely converted the land of Wales previously subject to us by feudal right with its inhabitants, unto a domain of our ownership … and has annexed and united it to the Crown of the said Kingdom as a constituent part of it … we … have caused to be rehearsed before us and the leading men of our realm the laws and customs of those parts used hitherto; which being diligently heard and fully understood, we have on the advice of the aforesaid leading men, abolished some of them, allowed some and corrected some, and some others we have decreed to be ordained and added thereto; and these we wish to be in future kept and observed in perpetuity in our lands….[6]

For nearly 20 years there was no Prince of Wales and the lands of the Principality were held directly by the King. When a Prince was created, however, all Welsh barons held their lands under him and the Principality was under his rule—personally, if an adult, or in his name if a child, as several princes were.[7] The system of government established in 1284, essentially a feudal lordship, was to remain largely unchanged until 1536 as individual Princes came and went, often with long gaps in between. Many were preoccupied with their own survival in volatile medieval courts—and they had reason to be.

When Edward of Caernarfon was created Prince he was already 17 years old, and he held the title for only six years before acceding to the throne. After he became King there was no Prince for over 30 years, Edward's son being catapulted onto the throne as Edward III at the age of 15 when his father was deposed in 1327.[8] Edward III's own son, Edward of Woodstock, was created Prince of Wales at the age of 13 in 1343. Known as the Black Prince, he was to hold the title for 33 years, until his own death in 1376—just a year before his father. In pursuit of his various military ambitions in France, Edward squeezed both men and money out of his patrimony, causing lasting damage to the goodwill so necessary for its smooth working.[9] By the time of his death Wales was supposed to be worth £4,600 a year to its Prince, a sum that reflected ruthless exploitation. The only thing that actually changed during these years was that some of the Marcher Lordships began to be held by the Principality rather than by the Crown. Richard of Bordeaux, the Black Prince's son, was Prince of Wales for about a year between the deaths of his father and grandfather. He was only nine years old, and his creation as Prince seems to have been to emphasize his position as heir to the throne. Edward III feared a challenge from one or other of Richard's uncles, but it did not materialize.[10]

Richard married twice but had no issue, and he was in turn deposed in 1399. His supplanter, crowned as Henry IV, felt impelled to make a similar gesture, and his 12-year-old son Henry of Monmouth was created Prince of Wales soon after his father's accession. Shortly after the whole area was convulsed by the Glyn Dŵr revolt, which sought, with French and Scottish help, to recreate the native and independent Principality of Llewellyn ap Gruffudd.[11] Eventually the rising was suppressed, and well before he acceded to the throne in 1413, Henry of Monmouth's princely regime was firmly re-established.[12] Henry V died in 1422, and his son, also called Henry, succeeded to the Crown at the age of nine months. After Henry VI took personal control of affairs in 1437, his power disintegrated: aristocratic feuding dominated both Wales and England, with many of the Marcher Lords leading their men to war in support of one party or the other.[13] Henry VI created his own son, Edward of Westminster, Prince of Wales about a year after his birth in 1453; he was to hold the title for 17 years, but for most of that time it was to prove empty. The Duke of York's son, Edward, who took the title Edward IV, deposed the king in 1460 and the Prince of Wales became a fugitive and exile for 10 years. The unfortunate boy was finally killed at the battle of Tewkesbury, following his father's brief readeption in 1471.

Edward IV's own eldest son — known as Edward of the Sanctuary — was not born until 1470, and the infant was created Prince of Wales immediately after the death of his predecessor. This time, however, an innovation accompanied the new Prince. Edward was given a special council, whose jurisdiction extended only to the Prince's lands in Wales, the Marches and the adjoining shires of England.[14] Any other lands appertaining to the Earldom of Chester or the Duchy of Cornwall (and these were scattered all over England) were managed separately.[15] The fact that the Prince was a child no doubt made this duality easier to implement and, like several other Princes, he never achieved his majority. His father died in April 1483 and he was duly proclaimed King Edward V, but only weeks later he was denounced as illegitimate by his uncle, Richard of Gloucester, who succeeded in seizing the Crown as Richard III. Shortly afterwards Edward and his younger brother, Richard, disappeared in the Tower of London, and the general supposition is that they were murdered. Richard promptly created his own 10-year-old son, Edward of Middleham, Prince of Wales, but seems not to have continued his predecessor's council. In any case the Prince died a year later, and Richard himself was overthrown and killed by Henry of Richmond at Bosworth in August 1485.

The Prince's council was certainly no longer in existence when the next Prince was created in 1489. This was Arthur, the three-year-old son of King Henry VII. The new King bore the Welsh surname of Tudor, was about one-quarter Welsh by blood, and was hailed by the Welsh bards as the *mab darogon*, or son of prophecy. He seems to have chosen the name of his heir with thoughtful reference to the legendary British hero.[16] Arthur was endowed with a full household, but it was to be some time before he was sent to Ludlow. However, the Prince's council was recreated and its main responsibility was the oversight of the Marcher Lordships. The makeup of these had changed over the centuries: the major Lordships of Glamorgan and Pembroke now belonged to the Crown, and were organized on the same lines as the English shires, using the English common law. No fewer than 22 other Lordships comprising the Earldom of March had also come to the Crown with the accession of Edward IV.[17] The council as constituted for Arthur was a royal council, exercising the King's rights as a Marcher Lord.

Arthur was carefully educated as heir to the throne, and after a protracted negotiation was married to Catherine, the daughter of Ferdinand and Isabella of Spain in 1501.[18] It was a remarkable achievement for the new Tudor dynasty to secure an alliance with the most prestigious ruling family in Europe. However, the Prince's health was poor, and in April 1502 he died at Ludlow, leaving Catherine a young widow and both his parents prostrate with grief. As early as 1490 his council had entered into a policy of indenture with the private Marcher Lords, binding them to exercise good justice within their jurisdictions, and after Arthur's death the council recommended that this policy should be extended to all the remaining Lords.[19] In 1504 the whole patrimony of the heir to the throne was conferred on the 13-year-old Henry, previously Duke of York, but the revenues continued to be paid into the King's chamber.

Henry VIII had two sons, one legitimate (at least by English law), and the other illegitimate.[20] Henry Fitzroy was born in 1519 and created Duke of Richmond in 1525. If the King ever thought of legitimating him, or making him his heir, he soon abandoned the idea as impracticable. Why Edward, who was born in 1537, was never created Prince of Wales is something of a mystery, especially with a father so preoccupied with his dynastic succession. There was, apparently, an intention to confer the title upon him when the King was seriously ill in 1546, but it was overtaken by events—Henry died in January 1547.[21] His elder daughter, Mary, is often referred to as 'Princess of Wales', and she was indeed sent to Ludlow with a household and council in 1525, when she was nine. However she was never created Princess, and eight years later was bastardized by the King's second marriage. When she succeeded to the throne on Edward's death without heirs in 1553, she was still technically illegitimate, although that was quickly rectified by statute.[22] The same applied to Henry's younger daughter, Elizabeth, when she in turn succeeded in 1558. Mary married, but bore no children, and Elizabeth never married, so the Tudor dynasty ended in 1603 with no further claimant to the title of Wales.

As far as the Principality is concerned, the sixteenth century was a hiatus—there were no Princes between Henry VIII's accession to the throne in 1509 and James I's son and heir, Henry Stuart, on 4 June 1610. Yet the century saw fundamental changes in the way that Wales was governed, which were to transform the role of future Princes in the region. Arthur's council had continued under Prince Henry, and after Henry became King it went on as before. However, by the time that Cardinal Wolsey as Lord Chancellor began to show an interest in the area in the early 1520s it was moribund, and central control was badly needed in a region now notorious for lawlessness.[23] The Chancellor sought to address this problem when he persuaded Henry to send his young daughter westward with a large and prestigious household—and a new council. His plan did not work.[24] Mary was recalled in 1529, and Wolsey fell from power in the same year.

By 1534 Thomas Cromwell had taken over the reins of chief minister, and he had also identified the problem of Wales. He had recently experimented successfully with statute law in producing a solution to the 'King's Great Matter', so perhaps the device that had solved one apparently intractable problem could be used for another.[25] In 1536, by the statute of 27 Henry VIII, cap.24, the whole structure of liberties and franchises, dating back to the Norman conquest, was dismantled and all jurisdiction was vested directly in the King.[26] At the same time another statute changed the structure of administration in Wales (27 Henry VIII, cap.26). The Principality had been divided into five counties since 1284, but the Prince had appointed its officers. Now these counties were brought within the English system, and all officers were to be appointed by the Crown.[27]

From that time onwards, the Principality had no governmental functions. At the same time the former Marcher lordships were 'reduced to shire ground' with the creation of seven new counties—Denbigh, Montgomery, Radnor, Brecknock and Monmouth. Meanwhile Glamorgan and Pembroke were brought under direct royal control. New Exchequers and Chanceries were erected in Denbigh and Brecknock to receive the accounts of the new counties, and all except Monmouth were placed under the supervision of the Great Sessions. Monmouth was not subjected to the Welsh legal system, but was attached to the nearest judicial circuit in England.[28] The changes were broadly welcomed by the Welsh gentry, particularly the creation of Commissions of the Peace which gave them a better opportunity to run their own affairs, and no attempt was made to inhibit the Welsh language as the language of everyday life. [29]

Only the Council in the Marches survived the reorganization, its existence and function confirmed by a further statute in 1543.[30] This covered not only the new and old shires of Wales, but also the English counties of Shropshire, Hereford, Worcestershire, Gloucestershire and (until 1569) Chester, becoming in effect a privy council with a local remit.[31] It came increasingly under attack as the seventeenth century advanced, and when the Civil War erupted in 1642, the Council in the Marches, together with the Star Chamber, Requests, High Commission (the body that governed the church in the name of the monarch) and the Council in the North were all swept away.[32] It was finally abolished by statute in 1689, following the dramatic aftermath of the Civil War—which saw a former Prince of Wales, Charles I, executed in London.

Such changes had many implications for the Princes themselves. Not least among them was money. Shorn of the profits of justice, the Principality's revenues in 1602 were deemed to be worth no more than

£1,900 a year—less than half what the Black Prince had received over 250 years earlier. A century later good management in the hands of the Crown's agents had raised the income to £6,887, but that was a gross figure and how much had to be allowed for standard deductions is not clear.[33] The royal finances in general were transformed by the Civil List Act of 1698 (9 and 10 William III, cap.23), which guaranteed the King an income of £700,000 a year for life, drawn from taxes and other duties, to defray the normal costs of his household, his family and the civil government. Parliament tacitly accepted responsibility for the armed forces.[34]

Since 1714, and in most respects since 1536, the title Prince of Wales has carried no responsibilities in the Principality and only an honorary connection with Wales. (The present Prince has chosen to establish and maintain contacts within the Principality out of personal inclination as well as a sense of propriety, but he is by no means bound to do so, and none of his immediate predecessors did as much.) When the future George II was created Prince of Wales, after a lapse of almost 80 years, a special enabling Act was necessary before he could be granted the revenues that went with the position. In 1727, when the erstwhile Prince became George II, the lands that still formed the notional Principality were vested in the Crown in perpetuity (what remains of the royal lands in Wales still forms a part of the Crown estate). Any further grants were thus made legally impossible. Frederick (created Prince in 1729) and his son George (in 1751)—neither of whom was on good terms with George II—were expected to subsist on their Civil List allocations. In 1760, on the accession of George III, the Civil List provisions were changed, and all those hereditary revenues that had continued to come to the King by virtue of his office were finally surrendered (except those of the Duchy of Cornwall) in return for an augmentation of the List.[35] Since 1727, therefore, all Princes of Wales have depended upon the Civil List for their income, except when they have also been Dukes of Cornwall. The constraints of the List were tight, and even the reasonably frugal George III needed a supplementary Act of Parliament to clear his debts in 1777.[36] His son, later George IV, who had been created Prince within a few months of his birth in 1762, found it quite inadequate for his flamboyant lifestyle. By the time he was 21, in 1783, 'Prinny' had become so deeply indebted that he also required a special Act to bale him out.

After George IV's accession in 1820, there was another lengthy gap in the succession of Princes, the next being Victoria's eldest son, Albert Edward, born and created Prince in 1841. Albert, known to his family as 'Bertie', succeeded to the throne as Edward VII in 1901; he held the title of Prince of Wales longer than any other incumbent to date, but made little impact upon public affairs during his mother's lifetime. Denied involvement in many affairs of state, he gained the reputation of a bon viveur, beloved of the ladies and relishing the delights of high society. However, he was demonstrably good at public relations, visiting the United States in 1860 and India in 1875–6, and would probably have done more if his mother had permitted it. Diplomacy remained a major strength when he eventually came to the throne, and he is best remembered for his efforts to improve relations with France—the so-called Entente Cordiale. Significantly, the King also maintained a good relationship with his son George, who he created Prince of Wales in November 1901. Already 36 when he received the title, George proved a highly conscientious Prince, albeit a less charismatic one than his father had been. Like others before him, he was precipitated into the role of heir to the throne after the death of his elder brother, Albert Victor, known as Eddy. A former naval officer, George was a happily married man to whom no scandal ever attached. He was immediately given access to Cabinet papers and encouraged to prepare for his administrative role as King. He was crowned George V in 1910 and followed what had by then become the custom by creating his own eldest son, the 17-year-old David, as Prince of Wales the following year.

David, who was Prince for 15 years, was undoubtedly one of the most charismatic figures ever to hold the title. He was particularly popular during the 1920s, not least for his involvement with social issues; he regularly visited deprived areas of Britain and spoke directly to the people living there. He also exuded a welcome glamour and, at a time when movie stars were first making an impression, has been described as the first royal superstar.[37] Nevertheless he lacked the stability of his father, with whom his relations were fraught, and when he came to the throne as Edward VIII in 1936 he swiftly became embroiled in a constitutional battle over his desire to marry Wallis Simpson, an American divorcee. Finding himself in an impossible political situation, he abdicated—after less than a year on the throne—

in favour of his younger brother, who became George VI.[38] Edward was himself childless, and George VI followed ancient tradition by refraining from creating his eldest daughter and heir, Elizabeth, as Princess. However, she was already married with a son when she came to the throne in 1952, and in 1958 the 10-year-old Charles became the latest Prince of Wales.

Some 11 years later, in an investiture at Caernarfon Castle modelled on that used for his great uncle in 1911, he was instituted and installed as Prince. Since then Prince Charles has enjoyed a high profile, and has used his unique position to address a wide range of social and environmental issues. As Prince of Wales he receives intense interest from the media all over the world, equipped with a technology of intrusion never previously available. It is interesting to speculate how well some of his less discreet (and less capable) predecessors would have fared under similar scrutiny.

★   ★   ★

So what links the Princes of Wales down the centuries, beyond the title itself? Each at the time of his creation was heir to the throne—of England before 1707, and of Great Britain since. But their circumstances varied considerably: 10 Princes were created as adults or adolescents and eight as children, while only a handful has held the title for more than 10 years. One or two have held the title for barely a year, one or two others for upwards of half a century. Nor has the position necessarily led to the throne. Of the 18 incumbents featured in this book, 10 lived to be crowned King and seven did not—while Charles still retains the role. As noted above, those who were created before the eighteenth century, and lived to achieve their majorities, received the revenues of the Principality, and of the Earldom of Chester. Since the eighteenth century these revenues have remained vested in the Crown, and a Civil List allowance has been paid instead. An adult Prince now only receives a direct income from the Duchy of Cornwall.

Both the characters and the positions of the Princes of Wales have varied dramatically over the centuries. The Black Prince was a soldier, Henry Stuart a 'Renaissance man', Bertie a charming leader of society and the present Prince an international environmentalist. Recent Princes have been important social and cultural figures, but since the eighteenth century their political significance has been entirely indirect.

The Hanoverian Princes were leaders of opposition to the governments of the day, but that has not happened since the early days of the Prince Regent. Princes of the later nineteenth and twentieth centuries inhabited a different political climate, and their interventions were strictly controlled. Prince Albert Edward, who served as Prince of Wales for 60 years, was familiar to most as a fashionable socialite, while his grandson Prince David sought to combine a flamboyant lifestyle with an individual concern for social issues. The present incumbent, Prince Charles, has created a unique position for himself as, among other things, a charitable entrepreneur, a pioneer of social enterprise and a patron of cultural, environmental and ecumenical causes. Yet whatever their role, those who have made the greatest impact have defined and reflected the age in which they lived. As Anthony Holden observed, 'The outstanding Princes of Wales in British History have been those in tune with the spirit of their time—patrons of the arts, public benefactors, inspirational and much loved figures, regardless of their private lives'.[39]

Such lives, of course, continue to be the source of great interest. An obvious thread of continuity is the importance of the relationship between the incumbent Prince and the monarch, usually his father. Both Edward of Caernarfon and Henry of Monmouth caused the King political anxieties—notoriously so in the latter case—while the Black Prince seems to have been everything that Edward III expected. After Henry, none of the next four Princes achieved his majority, and although Arthur was the apple of Henry VII's eye, we know nothing of his attitude in return. Henry Stuart enjoyed excellent relations with James I, but his brother Charles was inclined to take an independent political line that caused tensions in the last years of the King's reign. All the Princes of the eighteenth century were at daggers drawn with their sires—so much so that the antagonism between the Court and Leicester House became a byword for confrontation and opposition. Between 1716 and 1727, and again in the 1740s, the Prince of Wales was the patron, and in a sense the leader, of the dissident Tories. This had one immense advantage, which the shrewder Whig leaders appreciated; it kept the opposition loyal in the sense of Hanoverian, because the 'reversionary interest' was always more promising than the Jacobite. The fact that disaffected Whigs also looked to the Princes confused the issues, but helped to keep politics 'on the island'. When the Tories eventually returned to power under George III, it was of course the Whigs who started looking to Leicester House. Even so, it was lifestyle and money rather than politics that set the future Prince Regent so frequently at odds with the King.

Bertie was the first Prince of Wales whose father was not the King, and in some respects it was Victoria's long-running disdain that afflicted him most. However, that attitude derived directly from Albert, who regarded his firstborn as a distinct disappointment, and it was exacerbated by the unfortunate circumstances of the Prince Consort's death (his typhoid fever developed after a winter visit to Bertie in Cambridge following revelations of the Prince of Wales's affair with an actress). When he came to the throne as Edward VII he proved to be an admirable constitutional monarch, and his relationship with his own son undoubtedly benefited from his bitter experience. The future George V and Edward VII were best of friends yet, perhaps by some mysterious behavioural law, George's attitude to his own son, David, was the very reverse. Doubtless there were faults on both sides, but the King could never come to terms with the latter's playboy image—epitomizing as it did a new generation that the King failed to comprehend. In a sense the outcome proved that the King was right. Having won golden opinions as Prince of Wales, the brief reign of Edward VIII inevitably failed to meet expectations. The current Prince of Wales enjoys excellent relationships with his sons and parents alike, reaping the benefits of maturity and mutual respect.

What has become increasingly obvious since the Second World War, although always present in one sense or another, is the importance of successive Princes of Wales for what might be broadly described as the 'public relations' of the Crown. In the Middle Ages the birth of a son, and his survival long enough to be created Prince, was itself a sign of divine approval, and an inestimable benefit to any King. This was true of Henry IV, Henry VI, Edward IV and Henry VII. Only in the case of Richard III did it fail to work to some extent in the King's favour, despite the lavish ceremony in York Minster. The Black Prince was a hero in his own right, and his feats of arms as a young man greatly enhanced his father's prestige, while we can perhaps trace the origin of the 'dissipated prince' back to the youthful antics of Henry of Monmouth. Although he was never created Prince, the birth of Edward VI in 1537 was seen as a blessing of the King, and so served much the same purpose as his medieval predecessors. 'God is English,' proclaimed the preachers when the news reached them. Both Henry and Charles Stuart, in their different ways, enhanced James I's image, in the first case as a Renaissance polymath and in the second by destroying his father's unpopular foreign policy.

It is, however, with the Hanoverians and the rise of Leicester House that public perceptions begin to engage more critically with reality. The satirists—playwrights, poets, and cartoonists—made formidable use of the 'reversionary interest', by criticizing not only successive ministries but also the monarchy itself throughout the eighteenth century. By the 1780s it would be hard to say who was the more despised, the dull and ailing King or his riotous and degenerate heir. By 1800 the Prince Regent was a byword for elegance, good taste and depravity, and after the Napoleonic War a focus for radical attacks of all kinds. By the time that he died the monarchy was in ill repute. In contrast, the gently dissipated Bertie was a natural corrective to Victoria's pomp and dignity, providing an unaffected good humour and affability that retained the monarchy's favour and esteem. As King he was popular and, along with his son—the competent and hard-working George— saw the monarchy reach a level of public regard that had not been seen for centuries. With the rise of democratic politics in the early twentieth century, this mattered as never before.

Prince David, however, was a different character altogether. He was the 'people's Prince' in a sense that none of his predecessors had been —not even Bertie—but he presumed too far. As a young man, his girlfriends were tolerated to a degree that had not been true of the Prince Regent, but he found that (like his predecessor) he was expected to play by different rules as King. His failure to understand that drove him to mount constitutional battles he could not win, and in the end it cost him the Crown.

The present Prince of Wales, born only 12 years after Edward VIII's abdication, has had to refashion the role for a very different age. He has boldly championed a wide variety of causes, many of which have now been adopted by the fashionable mainstream, and used his position to generate discussion, action and international attention. The Prince has woven social, environmental and ecumenical concerns into a powerful personal philosophy and this, together with the remarkable achievements of his charitable foundation, has won widespread interest and acclaim.[40] Relations with the media have not always been easy, but as Charles draws closer to becoming the longest serving Prince of Wales, he and his family are held in high regard.

The Prince's collection of titles—Wales, Chester, Cornwall and Rothesay—forms one of the oldest noble presences in existence anywhere in the world, and reflects the position's evolution over seven centuries. The monarch's eldest son has automatically received the title Duke of Cornwall since Prince Arthur in 1489, but a Prince of Wales has to be created and there have been some surprising omissions—such as Prince Edward, later crowned as Edward VI. Traditionally female heirs have not held the title, although the young Mary Tudor was regarded as the unofficial Princess of Wales during her period at Ludlow; it has rather been reserved for the wife of the serving Prince. The Prince of Wales is the recognized designation of the heir to the throne, but several monarchs have acceded without having ever held it, from Edward III, Henry VII and James I to George I and, in more recent times, George VI, abruptly elevated from Duke of York. As a result frequent gaps have occurred in the use of the title—in the 750 years since the Principality was first bestowed in this way, there has been no Prince for more than 400.

Once linked with the Principality's distinctive form of government, the position changed radically after the statutes of Henry VIII's reign. The diverse Princes of more modern times, no longer rulers of a feudal lordship, have brought a very personal stamp to the title. In balancing established precedent with innovation, private interests with public demands, they sought to show kingly potential and to shape the tenor of the age. *Princes of Wales* offers a fascinating portrait of men—and boys—at the heart of history, and shows how they responded to this privileged yet demanding role.

CHAPTER I

The First Princes of Wales

In a sense the first three Princes of Wales, Edward of Caernarfon, Edward the Black Prince and Richard of Bordeaux, are shadowy figures. They left no personal correspondence, and we are dependent for our knowledge of their careers on record sources, particularly financial accounts, and on contemporary chronicles. The latter were often monastic, or at least clerical in origin, and were heavily influenced by their subjects' attitude towards the church. Moreover two of the first three Princes held the title only briefly—very briefly in the case of Richard—and most of what we know about their characters and actions relates to their subsequent reigns. The Black Prince was different. He held the title for over 30 years and never became King. Unfortunately he was a hero, or became one, and the stories of his life are heavily coloured by that perception. Consequently we cannot get much closer to him than we can to the others. In comparison to more recent Princes, particularly those who have had to cope with democracy and an intrusive press, these fourteenth-century predecessors appear two-dimensional. They were great magnates and their peccadilloes were tolerated (even by the church). What they could not afford to do was to flout the moral and political customs of the time.

The future Edward II was born at Caernarfon on 25 April 1284, the youngest of the four sons born to Edward I by his first wife, Eleanor of Castile. The King and Queen were in northwest Wales at the time of their son's birth because Edward was still settling the affairs of the Principality, which he had conquered from Llewellyn ap Gruffudd two years earlier. Eleanor was not confined in the present castle, the building of which had only just commenced, but either in its timber predecessor or in some unrecorded lodging in the town. The baby Edward was the latest of some 14 children conceived by the royal couple, of whom seven, including their two eldest sons, Henry and John, were already dead, which was an unusually high mortality rate for a royal family. Alfonso, their third son, was aged 11 at the time; he died a few months later, leaving young Edward as his father's heir.

The same year also [1284] the King held a parliament at Acton Burrell wherein these statutes were ordained which unto this day bear the name of the place where they were made. In the twelfth year of this King's reign his eldest son, Alphonse, departed this life at Windsor, and on St Mark's day [25th April] his son Edward, that after succeeded him in the kingdom, was born at Caernarfon, where the King had builded a strong castle, and was come thither with his Queen to see the same. Also in this year in the quindene of St Michael, the justices itinerants began to go their general circuits....[1]

In the sixteenth century a story became current that the King had presented his newborn son to the Welsh people in fulfilment of a pledge that he would give them a Prince who 'spoke no word of English', but there is no contemporary evidence for any such event; it was probably a tradition resurrected by the linguistic sensitivities of the 1580s.[2] When Edward was created Prince of Wales 17 years later, some emphasis was placed upon the fact that he had been born in Wales, but that seems to have been as far as the association went. Not very much is known about Edward's childhood. His sisters, Joan, Margaret and Elizabeth married and left home while he was still an infant. His mother died when he was six, and his grandmother when he was seven, so although he may have spent the first few years of his life 'among the women', that phase would have been cut short a little earlier than was normal. His first wet-nurse appears to have been a Welsh woman named Mariota Maunsel, and she was succeeded by Alice, the wife of Reginald of Ley-grance, but apart from the fact that they were later well-rewarded for their services, nothing much is known about either of them.[3] Edward was baptized, and spent about the first four months of his life at Caernarfon. He then returned with his parents to England, and is not known to have had any further contact with Wales until 1301.

Towards the end of 1284 a large and 'comfortable' household was created for him, run at first by Giles of Oudenarde as Keeper. Some accounts survive from this establishment, which show its expenses running at £2,140 a year, rising to £3,200 by 1292–3. It included seven knights, nine sergeants at arms, and an unspecified number of children 'by the King's command', presumably as company for his son.[4] Between the death of Eleanor and the King's second marriage to Margaret of France in 1299, the King's own household would not have been designed for children, and the evidence suggests that young Edward spent only a limited amount of time in his father's company as the King struggled with the military and political problems that confronted him. The boy's movements can be traced from the accounts, and he seems to have spent most of his time (at least during the winter) at the royal manor of King's Langley in Hertfordshire, with much rapid movement during the summer and month-long stays at the King's hunting lodge at Mortlake.[5] The overlap with his father's known itinerary was very limited. The responsibility for paying his substantial bills was transferred from the Royal Wardrobe to the Exchequer in 1295, and an attempt seems to have been made to cut them back—with only limited success. By 1299 the allowance was down to £1,100, but the debts that had been accumulated amounted to nearly £11,000, and how this problem was resolved we do not know. At one time it was alleged that his officers were simply taking provisions without paying for them, but if that was ever true it cannot have been used as a regular expedient.[6]

Edward never acquired much 'book learning'—something not at the time considered suitable to a gentleman, let alone a Prince. He could read and write in English and in French, and speak the latter fluently, but it is still uncertain whether he could read Latin, and he certainly could not write it. In short he had a very conventional chivalric education, with much emphasis upon field sports, riding and dancing. The Magister who was responsible for this aspect of his training was Sir Guy de Ferre the elder, who was probably in his service from 1293, and took over this position in 1295. Only in one respect was young Edward unusual—although he grew into a fine athletic youth, and had a skilled teacher in Sir Guy, the Prince never acquired a taste for the martial arts. He did not joust, and as far as we know, in spite of the training that he must have received, never took part in tournaments.[7] This lack of warlike potential may well have cast a shadow over his relations with his father and helped to fuel later quarrels between them, because the King spent most of his life at war, and never shirked a personal appearance on the battlefield. He would have expected his son to show a similar aptitude in preparation for his responsibilities as King, and his peers would have shared that expectation. Edward instead seems to have developed a more than conventional piety, exemplified as early as 1290 in an ostentatious devotion to St Thomas Becket, and he seems to have been much influenced by the Dominican friars, who were a significant presence both in his household and at court, where they featured ostensibly as confessors, but in reality as councillors. Sir Guy probably found Edward a very frustrating pupil.

The marriage of Princes, no less than Princesses, was part of normal diplomatic practice, and Edward first entered that arena in 1290, when Eric of Norway suggested a match with his daughter Margaret. Alexander III of Scotland then died childless, and Margaret was his heir, which greatly increased the attractiveness of the proposal to Edward I. However Margaret died on her way to Scotland in October 1290, and an opportunity of uniting the realms was lost. The residual advantage from Edward's point of view was that he was left to adjudicate between the conflicting claims of no fewer than 13 rivals, which he did as the acknowledged overlord of the Scots. He chose John Balliol, and then deposed him six years later for becoming too independent, and took the government into his own hands. He also removed the Stone of Scone, which provoked a sea of troubles in that land, and resulted in the emergence of Robert the Bruce.[8]

The next bride proposed for the young Edward was a daughter of Guy, Count of Flanders, the object being to strengthen the alliance against France. They were betrothed in 1297, but Guy turned out to be a broken reed as an ally and nothing came of the idea. Edward I then changed his strategy, and decided to settle with France to devote all his energies to dealing with the recalcitrant Scots. By the Treaty of Montreuil in 1299, the Prince was therefore betrothed to Isabella, daughter of Philip IV. She, however, was only three at the time, and their actual union had to wait for her to reach the canonical age of co-habitation (which was 12) in 1308. By that time Edward was King and 24 years old, but he seems to have shown little interest in other women.

Quite apart from his betrothal, by 1299 young Edward was acquiring a high political profile. He played no part in suppressing the revolt that flared up in North Wales in 1294–5 (because he was not old enough for any official responsibility), but when his father decided upon a last campaign against France in 1296, he left the 12-year-old Prince as his regent in England—a traditional gesture of dynastic continuity. If he had been only a little older this could have been a difficult assignment, but as it was his leadership was purely nominal.[9] The trouble was that the King had left a smouldering resentment behind him, led by the Earls of Hereford and Norfolk. A great council was summoned in the Prince's name in September 1296, and a *confirmatio cartaria*, addressing some of the grievances, was issued on 10 October. This was confirmed by the King (who was in Ghent) on 5 November.[10] If these protests were intended, as they seem to have been, as an objection to Edward I's continual wars, then in spite of the charter they went unheeded. On 21 October, before it had even been confirmed, writs were issued for another large army to go against the Scots, 'with the King's son', and levies were called up from Wales, Chester and 11 English shires. However, this never happened as hostilities were suspended with France in January 1297 and the King countermanded his orders, intending to lead his own army north. He returned to England in March 1297, and Edward of Caernarfon again faded into the background. Edward I campaigned against Scotland later in the summer, and again in 1298, when his armies won a considerable victory at Falkirk, forcing Bruce to take to the hills.

The Prince spent a good deal of time in his father's company during the winter of 1298–9, far more than had been customary in the recent past, and there are several signs that at the age of 15 he was being groomed for adulthood. He made his own offering at Canterbury in February 1299—a small but significant gesture—and when the new campaigning season opened, he was required to accompany the King. As the army advanced into Galloway at the end of June, the young Edward, 'newly bearing arms' as the chronicler significantly observed, was given the honourable but not particularly dangerous position of commander of the rearguard.[11] The campaign was inconclusive, and notable for only one thing—the appearance of a certain Piers (or Peter) Gaveston as a scutifer (squire) in the Prince's entourage. Gaveston was to prove a name of ill omen. The following year he was noted among the *pueri in custodia* in the young Edward's household, and also seems to have been one of the King's squires.[12]

Edward campaigned again with his father in the summer of 1300. He was noted as being present at the siege of Caerlaverock Castle, south of Dumfries, but did not in any way distinguish himself. In October 1300 he represented his father at the funeral of Edmund, Earl of Cornwall, and was then summoned to the parliament held at Lincoln in January

1301 in his own right, a singular mark of favour and a portent of what was to come. On 7 February a charter was issued, granting to him the Principality of Wales and the Earldom of Chester. (Unlike the Principality, the latter was well established, going back at least to 1070, and had been part of the dower of the Prince's mother, Eleanor of Castile.) The grant was straightforward, but detailed. It conferred upon him all the royal lands in North Wales, 'Anglesey, Hope and the Four Cantrefs', together with lands in West Wales and South Wales, including the counties of Carmarthen and Cardigan, the castles and manors of Haverford and Builth, and all the lands recently forfeited by Rhys ap Maredudd (who had been responsible for a rising in 1287). Only the castle and town of Montgomery were temporarily withheld. [13]

The 'four Cantrefs' were in a state of flux at this point. They consisted of Rhos (present day Conwy) and Englefield (Colwyn Bay) on the coast, and Rhovaniog and Duffryn Clwyd inland. Shortly after the grant, Rhos was absorbed into Caernarvonshire, and Englefield combined with Hope to form Flintshire, which was then attached to Chester rather than the Principality. Rhovaniog and Duffryn Clwyd combined to form Merioneth. The lands of Rhys ap Maredudd were absorbed into Carmarthenshire, and the castle and town of Montgomery were added to the grant about three months later.[14] Overton and Maelor Saesneg (Wrexham) were already part of its lands, but were absorbed into Flintshire when that county was created. The title of Prince was not actually used in the charter of creation, but this seems to have been no more than an oversight because it was being used in official documents only a few days later.

> The King, Sir Edward, at that Parliament,
> Gave fully to his son Edward
> The Lordship of Wales without reserve,
> The County of Chester with its appurtenances,
> And Pontivy and Montreuil, with the honours belonging,
> The son is prince and earl and takes the homages;
> He prepares himself earnestly towards the war of Scotland
> With thirty thousand Welshmen, besides other good men
> Earls and barons, knights at will....[15]

On 6 April Edward set off on a tour of inspection of his Welsh lands, visiting (among other places) Hope, Rhuddlan and Conwy. He did not visit his birthplace, probably because the castle was still being repaired after the depredations of Madoc ap Llewellyn in 1294–5. We do not know how Edward was received, but later stories suggest that it was quite well. In view of the bad 'press' that he later received as King, silence about this tour suggests that it was positive rather than the reverse. At the age of 17 Edward was now an important magnate, with his own council, court and entourage. He had become Count of Ponthieu when he inherited that province from his mother in 1290, but the French had taken it in 1294, and when it was returned by the terms of the peace of 1299 it was not restored to Edward. Instead the King took the unusual step of calling in the Italian banking house of Frescobali to administer it. He probably owed them money, and allowed them to collect these revenues as a convenient method of repayment. They retained that function until 1308.[16]

Relations between the Prince and his father fluctuated violently during the last few years of the old King's life. Edward campaigned alongside the King in the summer of 1304, and was present at the capture of Stirling Castle in July, but they fell out bitterly a year later over words that young Edward was alleged to have spoken to Walter Langton, the King's Treasurer. It is probable that Langton reproached him for an extravagant lifestyle that was outrunning his resources, so that the Treasurer was constantly being called upon to bail him out. If that were so, and the accounts are not clear on the point, it would be an interesting precedent for a situation frequently to recur in the histories of subsequent Princes. Edward I sided with his minister, and banished the Prince from court.[17] He was virtually confined to within a few miles of Windsor, and it seems that the revenues of the Principality were sequestered, because he was apparently constrained to live on an allowance of £66 13s 4d a week. Although a 'sufficiency of essentials' was guaranteed, he was forced to reduce his household, and the humiliation must have been acute. Father and son were ostensibly reconciled in October of the same year, but it seems that their former level of trust and mutual respect was not restored—which is hardly surprising.[18] Nevertheless the King was getting old, and the position of his heir was becoming increasingly important.

Continued upheavals in Scotland resulted in Robert the Bruce being recognized as King, in defiance of Edward, and crowned on 25 March 1306. This of course required a fresh campaign, and the Prince of Wales was very much in evidence. With many others he was knighted in a grand ceremony at Westminster Abbey on 22 May, and the King granted him the province of Aquitaine, with Oleron and the Agenais 'for the maintenance of his state'.[19]

> Grant to Edward, the King's son, whom the King caused to be decorated with the belt of knighthood last Whitsuntide, of the Duchy of Aquitaine for the maintenance of his state, to be held to him and after him to the Kings of England reigning by hereditary right, on condition that he may not alienate it, or any part of it, or detach from it, or diminish it in any way.
>
> Like grant to him of the said Duchy, and of the Isle of Oleron.
> Like grant of the land of Agenais....[20]

The subsequent campaign was successful up to a point. Bruce was defeated at Methven by an army jointly commanded by the Prince of Wales and William de Valence, but neither killed nor discredited, and at the end Edward, who was beginning to find long journeys burdensome, retired only as far as the Abbey of Lanercost in Cumberland. The Prince went back to Langley. The King is alleged to have rebuked his son for allowing his soldiers to kill Scottish women and children during the campaign—a charge that cannot be substantiated—and that may have been preying on the younger man's mind through the winter. For whatever reason, he seems increasingly to have sought comfort in the companionship of Piers Gaveston. The relationship between these two young men is often thought to have been homosexual, and it seems that that is what the King thought at the time, but the evidence is far from conclusive. Both subsequently married and begot children, but Edward at least fell out seriously with his wife, and she took a lover. What is clear is that Edward's relationship with Gaveston provoked further conflict with the King at the beginning of 1307. The Prince wished to confer his hereditary rights in Ponthieu upon his friend, and to this the King objected in the strongest possible terms, not least because at the time it was not his to give. In Edward I's eyes the proposal was symbolic of the influence that he believed Gaveston was having over his son, and in April 1307 the King expelled Piers from England.[21] As a result he quarrelled violently with his son, and is alleged to have pulled out handfuls of his hair in a physical assault, until the pair were parted by their servants.

The Prince was in many ways an unconventional young man, and that seems to have both puzzled and angered his extremely conventional father. He liked horseplay, and allegedly kept low company, a charge appearing with significant frequency in the subsequent histories of the Princes. That description could hardly have been applied to Piers Gaveston who—although not sprung of the higher nobility—was every inch a gentleman. It probably applied to the jesters whom the Prince kept, to his gambling companions, and above all to those who taught him the humble skills of swimming, rowing and thatching in which he took great delight. The thought that any son of his could prefer thatching to 'feats of arms' probably drove the old King apoplectic with fury.

There was also the undoubted fact that the Prince overspent his income. Even in 1293 his household was costing over £3,000 a year, and it is not to be supposed that this figure diminished greatly over the next 10 years as he grew to adolescence, while the net revenue from all his lands was no more than £1,648 in 1305.[22] Every so often the King reined him in, but the effects did not last. As soon as relations were more or less restored, his extravagance took off again. It may well have been the thought that he was proposing to reduce his income still further by granting away Ponthieu, and thus increasing his dependence upon the Wardrobe or the Exchequer, which caused the old man to lose his temper so spectacularly in 1307. Needless to say, after this falling out, the Prince did not accompany his father when he set out on his last campaign about a month later, and was not with him when his exertions finally overcame him near Carlisle in July. However, once his funeral rites had been duly observed, the new King did feel obliged to discharge his father's obligation, and picked up the latter's intended campaign into Scotland. He was near Dumfries on 6 August when he recalled Piers Gaveston from his brief exile, and created him Earl of Cornwall. It was to prove a serious mistake.[23]

Edward's reign was to prove a personal disaster, as he repeatedly misjudged the circumstances in which he found himself. At first there was optimism. He abandoned the campaign in Scotland without any serious fighting, and in the short term this was a popular move with his barons who had become tired of his father's incessant warfare. The parliament held at Northampton in the autumn granted him a small tax, known as a fifteenth, without protest—which was traditional at the beginning of a new reign. In January 1308 he crossed to France for his marriage to Isabella, and to perform his homage for the Duchy of Aquitaine. Trouble, however, was not far away, because Piers Gaveston, his youthful companion, had immediately become a grievance. While the King was in France, a group of important magnates drew up a formal document known as the Ordinances. These constituted a vague but pointed statement about 'things done contrary to the King's honour' and 'the oppression of the people'. The signatories expressed their loyalty to the King, but were clearly demanding changes in the administration, and particularly the removal of Gaveston, who they (like Edward I) regarded as a malign influence.[24] There were even threats to delay the King's coronation if action was not taken.

It did not come to that, and Edward was duly crowned on 25 February 1308, but he was required to swear 'to maintain and preserve the laws and rightful customs which the community of your realm shall have chosen'—the community of the realm being the self-selected image of the nobility, or that part of it which was actively engaged. The Gaveston issue, however, did not go away, and it is not clear quite why. His extravagance and taste for display were resented, as was his prowess in tournaments, but there is no contemporary evidence that a homosexual relationship was suspected. It was probably Gaveston's influence over the Crown's patronage that was most deeply resented, and this was to be a recurring theme with the friends of the former Princes of Wales. In a further parliament at Easter 1308 his removal was explicitly demanded. Edward felt that he had no option, so he sent his friend to govern Ireland, which was not quite what his enemies had in mind. Gaveston was also a bargaining counter. In a parliament held at Stamford in July 1309, the King agreed to a whole range of explicit reforms in return for a further grant of taxation and a confirmation of the Earldom of Cornwall to Piers, who was allowed to return from Ireland.[25] It looked as though a tricky corner had been turned.

This, however, turned out to be over-optimistic. Edward was deep in debt, and had conspicuously failed to cope with the challenge of Scotland. Forced into a corner, in March 1310 the King agreed to the appointment of a committee of Ordainers, with full power to reform the state of the realm. A series of ordinances were duly issued, and confirmed by the King, but when the final version was published in October 1311 he discovered that the ground had shifted.[26] The objective was still to dismantle his preferred system of household government, but no attempt was made to impose a restrictive council upon the King. Gaveston, however, had again become a representative figure, and on that issue Edward had no intention of submitting.[27] By January 1312 the country was on the verge of civil war. It seems clear that the King was in no position to fight, and Gaveston surrendered Scarborough on terms of safe conduct. These terms were dishonoured, and he was murdered in Warwickshire on his way south. This flagrant abuse split the Ordainers, several of whom now joined the King. More importantly, on 13 November 1312 when she was still only 16, Queen Isabella gave birth to a son and heir. His arrival immediately restored cordiality with the French court and appeared to answer those questions that had been asked about Edward's relations with his wife over the previous four years.[28]

A showdown was thus avoided for the time being. Neither side, in any case, could afford to fight a civil war. Disaster still stalked Edward, however, whose competence everyone was by now beginning to question. An attempt to impose himself on Scotland came to spectacular grief at Bannockburn in June 1314, not least because several of his most powerful lords boycotted a campaign about which they had not been consulted.

> If he [Edward] had followed the advice of his barons, he would have humbled the Scots with ease. Oh, if he had practiced the use of arms, he would have exceeded the prowess of King Richard [the Bruce]. Physically this would have been inevitable, for he was tall and strong, a handsome man with a fine figure. But why linger over this description of him? If only he had given to arms the attention which he expended on rustic pursuits, he would have raised England on high; his name would have resounded through the land. Oh what hope he raised as Prince of Wales! All hope vanished away when he became King of England. Piers Gaveston led the King astray, threw the country into confusion, consumed its treasures, was exiled three times and then returning lost his head....[29]

In a parliament at York in September, a strict adherence to the Ordinances was demanded and conceded. Several officers were replaced, and Hugh Despencer, the King's new favourite, was expelled from the court.[30] Just about everything went wrong, in spite of honest attempts to adhere to the Ordinances. After the parliament a new commission was set up to reform the royal household, but the King would not co-operate.

Tensions and disputes were now endemic, and civil war again seemed likely, until heroic efforts at mediation were finally successful in the so-called Treaty of Leake in October 1318. This time a council of 17 was imposed upon Edward, but the younger Hugh Despencer became Chamberlain, and that was a portent for the future. The treaty lasted barely a year, thanks largely to Despencer's pushy acquisitiveness, and the King's indulgence.[31] When Edward seized the Lordship of Gower into his own hands with the intention of bestowing it upon Hugh, it was regarded as a gross violation of March custom.[32] Within weeks all the Marcher Lords were up in arms, and baronial retinues threatened the parliament that met at Westminster in July and August 1321. It decreed the exile of the Despencers, both father and son, but this time the King fought, and at Boroughbridge in February 1322 won a notable victory. The Despencers returned in triumph, and in May 1322 the Ordinances were annulled. However, Boroughbridge was Edward's last success, and the regime of the Despencers declined from failure to disaster. Their real mistake was to become embroiled in war with France in 1324–5, and then to send Queen Isabella to her home country to negotiate peace.

Isabella had borne her husband four children, but the last had been in 1321, and their relationship had subsequently gone from bad to worse. In France, Isabella formed a liaison with the exiled Roger Mortimer, and swiftly gathered a powerful group of other exiles determined to destroy the Despencers, who had become every bit as unpopular as Piers Gaveston.[33] Supported by the Count of Hainault they mounted an invasion in 1326, which swiftly rallied the malcontent forces of England—including the City of London. The Despencer regime collapsed without any serious fighting, and both they and the King fled westward into Wales, where Despencer power was supposed to be great. But Wales did not stir in Edward's support, and he and the younger Hugh Despencer were captured at Llantrisant on 16 November and taken to Monmouth.[34] Any attachment that Welshmen may have felt to the man who had once been their Prince had long since evaporated, and the fact that he attempted to take refuge in the Lordship of Glamorgan was no recommendation. Despencer was taken to

Hereford where he was hung, drawn and quartered, and Edward was taken back to Kenilworth where he was imprisoned, and deposed by a parliament called to Westminster in his name in January 1327.

There was little to distinguish the government of Wales during this turbulent reign from the periods before and after. Wales continued to be exempt from parliamentary taxation, and although members were summoned from the Principality in 1322 and 1327, that experiment was not repeated.[35] All the King's lands in Wales were taxed at his own discretion. In fact the King largely took over the taxation system put in place by Llewellyn after 1267, and that was rightly seen as having been oppressive. The situation actually deteriorated while there was no Prince, and by 1326 Wales was being governed in the interests of the English minority, while its taxes went, directly or indirectly, into the Exchequer at Westminster.

Edward II's eldest son, also Edward, never held the title Prince of Wales, although he was created Earl of Chester within weeks of his birth and was granted the counties of Chester and Flint on 24 November 1312. Presumably his father's promotion did not constitute a tradition at this early date. His household was partly supported by revenues drawn both from Wales and from the Earldom of Cornwall, although he never held that title either, and these allocations must have been decreed by the King as a matter of convenience.[36] The future Edward III was betrothed to Philippa of Hainault in 1326, and the couple were duly married on 24 January 1328, when he was 15-and-a-half and she a little younger. Their first child was born at Woodstock on 15 June 1330, when he was a few months short of his 18th birthday.

The year 1330 was to prove a momentous one for Edward. Although he was in theory the King, and had been since the age of 14, his mother effectively acted as regent. She was supported by Mortimer—now her lover and Earl of March—who made the mistake of treating the young man with contempt. Reports suggested that Mortimer was planning to seize the throne for himself, and the unborn child that Isabella was carrying might well prove a threat to Edward's own newborn son. With the aid of a small group of loyal supporters, the King infiltrated the castle at Nottingham, where Isabella and Mortimer were staying, and surprised them in the royal apartments. After a brief fight, Mortimer was overpowered. The next morning the King declared his personal rule, and summoned a parliament to meet at Westminster on

26 November. There Mortimer was swiftly condemned to death, and he was duly executed three days later.[37] Isabella was confined to her dower lands, where she reportedly miscarried, and lived in political eclipse until 1357.

Meanwhile the King's son, Edward of Woodstock, grew and thrived. He was recognized as Earl of Chester from his birth, and the revenues of the earldom were assigned to Queen Philippa for the boy's maintenance in 1331. This was an original idea, and suggests that Edward had a great deal of faith in his wife's abilities. When the child was actually created Earl in 1333, however, this special arrangement seems to have come to an end and to have been replaced with a normal set of household officers. On 9 February 1337, Edward was also created Duke of Cornwall (the earldom having been elevated for his benefit) and, on 12 May 1343, Prince of Wales.[38] He was the first to hold these two titles together, and they have travelled in company ever since. His formal investiture took place in the context of a parliament, when a coronet was place on his head, a ring on his finger, and he was given a silver rod of office. All this was described as having been 'according to custom', but the only previous investiture had been that of his grandfather 42 years earlier—and of that no record survives. A few months later he was granted all the debts and arrears due to his father in Wales.

> Grant for the better maintenance of his estate, to Edward, Prince of Wales, Duke of Cornwall and Earl of Chester, of all debt and arrears of farms rents and accounts, whether of the time of the King's progenitors, or of the King's time, down to the time of the grant to the said Edward of the Principality, due to the King in North Wales and South Wales, and all the accounts due thence in the said times. Also of all victuals and stock, alive and dead, and other things now being in the castles of those parts, which he holds of the King's grant....[39]

By this time the Prince was 13, a young adolescent by our standards, but on the threshold of manhood in fourteenth-century terms. Not very much is known about Edward's formal education, but it seems to have been along the same lines as his grandfather's—strong on chivalry, but less so on literacy. In later life he could read and write in English and in French, but it is uncertain whether he could read Latin, and his familiarity with both history and theology was sketchy. Unlike Edward II at the same age, there are no signs of overt piety, but plenty of his later enthusiasm for the martial arts and some signs that he gambled heavily. As Prince of Wales, Edward was also thoroughly accustomed to being used as political stand-in. When his father was abroad in 1338, in 1340 and again in 1342, he was named as *Custos Anglie*, and paid an additional £1,000 for his expenses.[40] This did not mean that he was actually called upon to make decisions—those would have been made by the officers of state or the council if the King could not be reached—but it does indicate a ceremonial role, in the performance of which he must have become fully familiar with the rituals of royalty.

The young Prince had also been used several times in matrimonial diplomacy: in 1331 he had been betrothed to a daughter of the King of France; in 1339 to Margaret, daughter of the Duke of Brabant; and (nearly) in 1345 to a daughter of the King of Portugal.

Appointment of Masters Andrew de Offord, Richard de Soham, Professors of Civil Law and of the Royal Household, and Philip de Barton, to treat with the King of Portugal and Algarves for a marriage between the King's first born son, Edward, Prince of Wales, Duke of Cornwall and Earl of Chester, or any other of the King's sons, and one of the daughters of the said King....[41]

Almost from his birth he therefore featured in his father's restoration of the royal authority, which had been so damaged by the events of 1327–30.[42] Where Edward II had failed on the battlefield and been indiscreet in his distribution of patronage, Edward III did neither. He defeated the Scots at Halidon Hill in 1333, which did much to establish his reputation as a warrior, and he carefully built up his own party by redistributing the forfeited Mortimer lands.[43] Edward displayed admirable good sense in assembling his government after the crisis that had preceded its establishment, with the result that when he resumed war against France in 1337, his magnates were (more or less) behind him.

This situation did not endure. While the King was in France in 1340, and the young Prince was nominally regent, the officers whom he had left to serve his son signally failed to deliver either the money or the supplies that he needed. According to one historian, an atmosphere of 'extraordinary malice and intrigue' prevailed in the administration—a malice with which the 10-year-old boy was quite unable to cope.[44] Edward returned unannounced on 30 November 1340, and proceeded to purge the government. Unfortunately he found himself opposed by one whom he could not easily remove, John Stratford, the Archbishop of Canterbury, who retreated to Canterbury and launched a blistering attack on Edward for listening to the counsel of indiscreet young men. That Edward should have consulted young men was hardly surprising, seeing that he was only 28 himself, and the real objection was to his policy of war. When the parliament met in 1341 several peers demanded a reissue of the charter of 1311.[45] Recognizing the political opportunism of this move, the King conceded and gained the taxation that he so much needed. Later, when parliament was no longer sitting, he used a Great Council to revoke his reissue of the charter, and when the estates reconvened in 1343 they proved unwilling to pursue the matter. By the summer of 1343 he had recovered the initiative, and celebrated by a reconciliation with Stratford. It was in this context that Edward of Woodstock was created Prince of Wales, a move that was clearly designed to reinforce the King's now dominant position.

It was also a gesture that indicated the Prince's impending manhood. When the King went on campaign in 1343 he took his son with him, not with the intention of exposing him to danger, but to teach him the rudiments of one of a monarch's most distinctive occupations —the making of war.

Power to John [Stratford] Archbishop of Canterbury, William [Edendon] Bishop of Winchester, and Thomas de Berkeleye, William de Shareshall, and Robert de Sadington, knights, and Peter de Guildesborough, clerk, or any three of them, the Archbishop or Bishop to be one, to have the rule and custody of all the lands and lordships of the King's first born son, Edward, Prince of Wales, Duke of Cornwall and Earl of Chester, within the age of puberty, who is to go with the King beyond the seas, until the return of the Prince....[46]

On 12 July 1346 the young Prince was knighted by his father in Normandy, and commanded the vanguard of the army that fought at Crécy —an army in which (incidentally) the only sizeable non-English-speaking contingent was the Welsh archers. It is alleged that at one point during the battle, being hard pressed, he sent to his father for succour and received the rather off-putting response 'let the boy win his spurs'.[47] However, not only would it have been very unlike Edward III to expose his first-born to unnecessary danger, but also all the indications are that it was the Earls of Warwick and Northampton who were actually sustaining that part of the battle. The Prince was certainly present on the field, but whether he ever sent any such message is uncertain. Knighton's chronicle account is full of hyperbole.

> And then, because Phillippe de Valois was moving thence with his army, King Edward went with his men into the forest of Crécy. And about mid-day new reports came to King Edward that King Phillippe was ready and arrayed in three lines of battle. King Edward rejoiced at the news, drew up his men and marched to the bridge at Crécy, and about the hour of vespers or a little before he saw the enemy approaching. The English had by now fasted a long time, having stood to so as to be ready for the French. At once the bugles and trumpets sounded, and there fell a flood of rain with terrible thunder, but that amazing storm soon passed.
>
> In the first line of battle [the vanward] there was Edward, Prince of Wales, King Edward's first born, and the earl of Northampton and the earl of Warwick with their men, who with divine aid fought off the first line of the French, and then at once withstood the second in which there were two kings and a duke, namely the King of Bohemia, the King of Mallorca and the Duke of Lorraine, with many other noblemen. And then a third time the Prince joined battle with the third line, in which was the King of France, with the King of Germany and Sire de Hainault, and them too by the grace of God he overcame and defeated. The King of France, King Phillippe, was struck in the face by an arrow, and his charger was killed, but he mounted another good horse and fled, and none of the English knew what became of him, and many others fled too....[48]

What we do know is that the Prince adopted his badge of the three ostrich feathers, and probably his motto 'Ich Dien', from the blind king John of Bohemia, who, according to John Ardenne, 'he killed at Cresse in France' fighting on the French side.[49] Both the badge and the motto have remained attached to the Principality of Wales ever since. The title 'Black Prince' seems to have derived from the colour of the armour that he wore in this battle.

In other respects, however, Edward showed little interest in his Principality, and seems never to have gone there, in contrast to the Duchy of Cornwall. Eventually he held four great Lordships, because Aquitaine was also added in 1362, and his council had jurisdiction over all four. So great were his revenues (nearly £10,000 a year) that a special Exchequer was created at Westminster in 1344 to administer them.[50] This presumably handled extraordinary income from the Principality, because Exchequers already existed in Wales to receive the normal revenues due from the sheriffs and other lesser officers. The Prince also had a variety of seals for the authentication of documents—a Privy Seal for general business, and local seals for Wales, Chester and Aquitaine.

Nothing changed in Wales's structure of government during Edward of Woodstock's long incumbency (1330–76), but all was not well. 'It is not easy,' observed that great royal servant Sir Gruffudd Llwyd, 'to control the Welsh save through one of their own men'.[51] This was probably special pleading on his part, but it was nevertheless true that many of the Prince's officials in Wales were Englishmen (or even Frenchmen), and their presence was resented. In February 1345 Henry Shulderford, the recently appointed Attorney for North Wales, was murdered near Caernarfon, and shortly after one of the Lordship officials in Monmouth met with a similar fate.[52] Nor was this simply xenophobia, because it was in the 1340s and 1350s that the pressures upon the Welsh lands became most acute. The Prince's right to tax at will led to exorbitant demands being placed on the justice system.[53] So severe did the pressures become that local officials (who were usually Welshmen) took the unprecedented step of bypassing their Lord to petition the King for redress, and so well substantiated were their complaints that Edward III actually intervened against his son, not once but on several occasions.

Nor was money the only problem. Men were demanded in large numbers for the Prince's interminable campaigns, and references to Welsh soldiers—particularly archers—serving in the armies in France or Scotland are frequent. Wales, however, was not alone in feeling exploited. In 1353 a major visitation was held in Cheshire with a view to identifying neglected rights and hitherto undisclosed revenues. With his expenses outrunning even his very large income, the Prince could not afford to be squeamish. However, the fact that Edward came to be regarded as 'no good lord' in Wales was to fuel the fires of that resentment which was to burst forth so strongly nearly 30 years after his death.[54] At the time resistance was little more than empty boasting. Some dissident Welshmen did take service with the French, and in

1372 one Owain 'of the red hand' gathered a bunch of similar malcontents around him in Paris and announced his intention to recover his fatherland. Nothing happened. Two years later another group with similar aspirations got as far as Guernsey, and in 1377 there was talk of a further attempt, this time with Castilian help, but that never materialized either.[55] Probably these alarms lulled the English regime in Wales into a false sense of security, because the resentment that they overexpressed was nevertheless real enough.

These rather obvious grievances were not the only grounds for discontent. Edward was also in the habit of presenting his (English) clerks to the best benefices within his jurisdiction, and that included the bishoprics of Bangor and St Asaph. In the last part of the fourteenth century only one man was appointed (Llewellyn ap Madoc to St Asaph in 1357) who would have been capable of conversing with his flock in the native tongue that was all that most of them spoke.[56] At the same time there was discontent of a quite different kind over the administration of the law of real property. By Welsh law all land was owned by the community, or Commote, through an instrument resembling a lease, and then for no more than four years at a time.[57] Welsh law also recognized partible inheritance rather than primogeniture. It might be thought that this was fine for the younger siblings, although hard on the first-born, but in fact it was equally unsatisfactory for all, because the end result was tiny holdings, far too small to support the family working them. By the early fourteenth century there was a strong demand among the leaders of the Welsh community for the adoption of English land law, but the Prince's council would not listen.[58] Perhaps they saw a diminution of revenue from the introduction of a more straightforward system, or perhaps they believed that they were defending the interests of 'ordinary' Welshmen. English officials' insistence on maintaining traditional Welsh law built up a major frustration, particularly among the Welsh gentry. There was also resentment over the privileges accorded to the English boroughs, such as Conwy and Beaumaris, which were colonies planted originally by force. The rules excluding Welshmen from residing in them were by this time only slackly enforced, but the principle was resented, as were the market rights that compelled the Welsh residents of the hinterland to sell their produce in the borough markets—and to pay tolls for doing so. The English burgesses held their tenements, both inside and outside the town, by English law, and if they succeeded in acquiring land from the Welsh, it also passed under English law. In fact these privileges were the minimum inducement required to persuade English settlers to come to such remote and precarious places—but the Welsh could hardly be expected to see it in that light.[59]

In spite of his title, Edward of Woodstock was every inch an English Prince, and while he was studiously ignoring his main lordship, he was exceptionally busy about other things. In 1348 he was heavily involved in the formation of the Order of the Garter, and indeed it may have been his idea rather than the King's. The story of the origin of the name is merely a fable, invented long afterwards. The real point of using the Garter as a symbol of chivalry was that it could be conveniently displayed on the outside of the glaive, or leg armour, where, unlike devices worn on the helmet, it was not likely to be dislodged by a casual blow. The inspiration behind the Order was largely political. It was intended to be a highly prestigious (and relatively cheap) way of rewarding distinguished military service, and at the same time to be an honour that could be offered to foreign dignitaries with whom the King wanted to remain on particularly good terms. It took advantage of the ideals of the Arthurian round table, and all its members were supposed to be chevaliers '*sans peur et sans reproche*'.[60] Edward III was far too pragmatic to want to send his knights out on romantic quests, but the spirit of his new creation was celebrated with elaborate tournaments that at least created the illusion of chivalry. 'Prowess', the contemporary chronicler Jean Froissart wrote, 'is so noble a virtue and of so great recommendation that one must never pass over it too briefly, for it is the mother stuff and light of noble men.'

This aristocratic culture of violence was one fully shared by the Black Prince. The whole ethos of the Garter is redolent of the Prince of Wales, and it is probably just as well that he did not live to succeed to a throne where other priorities would have had to be taken account of. For when he was not playing at war, he was waging it in earnest. Both he and his father were present at the great sea battle fought in 1350. Unlike Sluys 10 years earlier, which had been largely accidental and in which neither the King nor his son had been involved, this battle was deliberately sought as a means of knocking the Castilians out of the war, and is usually known as '*Espagnols sur mer*'.[61] This was an unusually imaginative move for Edward III, who did not normally believe in anything (least of all fighting) that could not be done on horseback, and again it is possible that the initiative of the Prince lay behind it.

As his father became older, Edward's role became ever more prominent. He was in command of the great campaign of 1355, which cut a swathe through central France, and it was his army that the French caught at Poitiers on 18 September 1356 as it was trying to extricate itself. Cardinal Talleyrand, who had been trying to mediate peace between the two sides, was present and kept up his efforts to the last, but to no avail. By all the logic of warfare the French should have won. They were fresher, better supplied and far more numerous. But that would have been to count without the extraordinary effectiveness of the English (largely Welsh, in fact) longbowmen and the military genius of the Prince of Wales. Not only were the French defeated, their King was captured and courteously but triumphantly taken back to England. When the war was ended at Brétigny four years later, King John was ransomed, but the whole of southwestern France, from Gascony to Poitou, was ceded to the King of England. In 1362 Edward III recognized his son's exploits by creating him Prince of Aquitaine.[62] Whether that or Wales then took precedence is a subject for debate.

In 1367 the Prince's warlike energies found a new outlet. Pedro the Cruel had been ousted from the throne of Castile by the Francophile Henry of Trastámara, and naturally looked to the English, and particularly to the Prince of Aquitaine, for support. Temporarily unoccupied in France, the Prince was only too happy to oblige.

King Pedro decided to go to Bayonne, in the hands of the English, and at Corunna there came to meet him [two noblemen] … sent by the Prince of Wales, to say that he should go to the domain of the King of England, his father, who would help him to recover his kingdom, and so he had sent this mission to promise help…. Thus it was that King Pedro arrived at the city of Bayonne … and the Prince assured King Pedro that he was ready to help him with all the might of the King of England his father, and to accompany him to recover his realm, and that he had let his father and lord the King of England know all this, and that he was very sure his father would be very glad that all his men should help Don Pedro … and the King of England sent his messengers to King Pedro, and his letters to the Prince his son, by which he declared that he was very pleased with all the aid that his men might give, and he sent to tell the Prince his son, and the Duke of Lancaster, another son, to help Don Pedro personally.....[63]

Although the Prince did win an important battle at Nájera, his restoration of Pedro turned out to be only brief, and the main consequence of the campaign was a long-term alliance between France and Castile. The Prince's health also began to decline. A severe bout of dysentery after Nájera was followed by dropsy, he grew increasingly bloated and by the end of the year his celebrated energy was visibly ebbing away.

Moreover Edward's government in Aquitaine was seriously unpopular, and the great Gascon houses of Armagnac and Albret appealed to the *parlement* of Paris. War was resumed, and between 1370 and 1375 the English lost just about all that they had gained at Brétigny. English raids met no opposition, but when pitched battles were fought, they were defeated. In 1375 the war was brought to a close again by a treaty signed at Bruges, which left England with only Calais and the coastal lands of Gascony.[64] Edward's principality of Aquitaine had disappeared.

Meanwhile the Prince of Wales had at last married. In spite of his father's desire to use his marriage for diplomatic purposes, he eventually proved indulgent to a personal choice that had no diplomatic significance. His bride was Joan, the sister and heir of John, Earl of Kent, who had died in 1352. This was a purely personal, even romantic, choice because Joan had a colourful history, and was known, perhaps ironically, as 'the fair maid of Kent'. In 1339 she had married Sir Thomas de Holland, but had abandoned him in obscure circumstances after about a year, and in 1340 married William de Montacute, Earl of Salisbury. Holland had not accepted this, and in 1349 he obtained an ecclesiastical verdict confirming the validity of the original marriage. Joan returned to her first husband and had several children with him before his death in December 1360. Some 10 months later, on 10 October 1361, Joan, aged 33, married the 31-year-old Prince of Wales.[65] By the time that their first child was born in 1364, his mother would have been about 35, and when Richard arrived in 1367, nearly 40. Edward, the first-born, died in 1371, but Richard survived to carry on the succession—and to become Prince of Wales in turn.

By 1376 Edward III's once triumphant reign was limping to its conclusion. Most of the French conquests had been lost and the country had been decimated by the plague; the disease remained endemic after the great outbreak of 1348–9, leaving severe social tensions in its wake.[66] The Crown and the nobility were at odds again about how the responsibilities for law enforcement should be allocated. Queen Philippa had died in 1359, and as he got older Edward fell increasingly under the influence of his mistress, Alice Perrers. He was regarded at the time, and has often been described since, as senile in the last two or three years of his life. This should have been the signal for the Prince of Wales to begin assuming some of the royal responsibilities, but the Prince himself was now a sick man. Whether his constitution had been undermined by years of relentless campaigning is not known, but by 1369 he could scarcely ride, directing the siege of Limoges in 1370 from a litter. In 1371, aged only 40, he retreated to his manor at Berkhamsted, where he lived a further five years in acute pain. He died on 8 June 1376, Trinity Sunday, without ever wearing the crown that had seemed to be his destiny for so many years.

With both the King and the Prince of Wales virtually out of action, early in 1376 the King's next surviving son, John of Gaunt, began to come to the fore, and it may well have been this fact that prompted Edward to create his nine-year-old grandson, Richard of Bordeaux, as Prince of Wales in November 1376. Jean Froissart describes the great Christmas feast held by the old King in the Palace of Westminster in 1376, which England's prelates and nobility were ordered to attend.

> And there Richard, the Prince's son, was raised up and carried before the King, who invested him in the presence of the lords just mentioned with the succession to the throne of England, to hold it after his death; and he seated him at his own side. He then required an oath from all prelates, barons, knights, officers of the cities and towns, of the ports and frontier-posts of England, that they would recognize him as their King.[67]

Richard was to hold the title for only about nine months as the King died in the following June, but it was sufficient to ensure his right to succeed, and he became King as Richard II. The young King's inheritance was not an easy one—in fact there were problems in just about every aspect of government, and as we have seen the Principality of Wales was no exception.

By the end of the fourteenth century, most Welsh baronial families had either died out or had faded into obscurity. Lordships held by prescriptive right, or *arylwyddieath* (the remains of the rights of the ancient *brenin*, or kings), no longer had a place in feudal Wales. Most of them had long since been converted into tenures in chief, held under English law, and the remainder had been reduced by *cyfran*, or partible inheritance, to insignificance.[68] The brief tenure of Richard of Bordeaux as Prince made no difference to the underlying confusions of Welsh government, which sprang from several roots. In theory the distinction between English law and Welsh law was clear cut, but in practice much less so, particularly the law of real estate.[69] It was also not always clear where pleas should be lodged, particularly in civil matters. The Exchequers at Caernarfon and Carmarthen had originally been merely revenue offices, without any judicial powers, or the ability to enforce payments. From 1339 they had been given the status of courts, but it remained uncertain as to which pleas should be pursued there and which at Westminster.[70] Most seriously of all, Edward III's constant demand for soldiers had led to the growth of private retinues in Wales as in England.

Whereas in England the link between a man and his lord was most likely to be 'cash and contract', in Wales it was frequently kindred. Their bonds of loyalty were consequently stronger, and they were closer to the hands of their leaders off the field of battle. This contributed significantly to Wales's reputation for lawlessness, where a right of private warfare (albeit not acknowledged as such) subsisted, particularly in the Marches. English merchants and officials venturing into the region had to know the lie of the land in order to avoid plunder or kidnap, although this should not be exaggerated. With due care many Englishmen traversed the Marches in safety, sometimes with significant quantities of goods or cash, although it probably cost them in protection money. The perception of lawlessness probably depended less upon the actual number of victims than upon the abstruse, and often ineffective, processes open to anyone who had been wronged.[71] Even when Lordships were in the hands of the Crown, there was not much improvement.

Young Richard was born in the abbey of St André in Bordeaux on 6

January 1367. English power in Aquitaine was at its height, and his father was keeping his court there at the time. The Black Prince's court was renowned for luxury and sophistication—admittedly funded by the inhabitants of Gascony and Poitou—and it was celebrated in glowing terms by the Herald of Sir John Chandos: 'Since God was born, never was open house kept so handsomely and honourably'. More than 'fourscore knights and full four times as many squires' would dine there, along with a vast retinue of pages, valets, huntsmen, grooms and servants. One story told that the Prince would only be served by a knight wearing golden spurs, while Joan wore rich furs, fabrics and jewels.[72] Richard, the second son of Edward and Joan (his elder brother, called Edward for his father, was born in 1364) spent the first four years of his life in Bordeaux, but in 1371 his brother Edward died and—with the English government under intense pressure—the Prince moved his family back to England.[73]

Not very much is known about Richard's upbringing, and it can be presumed that he was mainly with his mother until about 1373. His household only begins to become visible when he was created Prince of Wales in November 1376, following his father's death. At that point Sir Simon Burley is described as his tutor and Chamberlain, and Sir Richard Atterbury as 'first master'.[74] What is otherwise known of these gentlemen suggests that he was educated along the same lines as his father and grandfather, with much emphasis upon chivalry and feats of arms, but it is also true that he showed little enthusiasm for such pursuits as a grown man. His household was independent alike of his mother and of the court, and moved, as was customary, around the royal residences in the Home Counties, but the Prince himself was mainly under tuition and public responsibilities were few. He presided at the parliament of January 1377, but that was a purely ceremonial function. When Edward III died in June 1377, Richard succeeded without dispute; he was crowned at Westminster on 16 July 1379. Both the coronation service and the state banquet were very long, leaving the exhausted boy king to be carried back to his palace by Burley, allegedly losing a slipper along the way. Despite his youth, no formal regency was declared, perhaps because his uncle John of Gaunt, who would have been the obvious candidate, was deemed to be too powerful already. Instead the King's council assumed the formal responsibility, and this was probably a mistake.

The result of having such a low-key executive was that the Household became too powerful, particularly in the distribution of patronage. Burley and Aubrey de Vere, who was emerging as the young
King's favourite, became Knights of the Household, and did virtually
as they pleased.[75] The parliament complained, and placed Sir Richard
Cobham to 'remain in the King's household' to check such excesses,
but his position must have been totally invidious, and nothing changed.
Part of the problem was that household largesse was being accompanied by ever-increasing demands for taxation to support campaigns in
France that were accomplishing nothing. The 'continual council'
effectively ceased in 1380, leaving the 13-year-old King in sole charge.
This had its advantages, because when the smouldering social discontent broke out in violence in the so-called 'Peasants' Revolt' of 1381,
the insurgents did not know quite who to blame. Respectful loyalty
was expressed to the King's person, and there were attempts to hold
John of Gaunt responsible for the grievances. As a result, Richard was
able to take the initiative in a series of confrontations with the rebels.[76]
They dispersed, and the charters that the King had issued under pressure were revoked on the July. It was the one undoubted success of
his reign.

From 1381 onwards, Richard made no secret of appointing his own
advisers, and he did not choose well. Robert de Vere, the son of
Aubrey, and Michael de la Pole, the son of a Hull merchant, emerged
first as Chamber Knights—in other words personal favourites.
Michael became Chancellor in 1383 and Earl of Suffolk in 1385.
Robert, described by his enemies as 'the new Gaveston', was created
first Marquis of Dublin and then (in 1386) Duke of Ireland.[77] Whether
the implications of homosexuality in the King's relations with Robert
were justified cannot be known, but probably not, because such innu-
endos were standard in the case of male favourites. Richard had married Anne of Bohemia, the sister of the Emperor Wenceslaus IV, in
1382 and their marriage appears to have been a happy one. He was
devastated when she died at the age of 28 in 1394. However, their
union was childless, and a doubt must remain. The English remained
on the defensive against France, and heavy taxation continued to be
demanded. The Commons continued therefore to complain, and in
October of the same year tensions between Richard and parliament
came to a head.[78] The Chancellor's dismissal was demanded—and

refused on the grounds that such appointments were a prerogative matter. Eventually Richard gave way—up to a point. De la Pole was dismissed and impeached, but the King remitted his punishment and he remained as influential as before.

Parliament had set up a committee to carry out the reforms that they were demanding, but Richard evaded it by setting off on a protracted progress or 'Gyration' around his kingdom, which lasted from February to November 1387. This cut no ice with the committee, or Lords Appellant as they came to be known,[79] and by the beginning of December an armed conflict was clearly impending. De Vere raised an army for the King in Wales and Cheshire, but his defeat by the Appellants at Radcot Bridge shortly before Christmas left the King totally exposed. He may even have been technically deposed for a few days, and would probably have been permanently removed if he had had a son to succeed him. He clearly had no support in the country, but the Appellants proceeded to fall out among themselves, and that saved him. De la Pole, de Vere and Alexander Neville (the Archbishop of York and another favourite) had all fled abroad after Radcot Bridge, and they were condemned and deprived *in absentia*, but many others of Richard's court were impeached by the Merciless Parliament and executed. Richard was powerless to prevent this, but never forgave the leading Appellants for their action.[80] Unfortunately for them, the Appellants' intervention had been totally negative. They had destroyed Richard's unpopular government, but had done nothing to replace it, and seem not to have known what to do next. As a result, during 1388, power gradually returned to the King, and on 3 May 1389, having now reached the age of 21, Richard formally declared his personal responsibility, and announced a fresh start.

For a few years there was relative calm. Richard built up the ceremony of the court, preferring to be addressed as 'majesty' rather than 'highness', and he began quietly to gather a following by retaining leading county gentry, thus undermining his magnates' attempts to do the same.[81] In 1395 he attempted (unsuccessfully) to get his great-grandfather Edward II canonized, and began to seek a settlement with France. At first this stumbled over the position of Aquitaine, but in 1396 a 28-year truce was agreed, a peace in all but name, and Richard married Isabella, the seven-year-old daughter of Charles VI. Meanwhile, in 1394, he had taken 5,000 men to Ireland, received the submission of the Gaelic chiefs and, in 1395, returned to England in triumph. In July 1397, however, without any warning, the King arrested the Earls of Arundel, Gloucester and Warwick. This has all the appearance of a pre-emptive strike—but against what? There is no evidence that any kind of conspiracy was in train, but the King was supported by his usually discreet and cautious uncle, John of Gaunt.[82] It is quite possible that the three Earls had talked of reviving the Appellants, but it is pretty certain that they had done nothing. Nevertheless all three were impeached of treason. Arundel was executed, Gloucester died in prison under suspicious circumstances and Warwick was eventually pardoned. Arundel's extensive lordships in northeast Wales were then annexed to the Earldom of Chester, which at the same time was raised to Palatine status.[83]

Richard had apparently got away with a gross breach of the provisions of Magna Carta, which guaranteed peers a trial by their equals. He then compounded his offence by conferring on the newly created Dukes of Aumale and Surrey (Edward of York and Thomas de Holland) the power to arrest and punish all traitors—without reserving any kind of legal process. The King's vision of his prerogative rights had thus disappeared off the political scale and become altogether unacceptable. The question then was—what could be done about it? And who could do it? Richard was childless, and married to a wife who was too young to procreate. Neither Roger Mortimer, Earl of March, who was his heir general, nor John of Gaunt, his heir male, was disposed to take a lead against him. But Richard was now living very dangerously, and when he decided in 1398 to take advantage of a quarrel between the Duke of Norfolk and Gaunt's son, Henry Bolingbroke, by banishing them both, he went a step too far.

From the manner in which he had survived earlier crises, Richard seems to have developed a sense of invulnerability, and that now betrayed him. John of Gaunt died in January 1399, and the King decided to take advantage of his son Henry's exile to disinherit him.[84] He could hardly have touched a more sensitive spot in aristocratic culture than the sacred right of heirs to inherit, because neither John nor Henry had been lawfully deprived. No sooner was Richard's back turned, on a visit to Ireland, than Henry Bolingbroke landed at Ravenspur on 1 July. He had some limited backing from the Duke of Orleans, but his greatest strength lay in the fact that all the King's staunchest allies were with him in Ireland. Henry cautiously played his strongest card first, claiming that he had come only to reclaim his lawful inheritance, but by virtue of being the second oldest grandson of Edward III he was also the heir male to the throne. Richard sent the Earl of Salisbury to North Wales to raise troops, and returned himself, probably to Tenby, at some time between 20 and 25 July. It soon became clear that his position was impossible.[85] If the men of Wales had rallied to him, the issue might have been different, but they did not, and this quickly became known in England. Even Edmund of Langley, Richard's surviving uncle, did not back him.

As Richard moved through Wales in late July 1399, his army melted away, including the men whom Salisbury had recruited. By the time he reached Conwy on 11 August, he had only a bodyguard of a few score archers, and a handful of friends who had nothing to gain by deserting him. Henry advanced to Chester, ostensibly to negotiate, but it was soon apparent that that would not be necessary. Holding all the cards, he took Richard prisoner at Flint and carried him off to London where he was deposed, according to Adam of Usk (who did not like him), on the grounds of his 'perjuries, sacrileges, sodomitical acts, reduction of his people to servitude, lack of reason and incapacity to rule'.[86] Like Edward II before him he had relied on the Welsh to dig him out of the hole that he had created for himself, and like Edward, he found them unwilling to oblige.

It is probable that the Prince's alleged sodomy was merely the figment of a malicious imagination, resulting perhaps from his reluctance to compete in 'manly' feats of arms. There was nothing wrong with his personal courage, and he hunted with enthusiasm, but tournaments and similar martial arts had no appeal for him. In spite of the apparent limitations of his formal education, his court later became something of a centre for the patronage of arts and letters, and, unlike his father, he could certainly read Latin. Richard had presided over a church that was embroiled in the Great Schism, and constantly at odds with the Pope, but neither his piety nor his orthodoxy can be seriously doubted.[87] The sacrilege, like the sodomy, seems to have been part of a contemporary Black Legend, designed to justify the actions of his supplanter. After his deposition Richard was taken to Pontefract, and there in the following year he met a suspicious death that was probably murder. Like Charles I after him, he had too lofty and logical a view of the royal prerogative for the untidy realities of English politics, and when he tried to impeach his opponents of treason and condemn them without due process, he committed the sin against the Holy Ghost.

The fourteenth-century Princes of Wales had been a mixed bag, the most interesting similarity being between Edward II and his great-grandson Richard. Each of them made the identical mistake of relying, when they succeeded to the throne, on personal favourites rather than on the established nobility, and each paid the same price. Each also sought as Prince to resist the 'martial arts' culture of the contemporary nobility, and was accused of sodomy in consequence. Edward seems to have been driven by a compulsion to be different from his father, and in that respect he set an agenda for Princes of Wales down the centuries. But Richard was too young, and was Prince for too short a span, for any such consideration to apply. His defiance of convention (and indeed law) was differently rooted, and may be traceable to the social and religious tensions among which he grew up. Someone certainly encouraged absolutist ambitions in the young man, but it would be hard to trace such influences to his brief spell as Prince of Wales. It may be that both Edward and Richard took after their mothers, but we do not know enough of the ladies' characters to be sure.

The Black Prince was quite different. He was his father's son, and made no secret of the fact. If anything, he was more accomplished in arms and chivalry than his redoubtable sire, and it is interesting to speculate what might have happened if he, rather than his son, had become King in 1377. He held the Principality far longer than the other two combined, but his legacy as Prince was a largely negative one. It was his ruthless exploitation of his position as Lord that led directly to the revolts of the early fifteenth century, and the regular government of Wales proceeded without his direct intervention. He was a soldier of the most conventional kind, and it is hard to see him upsetting his peers, as his son was to do. He did, however, upset the Welsh.

CHAPTER II

A Dangerous Inheritance

The fifteenth century was not a good time to be Prince of Wales. Of the four who were created only one, Henry of Monmouth, lived to become King in any real sense. Edward of the Sanctuary, the son of Edward IV, was rejected as soon as he acceded at the age of 13, and probably died a few weeks later. Edward of Westminster, son of Henry VI and Margaret of Anjou, spent most of his notional principate in exile and died at the age of 17, while another Edward, the son of Richard III, was probably 11 when he died in 1484. The last three were all, in a sense, victims of the civil strife that tore the country apart between 1450 and 1490. One Prince died in battle and another was almost certainly murdered. The century saw two depositions, the death of a King in battle, and an intense power struggle that involved virtually the whole nobility. There was also rebellion in Wales and war with France. The century has been much mythologized, partly because the Tudors used it as a dreadful warning of what would happen if the Crown were allowed to lose its grip, and partly because William Shakespeare set most of his history plays within its years of turmoil. Only recently have historians developed a more positive view of this period, and established some perspective on its celebrated disasters — but they have not been able to do much to redeem the Princes of Wales.

Henry of Monmouth was born in the castle of that town in either 1386 or 1387, the eldest son of Henry of Bolingbroke, Earl of Derby and of Mary, the daughter of Humphrey Bohun, Earl of Hereford.[1] His mother produced three more sons over the next six years and died (probably of exhaustion) in 1394. We know virtually nothing of her influence over her offspring, and given that the oldest of them was no more than seven or eight at the time of her death, that is not surprising. The woman who seems to have guided his early steps was his nurse, Joan Waryn, who was paid the modest sum of 40 shillings a year for her services. It is pleasant to record that nearly 30 years later, when he had become King, Henry V granted her an annuity of £20, so his recollections must have been very positive.[2] We know nothing about his upbringing, not even the names of his tutors, who were probably among his father's household clergy, and the tradition that he spent some time at Oxford can be discounted. His whereabouts from 1399 are known, and before that he would have been too young. Rather surprisingly, at the time of his father's exile in 1398 and of his grandfather's death in January 1399, young Henry seems to have been at court. Whether Richard favoured him or wanted to keep him within reach is not clear, but probably the former since he gave the boy an annuity of £500 a year.[3] If he was one of the 'henchmen' (sons of nobles customarily retained at court), then he was a very expensive one. Ironically, he went with the King to Ireland on his fatal visit in May 1399, and was knighted by him at the age of 12 or 13. Whether he was still with the King when the latter reached Flint, and the end of his political tether, is not clear. If he was, he must then have rejoined his father, but no one noticed or commented. Enjoying the charmed life of the young and unobserved, he was able to share in the Duke of Lancaster's popular and virtually bloodless triumph over his recent patron.

Henry IV's usurpation was later to provide the pretext for a generation of civil strife in England, but at first it was only the Scots who refused to recognize his title. A campaign into Scotland was therefore launched in August 1400, but it was a mere gesture and accomplished nothing. On his way back from the north, however, Henry was appraised of a potentially much more serious threat in North Wales, where one of the last Welsh barons, Owain Glyn Dŵr, had launched what was in effect a private war against his neighbour, Reynold, Lord Grey of Ruthin.[4] Reynold was one of Henry's staunchest supporters in Wales, and it is possible that the trouble may have originated in some action that he had taken against Richard in the previous year. However, Richard's cause played no overt part in the actions of either Glyn Dŵr or his friend Gruffudd ap David, who were objecting to other ways in which Lord Grey had conducted himself. As a reprisal, they camped on his land at Ruthin and stole some of his horses. Reynold reacted fiercely, denouncing Gruffudd as a thief in intemperate language, so that what should have been a trivial affair soon became much more serious. On 16 September 1400 Owain and nearly 300 of his kinsmen attacked the town of Ruthin and set it on fire. A few days later they attacked other English settlements at Denbigh, Harwarden and Holt, and on 22 September they assailed the border towns of Oswestry and Welshpool.[5] The local authorities reacted swiftly, and two days later the insurgents (as they had now become) were caught and defeated; 10 of them were executed at Ruthin on 28 September. It was at about that time that Henry reached Shrewsbury, and decided that the situation called for a show of force. A few days later he led part of the force that he had brought back from the borders on a sweep through North Wales, taking in Bangor, Caernarfon and Harlech. He met no resistance because the surviving rebels had taken to the hills, but he did succeed in making an explosive situation worse.

The guerrilla warfare that was triggered by these events was to go on for almost a decade. However, the King's direct involvement was to some extent screened as nearly a year before these events, on 15 October 1399, parliament had petitioned that the 12-year-old Prince Henry, his eldest son, should be created Prince of Wales.[6] So Henry of Monmouth became Prince of Wales, Duke of Cornwall and Earl of Chester in what was clearly a collusive arrangement.

A nd the same day, Harry, the King's son, by the assent of all the estates in the parliament, was chosen and made Prince of Wales, Duke of Cornwall and Earl of Chester, as heir apparent to the King and to the Crown of England; the which prince was brought before the king. And the king sitting took a coronell of Perry, and put it on his head, and kissed and blessed him. And took him a rod of gold. And so he was made Prince.[7]

A few days later he was also given the titles of Duke of Aquitaine and of Lancaster. These imposing titles should have carried a revenue of £8,500 a year, but Aquitaine was largely notional, most of it being in French hands, and the trouble developing in Wales drastically reduced income from that source as well. In any case, Henry was too young to administer his own estates.[8] He was not, however, too young to perform his formal duties.

T his year [1399] upon the morrow next after that the mayor had taken his charge at Westminster … my lord Prince was received into the city … whom the mayor with his brethren met at Cheapside upon horseback, standing in order from Friday Street to the old change … and all the fellowships in their best liveries standing from Bishopstreet to Cornhill, and from Cornhill unto Chepe … and the said Prince being in crimson velvet bordered with cloth of gold. And his vi [six] followers clad in crimson velvet without borders; and after the proposition made unto him by Mr. Recorder, he gave unto the mayor wise and discreet answer and thanks to the great comfort of the hearers and so departed unto Westminster.…

And upon Wednesday next following the mayor with his brethren … went unto the bishop's palace of Salisbury in Fleet Street, where my said Lord prince was lodged. And there within his Chamber of Estate, the mayor presented him with a pair of gilt basons weighing Ciiiixxviii ounces di [188 ½ oz.] and a pair of large gilt pots weighing CCCCix ounces [409 oz.], which when the Recorder had brought his grace to accept that little and poor gift, trusting that they should remember his grace with a better, said these words following: 'Father mayor, I thank you and your brethren here present of this great and kind remembrance, which I trust in time coming to deserve. And for as much as I cannot give unto you according thanks, I shall pray the King's grace to thank you, and for my part I shall not forget your kindness.'[9]

The Prince grew up with the wars in Wales, which absorbed all, and more than all, of the resources that were theoretically his. He also found himself frequently on campaign when he should really have been at his studies. At first, because of his youth, he served under the command of the Justice of Chester and North Wales, Henry Percy, the son of the Earl of Northumberland, known as Hotspur. However, in July 1403 Hotspur decided to run his own rebellion, and the 16-year-old Prince was suddenly left exposed.[10] Although Shakespeare famously presents the two men as military rivals of similar age, Hotspur was 23 years older—an experienced leader from whom Henry had learned much on campaigns. His revolt did not last long—he was defeated and killed at Shrewsbury before the end of the month—but the Prince of Wales had been given a harsh lesson in the realities of contemporary politics.

The Glyn Dŵr revolt was the most dramatic and significant event in the history of Wales after the conquest of 1282.[11] His rebellion is doubly perplexing to the uninitiated, because nothing in Wales was ever quite what it seemed. Gwilym ap Tudor, for example, was supposed to be on the side of law and order, but in fact he was adept at using small-scale military coercion to get his way in local disputes without attracting the attention of his English superiors. With men like Gwilym in positions of authority, it is not surprising that security deteriorated in the 1390s, when there was no Prince, and the King's mind was elsewhere.[12] Owain's dispute with Lord Grey was a 'local difficulty' that got out of hand. The authorities could (and should) have dealt with it on the spot, but unfortunately it attracted the attention not only of the King but also of the English parliament. Anti-Welsh laws dated back to the conquest, but they had never been rigidly enforced. Now, in 1401 and 1402, new penal statutes were enacted that were intended to be enforced. No Welshman was henceforth to hold any burgage tenement within an English town, or to hold any land or other property in England. If an English woman married a Welshman, she forfeited her Englishry.[13]

There was a great surge of anti-English feeling, but to apply modern terms such as 'war of independence' to what happened is to misunderstand the fifteenth century. An incident in April 1401 serves to illustrate the point. Rhys and Gwilym ap Tudor were powerful men in North Wales, and relatives of Glyn Dŵr. They had been involved in the original attack on Lord Grey in the previous year, and what they wanted was a pardon for that offence—not some grand stand for Welsh liberty. Because the government in London was reluctant to oblige, they seized Conway Castle as a bargaining counter.[14] This was a major embarrassment to the King and the Prince, exposing the limitations of their power. A deal was consequently struck. The King got his castle back, and the Tudors got their pardons.

However, from the government's point of view the security situation continued to deteriorate during the summer of 1401. Although he had no base, and no settled military establishment, Owain proclaimed himself Prince of Wales. Risings flickered and erupted unpredictably all over North and Mid-Wales. In Cardigan and Carmarthen local leaders sought the King's peace, and courts could be held as normal; in other places not. Flint and Denbigh were as yet untouched by the revolt, but Owain raided around Ruthin in January 1402. In April 1402, in a classic guerrilla operation, Owain captured his arch-enemy Reynold Grey in an ambush, thus gaining an important bargaining counter, and in June he won a small pitched battle at Bryn Glas in

Radnorshire. The victims were the Herefordshire levies, and many of the gentlemen of western Herefordshire fell on the field. He also captured Edmund Mortimer, brother of the late Earl of March. In November, Mortimer changed sides, marrying Glyn Dŵr's daughter, and bringing the resources of his Marcher Lordships to the rebels' assistance.[15]

By the beginning of 1403 the situation was one of total confusion. Although English authority had not broken down entirely, large parts of Snowdonia were effectively 'no go' areas, and the rebels were raiding almost as far as Chester. In July the men of the Twyi valley rose in Glyn Dŵr's support, and he was beginning to acquire the aura of a national leader. The castles of West Wales were all under siege, and under-garrisoned places such as Carmarthen and Newcastle Emlyn had already fallen. The initiative undoubtedly lay with Glyn Dŵr by the time that Henry Percy also raised his standard of revolt on 10 July.[16] As we have seen, he did not last long, but his legacy was that the Welsh of Flint and Denbigh were now committed to the revolt. Shakespeare's dramatic reconstruction of the battle of Shrewsbury, at which Hotspur was killed, should be regarded as fiction, but it does give an insight into the heroic imagery that by 1600 had come to surround Henry of Monmouth. In the heat of battle he exchanges noble challenges with Hotspur, recognizing that 'Two stars keep not their motion in one sphere/ Nor can one England brook a double reign/ Of Henry Percy and the Prince of Wales'. Although only 16 at the time, the Prince is also depicted as shrugging off an injury to lead the fatal charge and even saving the King's life as he grapples with the Earl of Douglas.[17] None of this need be taken too seriously, but it forms an interesting counterbalance to the 'black legend' of youthful debauchery and irresponsibility that had also gathered about the young Prince. A near contemporary Italian in the service of his uncle, Humphrey of Gloucester, described him (in about 1437) as having been in his youth 'a diligent follower of idle practices, much given to instruments of music, and fired with the torches of Venus....'[18] It was, of course, the noble side that won out in the end!

Already in March 1403 the Prince had been appointed to represent his father in Wales, an interesting comment on the perceived status of his title, and on 1 April he was placed in overall command. However, the force of 2,700 men allocated to him would have been quite inadequate for any serious campaign. It could have been used only as a rapid response force, and the strategy seems to have been one of continued negotiation. The military situation in the Marches remained fluid and unstable, and some French troops were noticed in an attack on Kidwelly in August, although this did not represent any large-scale commitment.[19] In spite of the Prince's appointment, it was the King himself who led his forces into Carmarthenshire in September. He regained control of that important town, but found few enemies to fight as the rebels knew better than to risk open battle with such an army. As a result he made little impression on the rebellion as a whole, and the sieges closed around the English outposts again as soon as he had withdrawn. At this stage it is uncertain quite what the Prince's command was intended to achieve, because in October the King appointed the Duke of York as his Lieutenant in South Wales, and the Earl of Warwick to take command of the Lordship of Brecon.[20] It seems that Henry of Monmouth's position was supposed to indicate some sort of normality, and that that had been abandoned by the end of 1403. The King was girding himself for a long haul.

By the beginning of 1404 Owain was tightening his grip on the whole of Wales. The English castles of the north and west began to fall, and Welsh forces were raiding all along the border from Shropshire to Hereford. Owain was confident enough by May to send a diplomatic mission to Paris. Two months later — and acting as an independent sovereign — he concluded a formal agreement with the French King, keen to build a bridgehead from which to operate against England.[21] Military success enabled Glyn Dŵr to tackle some of the problems of civilian government. He called a parliament (which had never happened in Wales before), and began to take over the existing administrative structure.[22] By the end of 1404 the great castles of Aberystwyth and Harlech had fallen to the Welsh, allowing Owain to establish his court and a centre of government at Harlech. Early in 1405 he signed the so-called 'triple indenture' with the Earl of Northumberland and Edmund Mortimer — a proposed threefold division of England that left Owain controlling most of the West Country. This was an insubstantial dream, and by April Northumberland had fled into exile, but it seems to have been seriously meant at the time.[23] In fact, during the summer of 1405 the war began to turn against Glyn Dŵr. In August he achieved the high watermark of his power, when a substantial French force landed at Milford Haven and enabled him to sweep irresistibly across South Wales. He called a second parliament and began to talk seriously about brokering a peace between England and France. However, the French were indulging in gesture politics. They had no intention of staying in Wales, and no interest in Owain's proposed talks. In fact his power was not nearly as strong as it looked.

The Prince's position meanwhile had been further defined. He had moved his household to the Marches in the summer of 1404 to signify his engagement with Wales, but as we have seen, his role was not clear. Nor were his resources adequate, and in the same year he was complaining to Archbishop Thomas Arundel that he had to pawn his plate to meet immediate expenses. Then in April 1405 he was appointed Lieutenant of North Wales, and given a force of 500 men-at-arms and 3,000 archers. This paralleled the Duke of York's position in South Wales, and made military sense if a two-pronged thrust was intended. However, the King was then distracted by a new revolt in Yorkshire and no such attack materialized.[24] Nevertheless the threat that the Prince now posed to the rebels in North Wales was understood, and support for Glyn Dŵr began to waver. The leaders of the revolt in Flintshire surrendered in August, and Anglesey was retaken by an amphibious operation from Ireland. In the south a royal victory near Usk brought the men of Caerleon to terms.[25] This was no great victory, but Glyn Dŵr's son was killed and his brother and brother-in-law captured. God, it appeared, was not pleased with the rebels, but for the time being Owain affected not to notice. On 12 January 1406 he solemnly ratified his agreement with the King of France 'in the sixth year of our Principate', and in March attempted to transfer the allegiance of the Welsh Church to the Anti-Pope in Avignon.[26] Meanwhile the prospect of French military help drizzled away in the spring of 1406, and the other English rebels, who had appeared to offer hope at least of distraction, were now fugitives themselves. By the end of 1406 the writing was on the wall.

Control of Anglesey was critical, and by early 1407 a new military governor had been installed. This enabled the important castle at Caernarfon to be recovered, and a start made with the restoration of civilian government on the island.[27] It also gave the Prince an advance base from which to attack the heart of Glyn Dŵr's support in Snowdonia. In June 1407 a Shropshire force led by Edward Charlton defeated the rebels in Powys, killing another of Owain's sons, and in April the rebels of Flintshire surrendered, having lost several of their more active leaders. In May the Prince's commission in North Wales was renewed, and £7,000 was allocated for his campaign against Aberystwyth. This did not succeed, and Glyn Dŵr relieved the castle in person, but that proved to be an isolated success for the rebels. Elsewhere Owain's tide continued to ebb remorselessly. Even in Snowdonia the Justiciar, Gilbert Talbot, was able to hold an Eyre—the first for several years.[28] As late as May 1408 Glyn Dŵr was still appealing to France for aid, but by then the war had reverted to what it had been in 1401, a series of guerrilla operations from remote strongholds in North and West Wales—irritating to the English authorities, but no longer threatening their control. Aberystwyth was finally taken in July 1408, and Harlech early in 1409, snuffing out the last of the 'alternative Principality'. By 1410 Owain had disappeared. He was offered a pardon in 1415, but it was not taken up, and the fact that it was reissued to his son Maredudd in 1416 suggests that Glyn Dŵr was by then believed (or known) to be dead.[29]

Thereafter he became the stuff of legend, but in reality, whatever euphoria he may briefly have generated, the legacy of the Glyn Dŵr revolt was long and bitter. This was not the Prince's fault. Having substantially restored law and order—at least to its previous level—he was inclined to be conciliatory, but he could not dictate economic recovery. Farms and settlements had been devastated by both sides in a war that was largely conducted in small-scale raids and punitive expeditions. It took a long time for rents and other revenues to recover.[30] Moreover, kindred had been set against kindred, and there were many dead to mourn on both sides. For a war that had seen so little large-scale military operation, it had been extraordinarily destructive, both physically and morally. For a generation at least the pragmatic needs of commercial and administrative co-operation were at odds with the rhetoric of mutual hatred between Welsh and English. As late as 1567, in his introduction to the first Welsh New Testament, Richard Davies could write:

> What destruction of books Wales suffered as a result of the war of Owain Glyn Dŵr may easily be understood from the townships, bishops houses, monasteries and churches that were burned throughout Wales at that time. What a pitiable condition for a people to be

despoiled and robbed of the light they had, and to be left like blind
men to journey and travel through the wilderness of this world....[31]

In 1427 and again in 1443 Welsh monks at Valle Crucis and Strata
Florida were accused of stirring up racial hatred against their English
brothers in Christ, and the Welsh bards continued to preach undis-
guised hatred of all things English.[32] The penal statutes were confirmed as late as 1447, and although they were by no means uniformly
enforced, as long as they were on the statute book they constituted a
perpetual source of grievance. Although in the aftermath of the conflict Marcher Lords such as the Earl of Arundel and Lord Grey sought
to tempt settlers back into the depopulated areas, it was long before
they yielded any return to their holders.

The Prince had learned his military trade in Wales. In his youth he
served under experienced commanders such as his father or the Earl of
Warwick, but even as a very young man he had held independent
command. In the course of gaining this experience, he emerged as a
gifted strategist. To what extent he actually had a say in the formation
of policy is, however, another matter. Many of the decisions that were
made in his name were probably taken by his father, or by his father's
council. As the war was coming to an end in 1406, and possibly when
he was turning 21, he became a regular attendee at the council in London. By 1409 the King was suffering from recurrent ill-health, and the
council was largely ruling in his place.[33] However, the council was not
united, and the King's somewhat mysterious illnesses left the Prince
and his Beaufort cousins seriously at odds with the Lord Chancellor,
Archbishop Thomas Arundel.

In December 1408 (while the war in Wales was still going on)
Henry and his brother Thomas were called to the King's bedside
because he was thought to be dying. It turned out to be a false alarm,
but it left the Prince of Wales in an impossible position—one that
Prince George would have appreciated four centuries later. He could
not be regent, because his father's lapses and recoveries were unpre-
dictable, and when he recovered he was both lucid and dictatorial.
Arundel was dismissed during one of these arbitrary spells in December 1408, and young Henry was left face-to-face with his father. In
spite of later legends, the tensions between them were political rather
than social, and seem to have involved drastically different visions of

the direction in which the country should be heading. Nor had the Prince, despite his maturity as a soldier, learned to bide his time and hold his tongue. In July 1411 he was appointed Captain of Calais and Lord Warden of the Cinq Ports, both offices of high trust, but in November the crisis between them came to a head. The King dismissed the majority of his existing council, including the Prince, and recalled Thomas Arundel.[34] It appears that he feared that he was being elbowed aside by his martial son and for the next two years preferred to rely on his younger son, Thomas, whom he created Duke of Clarence in 1412. There was no question of his seeking to disinherit Henry, and indeed he was actively promoting a marriage between the Prince of Wales and Anne, the daughter of John the Fearless of Burgundy. Nothing came of the marriage, but relations had obviously not broken down entirely. The Prince clearly had his enemies, and that may explain their somewhat ambiguous relationship. The stories of his low-life exploits, some of which appear to be contemporary, seem to have arisen from such a source, because there is no substantive evidence for any of them. Much later Holinshed was to tell a story of how Prince Hal appeared before his father in tattered clothes (a 'gowne of blew satten full of small oilet holes') to apologize for some scrape or other—but again no contemporary alludes to such a thing.

More seriously, in the summer of 1412 he was accused of peculation in his office at Calais, and brought an armed force with him when he came to London to answer the charge. This may have been no more than an enhanced retinue and he could hardly have intended to use it against the King. The Prince seems to have needed to outface some personal enemy, but who that may have been is not clear. He was exonerated of the charges, the source of which seems to have been known to the King. Outside the court, sympathy seems to have been generally with the Prince, and when Henry IV finally died on 20 March 1413 there was a general air of expectancy. The new King was a skilful and proven soldier in the prime of life. He had, apparently, a clear complexion, fresh and fair, good teeth and a fine head of hair. So much, together with his cleft chin, can also be confirmed from his surviving portraits. He started with gestures of reconciliation. Richard II was re-interred at Westminster Abbey and Henry Percy, son of Hotspur and grandson of the rebel Earl who had died in Scotland in 1408, was recalled and pardoned. He was to be restored to the earldom in

1416.[35] More importantly, like his father, Henry V needed the support of the church, and distanced himself from the Lollard network that was represented among his followers by Sir John Oldcastle. Oldcastle was cited for heresy, escaped from prison, and was eventually captured in Wales in 1417. Charges of rebellion were levelled against him, and he was executed for both heresy and treason.[36] Henry V's credentials with the church were then well established.

It seems that from the start Henry had it in mind to 'busy giddy minds with foreign wars'. He began to cultivate the Welsh Marcher kindreds, knowing that he would need their services in either France or Scotland, or both. He also took an aggressive line in negotiations with the French, demanding the return of all those provinces that had been gained at Brétigny and subsequently lost. Realizing the uncertain mental health of Charles VI, and the feuds and divisions paralyzing the French court, he also began to press for a marriage between himself and Charles's daughter Catherine, anticipating the benefits of such a match. He also needed to rebuild the allegiance of his own aristocracy, which had been damaged during his father's declining years. The urgency of the latter was demonstrated when a (not very serious) conspiracy was disclosed to replace him on the throne with Edward III's heir general, the Earl of March.[37] The Earl was not a party to the plot, but it cost Richard, Earl of Cambridge his head. It was, however, by successful war in France that a real sense of unity and purpose was to be restored, and that became the King's immediate objective. Seizing upon a pretext, he mustered an army and landed near Harfleur on 14 August 1415. Within a few days he had taken the town, and proceeded to win a resounding victory at Agincourt on 25 October—a victory that redefined Anglo–French relations. An impressed parliament voted him tonnage and poundage for life, followed by a double subsidy. There was no settlement in France, largely because it was not in Henry's interest to accept one, and the steady conquest of Normandy followed, culminating in the capture of Rouen in January 1419. Negotiations were attempted in March but came to nothing because the French were unwilling to accept the weakness of their position.[38]

Meanwhile, their divisions deepened, and the English overran Pontoise. Then, on 10 September 1419, Duke John the Fearless of Burgundy was murdered at Montreuil—not quite in the presence of the Dauphin, but certainly with his connivance. Unsurprisingly his son and heir, Philip the Good, immediately allied with the English, and his defection forced Charles's council to come to terms. A general truce was agreed at Christmas, and on 2 May 1420 the treaty of Troyes was signed. This effectively disinherited the Dauphin, making Henry V the heir to the French throne. He was also betrothed to Catherine, and they were married at Troyes on 2 June.[39] As a peace treaty this was a failure; it was inevitably rejected by the Dauphin, who remained unsubdued with considerable backing, and fighting consequently continued.

In February 1421 Henry took time off from the battlefield, for the first time in four years, and brought his bride to England. She was crowned at Westminster with full ceremonial, and then paraded around the country, her beauty winning her many admirers. More important, by the summer she was pregnant. Having done his duty, the King returned to the battlefields of France. Catherine moved to Paris, where their son was born on 6 December 1421. Henry visited his wife, but soon returned to campaigning. It was a fatal decision because he caught typhoid and died at Vincennes on 31 August 1422, leaving his throne to a nine-month-old baby. When Charles VI followed him to the grave on 11 October, the infant Henry became King of France as well as England. With the demise of her warrior king, the odds shifted against England in her war with the Dauphin, but for the time being the Duke of Bedford, acting as regent in France, continued to have the upper hand. There had scarcely been time to think of young Henry's titles, but he appears to have been accepted as Duke of Cornwall from birth. The titles of Wales and Chester were never conferred.[40] Throughout his long minority, and well into his personal rule, the Principality remained in the hands of the King, and became deeply enmeshed in the struggles of York and Lancaster which began about 1450.

By the time that the next Prince of Wales was born in October 1453, the government of his father, Henry VI, was in terminal decline. Failure of the siege of Orleans in 1428 had turned the tide of war against the English. Henry VI's coronation had taken place in Paris in December 1431, but it proved a hollow victory when, a few days later, the Duke of Burgundy—on whose alliance so much depended—came to terms with the newly-crowned Dauphin, Charles VII. In November 1432 Philip's sister Anne (wife of the regent John, Duke of

Bedford, the young King's uncle) died, and her death destroyed what was left of Anglo-Burgundian amity. In 1435 Duke John himself died, and the English position fell apart. Attempts to find an adequate replacement failed, and sporadic attempts began to be made to end the conflict on acceptable terms. It was to reinforce one such truce in 1445 that Henry contracted to marry Charles's niece, Margaret, the daughter of Renée of Anjou. [41]

In November 1437, when Henry was 16, he announced his intention to assume personal responsibility for the government, and to reorganize his council.[42] This led to the increasing ascendancy of Cardinal Beaufort, and to conflict between Beaufort and Humphrey, Duke of Gloucester, who had been Protector during the King's minority.[43] Over the next few years, the King made a number of changes which brought his council and his household closer together, and in particular brought the Lord Steward, William de la Pole, Earl of Suffolk, into prominence. By 1445 the council had become a clique of Suffolk and his friends, telling the King only what was in their own interests. It was against this background that the negotiations that resulted in Henry's marriage to Margaret took place. Suffolk led the English delegation, but apart from the marriage itself gained nothing beyond a truce and an agreement to go on talking. It was the failure of these subsequent negotiations that placed the new Queen in such an invidious position, and led to a steep rise in the unpopularity of the recently elevated Marquess of Suffolk. The royal couple were married on 28 May 1445, and she was crowned at Westminster Abbey two days later.[44]

Henry's sexual orientation appears to have been unquestioned, but it was to be nearly eight years before the Queen conceived a child. Meanwhile, in pursuit of an illusory alliance with his father-in-law, Renée of Anjou, Henry effectively surrendered his claim to Maine, and the English troops withdrew.[45] Suffolk was principally, and not unfairly, blamed for this, and for other disasters that befell the English in France.[46] Rouen fell to the French in October 1449, and at the beginning of 1450 a further defeat at Formigny spelled the end of English Normandy.[47] When parliament reassembled on 22 January, Suffolk, who had been raised to a Dukedom by a grateful King in 1448, was called to account. On 7 February he was formally impeached for treason, and in an attempt to frustrate the guilty verdict that was clearly impending, Henry banished his favourite for five years. However, on

30 April, on his way into exile, his ship was intercepted and he was summarily beheaded. A few weeks later, on 20 June, his friend Adam Ayscough, the Bishop of Salisbury, was dragged out of mass and lynched. It is likely that Suffolk's enemies were responsible for both these crimes. With no obvious way of calling either the King or his favourites to account, this must have seemed the only available method of redress.

Jack Cade's rebellion of 1450 was less a 'peasant revolt' than a calculated protest by the more substantial section of the community against a regime of lawless oppression. Cade used the name 'Mortimer', the family name of the Earls of March whose claim to the throne had been advanced against Henry V. That line was represented in 1450 by Richard, Duke of York, who in September 1450 returned unbidden out of Ireland in an attempt, as he claimed, to force the King to adopt a more responsible attitude to counsel. Making no progress, early in 1452, he decided to force the issue. A complex negotiation followed, during which York protested his continuing loyalty to Henry, and the King agreed to imprison his rival the Duke of Somerset while charges against him were investigated. York dismissed his force and returned with Henry to London, where it quickly transpired that he had been duped.[48] Somerset was not imprisoned, and instead York found himself under arrest. On 10 March he was released after swearing a solemn oath never again to appear in arms against the King, and on 13 March he and Somerset entered mutual recognisances to keep the peace against each other. It was at this time of (relative) euphoria that the future Prince of Wales was conceived. However, before his birth in October the King had suffered a complete mental collapse.

The nature of this illness is unclear—catatonic schizophrenia has been suggested—but it left him completely helpless and unresponsive. It came on in August, while he was at Clarendon, near Salisbury, and he was swiftly moved back to Windsor where he was to spend the next 17 months in virtual seclusion. Once it was clear that his son was healthy, and the Queen had been safely churched, it was decided to try the therapeutic effects of an encounter.

The Duke of Buckingham took him in his arms, and presented him to the king in godly wise, beseeching the king to bless him, and the king gave no manner answer ... the Queen [then] came in and took the prince in her arms, and presented him in the like form as the Duke had done, desiring that he should bless it, but all their labour was in vain....[49]

Politically a crisis could not be avoided, for the situation was unprecedented. Royal indispositions in the past had been for known reasons, and usually of short duration, but this was indeterminate in every sense. Queen Margaret put in a bid for the regency, which was clearly necessary, but the parliament that reconvened on 14 February 1454 rejected her claim, and conferred the protectorate instead upon the Duke of York.[50] Prince Edward had been baptized within days of his birth, at Westminster Abbey, one of his godfathers being, significantly, the Duke of Somerset. He was recognized as Duke of Cornwall from birth, and was created Earl of Chester and Prince of Wales in parliament on 15 March 1454. This was almost certainly intended to signal his right of inheritance, and when the Duke of York became Protector, his position was carefully safeguarded—a necessary precaution in the circumstances.

Commission to William [Booth], Archbishop of York, William [Waynefleet], Bishop of Winchester, Thomas [Bourgchier], Bishop of Ely, Walter [Lyhert], Bishop of Norwich, Reginald [Boulers], Bishop of Coventry and Lichfield, John [Chedworth], Bishop of Lincoln, and to Richard, Duke of York, John, Duke of Norfolk, Humphrey, Duke of Buckingham, Richard, Earl of Warwick, John, Earl of Oxford, Richard, Earl of Salisbury, Chancellor, John, Earl of Worcester, John, Earl of Shrewsbury [and others] ... [because] ... the king by charter dated 15th March last created Edward his first born Prince of Wales and Earl of Chester, which charter has not yet been executed ... appointing the said commissioners to create him Prince of Wales and Earl of Chester, and to invest him therewith with a circlet on the head and a golden ring on the finger [and] a golden rod....[51]

A household, which was really a glorified nursery, was created for him almost at once, limited in size to 39 persons, but there is no suggestion that he was parted from his mother during these first few months.[52] The name of his wet-nurse, or nurses, is not known. As Protector of the Realm, York was not a great improvement on his predecessor the

Duke of Somerset, whom he promptly imprisoned. It was just that it was now the Yorkists who were abusing the system rather than the Lancastrians. Of impartial royal authority there was still no sign.[53] Consequently when Henry suddenly recovered his wits at Christmas 1454, there was no great sense of either euphoria or despair. York surrendered his Protectorship, Somerset emerged from prison, and the King recognized his son and heir—approving all that had been done on his behalf. Otherwise it was business as before, and York and his followers were back in opposition.

For the next six years the political pendulum swung back and forth. In May 1455 there was an armed confrontation at St Albans. The Duke of Somerset was killed, and the King passed back under the control of the Duke of York. In November York again became Protector, but faced with the implacable hostility of the Queen, and clear evidence that Henry was *compos mentis*, he was forced to resign at the end of February 1456.[54] Up to this point Prince Edward's position had not been affected. As a young child he remained under his mother's care, and his political role was purely symbolic. When the court moved to Coventry, where Margaret was particularly strong, in August 1456, Edward went with them, and on 12 November his household was allocated £1,000 a year out of the revenues of his patrimony. The balance continued to be paid into the royal coffers, but this is the first sign that his creation as Prince of Wales was anything other than a gesture.[55]

His mother, however, was not satisfied, and on 28 January 1457 a council was appointed to manage the Prince's patrimony, which suggests that financial control was transferred at that point. Margaret remained the driving force behind this council, and it would appear that she was using her four-year-old son as a screen to cover the build-up of her own political power—a process that the King's feebleness rendered justifiable, if not necessary. Armed confrontations continued, and at the battle of Blore Heath in September 1459 the men of the Prince's affinity from Wales wore his insignia for the first time. The Coventry parliament in November of that year, which condemned the Yorkist leaders, also recognized the young Edward as the future King.[56] Early in 1460, when Edward was in his seventh year, his name began to appear on Commissions issued for Wales and Cheshire, a formality that would have been readily understood.

Fighting continued. In September 1460 the Duke of York again returned from Ireland, whither he had retreated after surrendering his Protectorate for the second time, and this time York was in so strong a position that when parliament opened on 10 October he marched in and laid claim to the throne. The Lords did not support him. Even some of his own followers were dismayed by his temerity, because although he had effective control over Henry, both Margaret and (more important) Edward, were still at liberty.[57] Eventually on 25 October a deal was struck, whereby Henry would remain King for his lifetime, but the Duke of York was recognized as his heir, and would succeed him. The loser by this botched arrangement was, of course, Prince Edward, whose whole patrimony in Cornwall, Chester and Wales was to be transferred to the Duke. There was no sort of logic behind this because if Henry was the rightful King, then Edward was his heir; and if Henry was not the rightful King, then he should have been deposed at once. The Prince's council protested at once against such an arbitrary decision, and there is no sign that the revenues, estimated at 10,000 marks a year (£6,666) were ever transferred.

Nor was the defiant Margaret prepared to accept defeat. Indeed her wrath became part of the Black Legend that she had acquired by Tudor times, and which Shakespeare took from Edward Hall: 'The fears they had of the Queen, whose countenance was so fearful, and whose look was so terrible, that to all men ... her frowning was their undoing, and her indignation was their death'.[58] No doubt the real Queen would have been only too pleased to have made such an impression in defence of her child and his rights! Despairing of her husband, she appealed to Mary of Gueldres, the Queen Regent of Scotland, and at Lincluden on 5 January 1461 Mary agreed to help the Queen in return for the cession of Berwick.[59] At the same time a marriage was agreed in principle between Edward and Mary, the year-old sister of the nine-year-old James III.

Neither side, however, was called upon to honour its agreement, because at about the same time that it was signed, the Duke of York was defeated and killed at the battle of Wakefield. As soon as the news of the Lancastrian victory reached her, Margaret and Edward hurried south.[60] At St Albans on 17 February she inflicted a further defeat upon the Earl of Warwick, now leading the Yorkist forces, and was reunited with Henry. The King was so delighted with her achievement that he knighted his young son immediately after the battle, so that the latter could transfer the honour to some 30 others who had taken part in the actual fighting; perhaps an indication of the role that the Prince would be expected to play in the future.[61] Warwick, however, rode the setback. London was strongly pro-Yorkist, and refused the Queen entry, forcing her to retreat to the north. Some 10 days later, on 27 February, the Duke of York's eldest son, Edward, Earl of March was welcomed into the city, and because there was no further point in dissimulation, proclaimed King as Edward IV. On 29 March the new King routed his Lancastrian enemies at Towton in Yorkshire, and Henry, Margaret and the Prince of Wales fled into Scotland. This victory turned out to be decisive, and Edward's brief tenure of the Principality effectively ended at that point. His council was dissolved, and such revenues as had been paid to him reverted to the Crown, along with all the other management functions that the council had carried out. He was attainted by parliament, along with all the other Lancastrian leaders, on 16 December 1461, and spent the next 10 years as an exile and a fugitive.

Henry remained in Scotland for the time being, but Margaret and Edward soon moved on to the Low Countries. From 1463 to 1470 they lived at his grandfather Renée's castle of Koeur, with a small retinue of fugitive Lancastrians.[62] Edward, unlike the future Charles II two centuries later, was at first too young to perform any leadership function, and in political terms looks very much like his mother's instrument. As he grew from 10 to 17, we know very little about his schooling, but he was apparently a very physical child, and in 1467 he was described as 'talking of nothing but making wars', and as 'giving himself entirely to martial exercises'.[63] Perhaps he felt that only by establishing a contrast with his father's pacific and supine image would he stand any chance of recovering his rights. In 1468 there was a proposal that he should marry Marguerite, the daughter of Louis XI of France, but that turned out to be too risky a step for so canny a monarch. Only the unexpected arrival of the Earl of Warwick in France in 1470 offered new hope. Warwick had fallen out with Edward IV, whom he had conspicuously failed to control in the way that he appears to have intended, and after an abortive coup in 1469 had decided to change sides.[64] It took a good deal of effort to persuade Margaret of his sincerity, but in July 1470 they finally met and concluded an agreement. Using his own and Margaret's connections in

France to provide the manpower, he undertook to restore Henry VI (then languishing in the Tower of London) to the English throne. One aspect of the deal was that Edward should marry his daughter Anne. They were immediately betrothed at Angers, and married (probably) on 13 December, after Warwick had returned to England. Gambling on the success of their venture, there was clearly a desire to secure the next succession as quickly as possible.

Warwick took Edward IV completely unawares, forcing him to flee to the Low Countries, and Henry was again proclaimed King on 3 October. However as Warwick struggled to put together a new Lancastrian administration, Margaret and Edward delayed in France. This proved fatal, because the ex-King wasted no time in mobilizing the support of his brother-in-law the Duke of Burgundy, and landed again in England on 12 March 1471. By a mixture of audacity and subterfuge he rallied an army, defeating and killing Warwick at the battle of Barnet early in April.[65] On 14 April, having overcome her doubts and apparently ignorant of Warwick's fate, Margaret eventually landed at Weymouth and the old Lancastrian peers and gentry of the South West flocked to join her. The Queen and the Prince moved north, apparently hoping to arouse Lancastrian sentiment in Wales, as both Edward II and Richard II had done earlier. They met with an equal lack of success. The Severn Bridge was held against them, and the town of Gloucester refused to open its gates.

After a hectic chase and forced marches on both sides, which left the Queen's army particularly exhausted, the two forces encountered at Tewkesbury on 4 May. The 17-year-old Prince had nominal command of the centre of the Queen's army, and Shakespeare gives him a rousing speech like that of his grandfather Henry V at Agincourt (for which there is no evidence whatsoever), but his troops were routed, and he died on the field of battle. It was a bloody and complicated conflict, in which the Lancastrians at first had the upper hand, until the tide was turned (allegedly) by the Duke of Gloucester – only a year older than Edward. The latter's attempts to rally his fleeing forces having failed, the flight turned into a massacre in which he also died. It was later claimed that even those who had sought sanctuary in Tewkesbury Abbey were not spared, and the story of Edward's death was dramatically embroidered. Margaret, having also attempted to find sanctuary, was captured three days later and eventually ransomed.

However, with her son's demise all the fight had gone out of her, and her husband Henry's death a few days later was almost an irrelevance.[66] Edward had not left his wife pregnant, and the main line of John of Gaunt came to an end at that point. It had been more than a decade since he had been in any real sense Prince of Wales, although he had continued to claim the title. Needless to say, throughout that time the management of the Principality and the control of its revenues remained vested in the government of Edward IV.

While these events had been reaching their tragic climax, Edward IV's wife, Elizabeth Woodville, had for some weeks been confined to the sanctuary at Westminster Abbey, whither she had fled on the news of Henry VI's re-proclamation. There, on 2 November 1470, she bore a son, who a few days later was baptized in the abbey, with the abbot as godfather. Confusingly, being named for his father, he was also called Edward. By April 1471 Elizabeth was restored as Queen, and on 26 June her son was created Earl of Chester and Prince of Wales.[67] In July the Dukedom of Cornwall was added, a new creation apparently being considered necessary because he had been born in the lifetime of his predecessor, and therefore could not be regarded as Duke from birth.[68]

17TH JULY 1471. Charter creating Edward, the King's eldest son, to be Prince of Wales and Earl of Chester. By the King and of the said date.

17TH JULY 1471. Charter granting to Edward, Earl of Chester, the Counties Palatine of Chester and Flint. By the King and of the said date.

17TH JULY 1471. Charter creating Edward, the King's eldest son, to be Duke of Cornwall. By the King and of the said date.[69]

The point of these rapid promotions was immediately made clear on 3 July when a special oath of allegiance to him as heir was demanded of all courtiers and royal servants. In spite of his extreme youth, Edward rapidly became a factor in his father's scheme of government. A household had already been established for him, and on 8 July it was decreed that until he reached the age of 14 the management of that, and the lands of his patrimony, would be in the hands of a council. His three uncles, the Dukes of Clarence and Gloucester and Earl Rivers, were all members of that council, but it was to be led, for the first time in such a formal context, by his mother the Queen.[70] On 17 July the lands of

Wales, Chester, Flint and Cornwall were handed over into the care of this council, although it did not become fully operational until the issues began to be paid in November of the following year.

Because Edward IV died before his son came of age, this structure appertained for the rest of the reign, and for the time being Elizabeth exercised extensive powers of patronage within the Principality. In fact her powers, and those of her council, continued at first to be augmented, because on 23 February 1473 the council was enlarged and given plenary authority to act in the Prince's name.[71] However, later in the year the management of both the Prince and his patrimony was reorganized to eliminate the role of the Queen, which had presumably become controversial. On 23 September a new set of ordinances was drawn up 'for the good governance of the prince and his household'. On 10 November John Alcock, the Bishop of Rochester, was appointed President of the Prince's council, which was relocated to Ludlow. Alcock was also given charge of the three-year-old Edward's education, which suggests that he was taken away from the 'women's side' at an unusually early age.[72] In more than one way the position of the Queen was ambiguous. When Edward was planning to invade France in 1475, he named his four-year-old son 'Keeper of the Realm', but left the effective regency in the hands of Elizabeth rather than any of the boy's uncles. At the same time he prepared his son for these formal duties by knighting him on 18 April, and creating him a Knight of the Garter on 15 May.

Elizabeth's displacement from the government of Wales may have been due to the fact that the lawlessness of the Marches had become a serious problem.[73] By the 1470s this was no longer a question of York and Lancaster, but simply of powerful men playing for their own advantage. William Herbert, the 2nd Earl of Pembroke, was still underage in 1471, but was nevertheless appointed Chamberlain and Justiciar of South Wales on 27 August. He turned out to be useless, and in the parliament of 1472 there were bitter complaints about the 'outrageous demeaning of Welshmen'. In 1474 a gang of aristocratic ruffians simply refused to appear before the King's council when summoned, and were still at large in 1478.[74] At first the Prince's council, even in its revamped form, had no jurisdiction in such matters, being responsible only for the patrimony, but in 1474 it was given a limited authority to deal with disturbances in the border lordships, and this proved to offer a way ahead.

The young Edward thereafter began to 'bear the King's presence' in the Marches, and his council became the focal point for the exercise of royal authority.[75] Initially this was done by tacitly transferring the King's rights as a Marcher Lord to his son's council, but in January 1476 the five-year-old Prince was given a general commission of Oyer and Terminer, not only within the Principality, but also in the Marches and the adjacent shires of Gloucester, Hereford, Salop and Worcester. This transformed the jurisdictional situation, and in March yet further powers were conferred, to enquire of all liberties and franchises which might be, or should be, resumed into the King's hands.[76] In December the Prince was given authority to appoint to all judicial commissions in Wales and the Marches, an important delegation of the King's direct power. By the end of 1476 the King's powers in the area were effectively delegated to a council resident at Ludlow, which operated in the name of the Prince. In December 1477 its position was further strengthened when the Lordships of the earldom of March (which was in the King's hands) were placed under its direct control, and in 1479 when the feeble Earl of Pembroke was constrained to exchange his title for that of Huntingdon, handing over his important offices in Wales to the Prince.[77] Edward's council still had no right to interfere with the day-by-day running of those Lordships still in private hands, but it now had a supervisory authority both there and in the border counties. Most importantly it had the same authority as the King's council itself to deal with failures of justice or official negligence; and, of course, it had complete power within the Principality.

In addition to representing his father in Wales and the Marches, Edward, like other Princes of Wales, had to play his part in the foreign policy of the reign. This meant mainly being placed on the marriage market, and in 1476–7 his name was being linked with that of the Infanta Isabella, the oldest daughter of Ferdinand and Isabella of Spain and the elder sister of Catherine of Aragon. That negotiation came to nothing, but there were similar proposals respecting a sister of the Archduke Maximilian of Austria and a daughter of Galeazzo Sforza, the Duke of Milan. Finally, in 1481, a firm agreement was reached with Brittany for a match between Edward, then aged 10, and the 4-year-old Anne, daughter of Duke Francis II. The marriage itself was not due to take place until Anne reached the canonical age of 12, which would not have been until 1489.[78] In the event, neither Edward nor his father was to live that long. Edward IV, having 'overmuch consumed his royal person' died on 9 April 1483, just a few days short of his 41st birthday, leaving his heir a minor and no clear instructions for a regency government. His death was unexpected, and probably the result of a stroke brought on by his famous overindulgence in food and alcohol. The last mandate he had given in writing related to his absence in France eight years earlier, and named his Queen, but it is reasonably certain that on his death bed he named his surviving brother, Richard of Gloucester, as Protector.[79]

The Prince of Wales (now aged 12) was at Ludlow when his father died, in the company of Anthony, Earl Rivers, his mother's brother. Richard of Gloucester was at Middleham in Yorkshire, and these locations indicate that the King's death was unexpected. There was no recent history of animosity between the Duke of Gloucester and the Queen or her kindred, and no warning signs of the storm that was now to break. The trouble was that young Edward was much closer to Anthony than he was to Richard, and the latter almost immediately developed a paranoid suspicion that the young King and his mother's kindred would conspire to deprive him of the Protectorate.[80] He may have been right, because while he was still in the north the council in London was discussing what the Protectorate should actually mean. Some argued that it should mean full powers until the King came of age at 18, others thought that those powers should be limited by the council, and still others that they should extend only until the King was crowned—a matter of about three weeks since that event had already been provisionally fixed for 4 May.

Whether there was really a 'Woodville conspiracy' to seize control of the government remains a matter of doubt. They had the resources, but whether they had the will is another matter.[81] Richard jumped to the conclusion that they had, and determined upon a pre-emptive strike. Mustering a portion of his northern affinity with great speed, he intercepted the King on his way to London on 29 April at Northampton. Earl Rivers, who was with Edward and commanded his modest escort, was taken completely by surprise, and in any case did not have the troops to put up a fight. After an initial display of friendliness, he was taken into custody, and the boy King (who must have been both baffled and frightened by this show of force) proceeded to London escorted by his other uncle. News of her brother's fate sent the dowager Queen and her remaining six children hurrying into sanctuary at Westminster, as she had done 13 years before, but Richard at first presented himself very correctly. He had come, he said, to make sure that his late brother's wishes were respected, and to assure himself of the Protectorship, which was his right.[82] The coronation on 4 May was quietly abandoned.

Having secured his initial position, Richard proceeded to use the Crown's powers of patronage to strengthen and consolidate his following, but he was still, as late as the beginning of June, planning Edward's coronation. At what point he changed his mind is not clear, but what is clear is that despite his success he remained deeply suspicious of many of those around him. It is very unlikely that Lord Hastings, Edward IV's Chamberlain, was really conspiring with the late King's mistress, Elizabeth ('Jane') Shore, but he was conspicuously loyal to Edward V, and therefore a potential obstacle in Richard's way. On 13 June the Protector, acting in collaboration with the Duke of Buckingham, denounced him in council for conspiracy and had him summarily executed without a shadow of judicial process. Cowed by this display of effective violence, the council raised no protest when, three days later, by a mixture of cajolery and the threat of force, he managed to extract Richard, Duke of York – the young King's brother – from the sanctuary at Westminster. Both boys were placed in the Tower of London—then a Plantagenet palace as well as a prison, but dangerously cut off from the outside world.

With both princes under his control, Richard showed his full hand. On 22 June, which was a Sunday, he commissioned one Ralph Shaw, a doctor of theology, to preach a sermon at Paul's Cross in which he denounced both the late King's sons as bastards, on the grounds that Edward had been contracted to Lady Eleanor Butler at the time of his marriage to Elizabeth. 'The said King Edward during his life, and the said Elizabeth lived together sinfully and damnably in adultery against the law of God and of his church…. It appeareth evidently and followeth that all the issue and children of the said King Edward, be bastards and unable to inherit….' On 25 June an assembly of peers and commoners—who had come together expecting the coronation of a new King Edward—found themselves instead confronted with a demand that they instead recognize the undoubted right of King Richard.[83] They did not constitute a true parliament, but Richard treated them as though they were, and claimed to have been accepted 'by the concord [and] assent of the lords and commons of this realm'. By a mixture of speed and ruthless determination, he had secured the Crown, his enemies temporarily scattered and intimidated. He was crowned with suitable pomp, and no shadow of dissent, on 6 July.

What happened to Edward and his brother has always been one of the great unsolved mysteries. According to the contemporary chronicler Dominic Mancini, they were seen alive in the Tower a few weeks after Richard's coronation—and then they vanished. Mancini cites John Argentine, a royal physician, to the effect that Edward was expecting death before his disappearance, but there can be no certainty, and Mancini was hostile to Richard. There were at the time, and have been since, many theories that postulated their escape and survival (often in some humble disguise), but the truth almost certainly is that they were murdered at some point during August or September 1483, and that the bones exhumed in the White Tower in 1674 were those of the princes.[84] Who was immediately responsible is again the stuff of conjecture, but the deed cannot have been done without Richard's knowledge and consent—and the chances are that he was responsible. Tradition ascribes the actual crime to Sir James Tyrell, but there is no contemporary evidence. When the Duke of Buckingham rebelled against his former friend in the autumn of 1483, he did so at first in the name of Edward V, but before his ill-fated venture was suppressed he had switched his allegiance to Henry of Richmond. Henry was an exile, and a shadowy figure by comparison with Edward, and the only plausible reason for the change is that by then Buckingham knew that Edward was dead. He had played no part at all in the events of his brief 'reign', except to express a fatal affection for his uncle Rivers. Similarly, as Prince of Wales he had been a potent symbol, but he was not old enough to make any effective input into the actions that were carried out in his name. The government of Wales was transformed, but whether he was even aware of the fact we do not know. He did not live to outgrow his schoolroom, and even the content and practice of that is shadowy.

In spite of the nature of his claim, Richard wasted no time in acting the part of a lawful King. He and his Queen, Anne Neville, had a son, Edward of Middleham, who at the time of his accession was either seven or nine years old. (There is some controversy over the date of his

birth because his parents were married in 1472, and it had been con-
jectured that he was born in 1474. All that can be said with certainty is
that he was born by 1476, and that he was his parents' only child.[85])
Very little is known about his upbringing, except that it took place in
Yorkshire, and that his nurse was a certain Isobel Burgh, later rewarded
by Richard out of the revenues of Middleham. As the son of a Duke,
Edward ranked as an Earl from birth, but he was specifically created
Earl of Salisbury on 15 February 1478, when the revenues of the earldom, then in the hands of the Crown, would have been granted to his
father in wardship.[86]

We know that Edward spent the whole summer of 1483 at Middleham, and indeed there is no conclusive evidence that he was ever anywhere else until his father became King. Richard wasted no time in
using him, and on 19 July he was given his first symbolic title, that of
King's Lieutenant in Ireland. He never went there, or as far as we know
interested himself in the affairs of the Lordship at all, but he was a convenient figurehead for the officers and council who carried out the
real tasks of government. More significantly, he left Middleham on 22
August to meet his father at Pontefract, and two days later he was created Prince of Wales. On 8 September he was solemnly invested as
Prince in York Minster, a ceremony that was followed by a procession
through the streets of the City.[87] At the same time his illegitimate
brother John was knighted.

> Setting forth that the land of Wales lies in a corner, and differs in
> language and manners from the other people of the realm, for
> which reason it requires a special lord immediately under the king,
> and that the said county of Chester borders on the said land. Creation,
> according to former precedents, of the king's first born son, Edward,
> with the counsel and assent of the prelates, dukes, earls and barons of
> the realm, to be Prince of Wales and Earl of Chester, and investiture
> by girding him with the sword and placing a coronet on his head, and
> a ring of gold on his finger, and a golden rod in his hand, the same to
> be held by him and his heirs, kings of England. By Privy Seal and of
> the said date.[88]

Having played his part in his father's calculated pageantry, he may then
have returned to Middleham, but he seems to have been with the
court at London over Christmas. In February 1484, in another act of

ritual self-assertion, Edward was formally declared heir to the throne. By that time he appears to have been back at Middleham, and there on 9 of April he died. Just as we know nothing about his education, so his character remains a complete mystery. We do not even know whether he normally enjoyed good health or whether his demise had been long expected. It appears that he had been granted the full patrimony of the Prince at the time of his investiture, because these revenues are described as reverting to the Crown at the time of his death. The only male member of the York family now surviving, apart from the King, was his nephew the young Earl of Warwick.[89] Anne did not long outlive her son, dying on 14 March 1485, aged 28. There were inevitably rumours of poison, but the likely culprit is pulmonary tuberculosis. With hindsight it looks as though Richard's whole regime was unravelling, but it probably did not look that way at the time. Premature deaths were only too common—even in royal families.

If Edward had a council in Wales, it appears to have been confined to the administration of his estates. It would in any case scarcely have had time to become established; of the three 'little Edwards' who held the title between 1454 and 1484, Edward of Middleham's incumbency was the most perfunctory as well as the briefest. Although Richard III set up a council in the north, presided over by John de la Pole, Earl of Lincoln, no similar solution was applied to the Welsh Marches. The King, little loved in Wales, initially relied for control on his ally the Duke of Buckingham, who held many Marcher Lordships, particularly in the southeast. When that position was forfeited by Buckingham's rebellion towards the end of 1483, Richard resorted to piecemeal appointments, and he did nothing to check the rise of great men such as Rhys ap Thomas. On the contrary, he seems to have relied upon them for the regular enforcement of law and order, making no attempt in his brief reign to continue the embryonic conciliar government established for the future Edward V. When the Principality reverted to the Crown on Edward V's accession, it appears that the council was simply stood down, never existing in the same form for Richard's son. Yet this regime did at least point the way ahead, and provide a model to be picked up by the next King who had a real interest in the well-being of the province, Henry VII.

There had been no adult Prince in Wales since Henry of Monmouth, nor was there another until the seventeenth century, by which time the whole structure of government had changed. The normal situation in Wales during the Middle Ages was that the Principality was a feudal liberty in the hands of the Crown, while the Marcher Lordships largely went their own ways — except when they, too, were in the hands of the Crown. Yet devolved government did not relieve the King of any part of his responsibility, as the prevailing confusion reveals.

For the Princes themselves, the situation was perilous and often way beyond their control. Children without a strong — and living — relative in power were symbolic figures at the mercy of events, and those surviving to adolescence had to grow into the position fast. Success on the battlefield was vital, but not in itself enough. As the fifteenth century shows, Princes and Kings needed not only to sire legitimate heirs quickly, but also to survive long enough to secure their inheritance.

CHAPTER III

The Tudor Princes

The sixteenth century was a hiatus in the history of the Princes of Wales. After the death of Arthur in 1502, his brother Henry held the title for just five years, after which there was no further Prince for the remainder of the century. Arthur's death was a shattering event in England, although overshadowed in the eyes of later historians by the achievements and eccentricities of Henry VIII. After the birth of Henry VII's sixth child, Edmund, in 1499, only one son who lived more than a few weeks was born in the Tudor line of succession. Why the future Edward VI was never created Prince of Wales remains something of a mystery, although it seems clear that he would have been so promoted if his father had not died when he was nine years old. Henry VIII's elder daughter, Mary, was treated as Princess for about four years, but never invested, while her younger half-sister, Elizabeth, was declared illegitimate from the third year of her life until she actually came to the throne. Perhaps the absence of a Prince assisted the process of change, because between 1525 and 1545 the whole structure of government in Wales was revolutionized. The Principality ceased to be a quasi-feudal Lordship, and the title 'Prince of Wales' became a badge of honour worn by future heirs of England.

Henry VII's title to the throne was slight. His mother, Margaret Beaufort, was the daughter of John, Duke of Somerset, himself the grandson of John of Gaunt through his third marriage to Katherine Swynford. Unfortunately, Katherine had been John's mistress long before they were married, and the son through whom the Duke traced his descent had actually been born out of wedlock. Their subsequent union had legitimated him for normal purposes of inheritance, but Richard II (and the Pope) had decreed that that did not extend to the Crown.[1] Strictly speaking, therefore, Henry had no claim to the English throne at all. He would have had a better claim to the throne of France, if it had not been for the Salic law, which forbade the transmission of any claim through a female line. His paternal grandmother had been Catherine, the daughter of Charles VI and widow of Henry V. In 1485 his title to the throne rested on three things: selective amnesia about the Beaufort inheritance, the fact that he was male, adult and of proven competence, and (most important) that he had defeated and killed a childless Richard III at Bosworth.

Henry strengthened his political position substantially by his marriage in January 1486 to Elizabeth, the eldest daughter of Edward IV. She had a far stronger claim than he did, and there was no Salic law in England, but she had not led a victorious army, and it remained the custom that a man would always be preferred to a woman if there were an eligible candidate in sight. It was to prove a fruitful and happy union, and when their first son was born on 19 September 1486 he was the undoubted heir to the houses of both York and Lancaster. He was also the heir to the bardic traditions of Wales, and for that reason was named Arthur after that legendary forebear who had ruled over all Britain, and beyond.[2] The name had not been used in the royal family since the ill-fated nephew of King John had borne it in the early thirteenth century, and its choice at this time was undoubtedly significant of the King's thinking.

Arthur was born at St Swithun's Priory, Winchester, and baptized on 24 September in the cathedral, that ancient seat of English royalty, amid great pomp and rejoicing. Significantly his maternal grandmother, the dowager Queen Elizabeth, stood as godmother. He was judged to be Duke of Cornwall from birth, and was created Earl of Chester and Prince of Wales on 29 November 1489. At first Arthur had no household in the proper sense, but rather a nursery, located at Farnham and headed by Dame Elizabeth Darcy, who had performed the same office for Edward IV's younger offspring. It was not until 1489 that male servants began to be mentioned, and it would appear that the creation of a full household was linked with his knighting and creation as Prince.[3]

A council was immediately established for him, along the lines of that which had existed for the young Edward V, only on this occasion it was not headed by the Queen, either formally or informally. It was led by Henry's uncle, Jasper Tudor, Duke of Bedford, who, in his capacity as Earl of Pembroke was a powerful man in the Marches in his own right, and who had been close to Henry since the latter's birth at

Pembroke in 1457. Beginning in March 1490, the King entered into indentures with the officers of the royal Lordships in Wales, whereby they were bound to suppress felonies, and the council was given the responsibility to see that these contracts were observed. All persons from the royal Lordships seeking redress of grievance were to address themselves to the Prince or his council.[4] By 1493 Arthur had been given the same judicial powers that his predecessor had exercised, with authority to appoint to all commissions in the Principality and the Marches, including those of Oyer and Terminer, powers of array, flight of criminals and enquiry into liberties claimed.

> Power during pleasure to Arthur, Prince of Wales, Duke of Cornwall and Earl of Chester and Flint to appoint the king's justices of Oyer and Terminer in the counties of Salop, Hereford, Gloucester and Worcester, and in the marches of Wales adjoining those counties, and in Wales; to array men at arms, archers and other fencible men there for the defence of his person and the resistance of ill doers and for coming to the king if he sends for them, for putting the laws in execution. Power to him also to have retainers of cloths or badges, or by oaths notwithstanding the statutes. Commission to him also to enquire what offices ought to be forfeited because of the non-lawful discharge thereof, with power to appoint to the same when so forfeited. Power to him also to substitute others under him to execute the premises....
>
> Commission during pleasure to Arthur Prince of Wales to be King's justice to enquire by jury of the marches of Wales, of all liberties, privileges and franchises in the possession of any person whatsoever which in future from any causes or defects ought to be seized into the king's hands; of all usurpations of liberties, privileges and franchises, and of all escapes of thieves and felons in the said marches, with power to substitute others. [20 March 1493][5]

At the same time most of the Crown's Marcher Lordships were transferred to the Prince, who thus became the greatest Lord in the region. As the Prince was only six years old at the time, it is to be understood that his council, which was, in effect, the King's council in the Marches, exercised these powers. In spite of his Presidency, and the trust in which he was held by the King, Jasper Tudor was bound by similar indentures. Jasper died in 1495, and Arthur did not take up residence at

Ludlow until after his marriage in November 1501, at which point William Smyth, Bishop of Lincoln, was constituted President. In spite of these apparently sweeping powers, the council did not resolve the problems of governing Wales, because it only operated between Lordships, or when a Lord's authority had manifestly broken down. It did not have the authority to intervene within Lordships, except by invoking the Lord's indentures, which it was clearly reluctant to do. It was in short a very conservative arrangement, trying to work with the grain of private interests, and not to supersede them. This was true even within the Principality, where it was normally very cautious in respecting the traditional rights of established officials. Although it was a step towards the establishment of greater central control, it was a very small step, and one that faltered seriously when the King was looking the other way.

Meanwhile, the Prince was also being used in other ways. In May 1490 he was appointed Warden General of the Marches against Scotland.[6] Like the Principality of Wales, this was a symbol rather than a function, and the man who really ran the Marches for the King was Thomas Howard, Earl of Surrey, ostensibly Arthur's deputy. The Prince was also named to a large number of special commissions, not because he was expected to sit on any of them, but as an indication of Henry's interest and concern with their proceedings. When the King went briefly to France in 1492, his elder son was named as tradition demanded, 'Keeper of England', a function that was in fact discharged by John Morton, his Chancellor and Archbishop of Canterbury. Fond as he was of his wife, Henry never gave her responsibilities of this kind, perhaps for fear of awakening inconvenient Yorkist sentiments.

P ower to Arthur, Prince of Wales, Duke of Cornwall and Earl of
Chester, as Keeper of England and the King's Lieutenant there,
to grant licences to elect to conventual, but not to cathedral, chapters,
to assent to elections, to make restitution of temporalities and receive
faculties on election of minor prelates, but not to the great prelates
without the king's command; and to present to benefices not exceeding the taxation of forty marks; churches of the taxation of twenty
marks and under to which the Chancellor is accustomed to present,
being excepted.

Appointment of the said Prince as Keeper of England and the King's

Lieutenant there, while the King is in remote parts. By the King.

Power to the said Prince to appoint a fitting person to hold the pleas of the Marshalsea, which the king wills shall be held in the presence of the said Prince. By the King. 2 October 1492[7]

Meanwhile Arthur, upon whom all these weighty expectations were focusing, was actually living in his extensive household, tracking the court around the Home Counties, and working at his books. John Rede, the former headmaster of Winchester, was his first tutor, appointed in 1491. He was followed after a few years by Bernard André (the poet laureate and a notable defender of the dynasty) and subsequently by Thomas Linacre.[8] There are no indications in the surviving evidence that the Prince was a particularly diligent or apt pupil, but he was very thoroughly taught.[9] We can probably get the best idea of the regime he followed by looking at his younger brother Henry, who in later life was an accomplished Latinist and a competent theologian and musician, as well as being a fine athlete. In 1499, when Erasmus visited Eltham Palace, the nine-year-old Henry did the honours, and provoked a celebrated ode from the distinguished visitor on the virtues of the royal family. Arthur does not appear to have shared his brother's athleticism, but their curriculum was no doubt much the same. How much interest the King took in the progress of his offspring we do not really know, and it is generally thought that the motivator behind this strict schooling was actually their paternal grandmother, Margaret Beaufort, who was both intellectual and forceful. This was an influence that the Queen is alleged to have resented.[10]

Education was intended to fit Arthur for the throne, and after about 1496 would have included lessons in statecraft, thinly disguised as classical history. However, an even more important rite of passage, under consideration since he was in his cradle, was his marriage. Henry had at first two main objectives in his foreign policy. The first was to secure the recognition of his dynasty by as many contemporary sovereigns as possible, and the second was to check the ambitions of France.[11] He was well aware that it had been French support that had brought Henry VI back to the English throne in 1470, and had no desire to see Charles VIII using Yorkist pretenders to put pressure on him. Consequently, when Breton independence came under threat after the death of Duke Francis in 1488, Henry signed the treaty of Redon on 14 February

1489 with the intention of frustrating Charles's intention to marry his heiress, Anne.[12] This failed, but the King did gain the implicit recognition of Charles VIII, and the latter's agreement to expel Perkin Warbeck from his territories.

Relations with Scotland were complicated by the unstable condition of that country. A three-year truce was agreed on 3 July 1486, and various marriage arrangements were discussed, but these were aborted by rebellion and by the assassination of James III on 11 June 1488. For several years the most that could be obtained were short-lived truces, and it was not until June 1495 that commissioners were appointed to negotiate a full peace, to be sealed by a marriage between James IV and Margaret, Henry's eldest daughter. These negotiations were stalled by James's support for Perkin Warbeck in 1496, but resumed in July 1497 when James had realized the error of his ways. The truce of Ayton resulted in February 1498, and a full treaty of peace (the first since 1328) followed in January 1502. In August 1503 James and Margaret were married, and the resulting friendship lasted for 10 years.[13]

Arthur had not featured in any of these negotiations, because as early as March 1488 he had been earmarked to seal a treaty of friendship between Henry and Ferdinand and Isabella of Spain. A Spaniard who had been sent to inspect the 18-month-old Prince reported him to be a child of exceptional promise. The Trastámara were one of the most ancient ruling houses of Europe, and the bestowal of a daughter upon the upstart Tudors would constitute the ultimate seal of approval. Ferdinand was in no hurry because his daughter Catherine was barely three, but an agreement in principle was reached at Medina del Campo in March 1489, and ratified in 1493. Henry's signed copy is now held in the National Archives, together with the magnificent seal of Ferdinand and Isabella (E30/615).

There the matter stuck until October 1496, but in the meanwhile Arthur could not be deployed in other negotiations for fear of disturbing the agreement. Finally the new treaty was ratified on 18 July 1497, but even then matters progressed slowly. The couple were married by proxy on 19 May 1499, at the Prince's manor of Bewdley and in the presence of the Spanish ambassador, Dr de Puebla. Arthur professed his 'deep and sincere love for the Princess, his wife'—who, of course, he had not yet met—and a further treaty of alliance was ratified on 10 July in London.[14] After another proxy marriage in November 1500, the 15-year-old Catherine finally reached England in October 1501, landing at Plymouth after a journey fraught with perils and delays. From there she progressed by easy stages to Exeter, and was greeted by the Earl and Countess of Surrey at Amesbury. In defiance of Spanish etiquette, the King and Prince Arthur met her on the way, declaring in response to protests that she was now an English subject. What Catherine made of this situation we do not know, but Arthur and the King seem to have been favourably impressed. No disputes were allowed to disrupt the plans, and she was (at last) personally wedded to Arthur on 14 November.

The ceremony was worth waiting for, because the City of London had been given plenty of notice that something very special in the way of pageantry would be required. As early as November 1499 a special committee of eight City dignitaries had been set up to talk to the royal officials about 'the receiving of the princess that by God's grace shall be coming out of Spain', and six 'stations' or pageants had been projected.[15] It is not known who choreographed these stations, but they were to prove the most complex and original ever staged in England.

The whole series was given a firm underlying plan. The theme was the quest for honour, and the material drawn from the forthcoming marriage, featuring the persons of the bride and groom. The first two scenes presented the quest, demonstrating that honour could be achieved only through a life of virtue. Pageant number one introduced the theme, and the persons of Arthur and Catherine, while number two concentrated on the latter, showing her proceeding in the company of Policy, Noblesse and Virtue, each represented by an actor.[16] The speech of Alphonse gives a flavour of the event.

> *Longa rescarcito Arthuri post tempore Regno*
> *Huc te ventuurum Sidera prodiderant.*
> Daughter Katherine, I, Alphonse remember
> Certain constellations passed many a day
> Showing a goodly princess young and tender
> Of mine own issue should from her own country
> Towards north west take a great journey;
> And to a noble Prince should there married be
> Aspiring to honour and dignity
> Daughter the same signifier of kings

Entering the saggitary and his triplicitie
To whose conjunction approximate is
Esperous and Arthur, the signifier as we see
For the more part in the same house to be
   [These are astrological allusions]
Lo! Lady Katherine these tokens signify
What dignities ye shall obtain, where and why.[17]

Number three consisted of favourable prognostications for the couple —long life and healthy children as well as honour—while number four built up the bridegroom in the same way as number two had built up the bride. The fifth pageant was in general praise of marriage, while the sixth emphasized again the link between virtue and honour. Each pageant was full of subtle allusions, and double and treble significances, which only someone with a first-class Renaissance education could possibly have followed. Although presented in the popular forum of the London streets, the whole series was an exercise in courtly intellectualism, and was deliberately designed to flatter the first-class education that the bride was known to have enjoyed.[18] Arthur may well have had difficulty in keeping up. Many of the concepts used were fundamental to medieval cosmological thinking, but were here presented with great ingenuity.

Although it could be argued that the thinking was not particularly profound—and much of the verse was execrable—the general effect was both clever and impressive. The question of who would have been impressed at the time is, however, more difficult to answer. Visually the meaning would have communicated itself readily to anyone with sufficient education, including most of Catherine's entourage. However, with the exception of scriptural citations all the dialogue was delivered in English, a language that hardly any Spaniard spoke, except for the merchants resident in London. In spite of the fact that she had long been destined for this country, it is by no means clear that Catherine herself had more than a few words.[19] Of the spectators who had the intellect to understand, very few would have had the language; and of those who had the language, very few would have had the intellect. Nevertheless it is clear that the effort was warmly appreciated, and no confusion was allowed to disturb the long prepared nuptials that followed.

The celebrations continued for nearly a month, and all those who recorded their impressions put the best possible gloss upon the occasion, one even commenting that the King looked old beyond his years, in an obvious reference to Arthur's hoped-for accession. He was, they all agreed, a youth of great promise, and far more popular than his father—a sentiment familiar to all those who have explored the history of the relationship between monarchs and their sons! Henry himself reported to Ferdinand and Isabella that the whole people were rejoicing. There were tournaments in the lists at Westminster, where the tree of chivalry was set up for the first time, processions of disguised knights, pageants, and even a Spanish acrobat for light relief. It was by far the most lavish celebration of the reign, and one which Henry (understandably) never had the heart to repeat.

After the wedding there may well have been some debate as to where the couple should live, but Arthur was now 15 and Catherine nearly 16, so there was no reason why they should not begin to cohabit immediately. The King, moreover, was anxious to link his son's new status with the imposition of his personal authority in Wales and the Marches, so it was decreed that the newlyweds should reside at Ludlow. Arthur had certainly visited the Marches before—he is known to have been in Shrewsbury in 1494—but he had not lived there for any length of time.[20] Now, however, his household became clearly detached from the court, and Sir Richard Pole, his Chamberlain, had a suitably independent command. Sir Richard was the King's kinsman of the half blood, and his wife Margaret was the daughter of the Duke of Clarence, niece to King Edward IV and sister of the ill-fated Earl of Warwick, an unfortunate inconvenience to both Richard III and Henry VII. There could have been no more appropriate person to lead the ladies now appointed to attend upon the Princess of Wales.

Arthur's household was appropriately enlarged, and his council reorganized to cope with the fact that he himself would now be expected to play a more dominant role. Alas for all such plans, and for the cheerful prognostications offered before their marriage! Not long after returning to Wales, and before his presence could make any significant difference to the government of the country, Arthur became ill, and on 2 April 1502 he died at Ludlow, probably of pneumonia. He was buried with great pomp at Worcester Cathedral on St George's Day, and his father built a magnificent chantry chapel for him on the south side of the high altar. He and Catherine had lived together long enough before illness overtook him to leave the question of whether the marriage had been consummated an open one. This was a doubt that was to return later like an ill-omened spectre, but it was not unnoticed at the time.[21] The Princess herself was less positive (or negative) on the subject than she later became, but that may have been simply because she did not want to cast any aspersions upon her late husband's virility. Immediately after Arthur's death it was even being speculated that he might have left her pregnant, but time soon resolved that uncertainty. Both his widow and his devastated parents were left to pick up the pieces. We do not (and cannot) know what the consequences might have been if he had survived, but if the Prince of Wales had become King, and if Catherine had borne him a son, England's whole subsequent history would have been very different.

Henry, who for a few weeks in 1500 had actually had three sons, now had just one.[22] His dynastic ambitions hung by that thread, and in spite of their distress and of Elizabeth's advancing years (she was now 36) they decided to repair the damage. The Queen became pregnant, but in February 1503 she was delivered of a daughter who lived only a few days, and died herself in the effort. The King was genuinely heartbroken, and his dutiful but somewhat perfunctory negotiations for remarriage are outside the scope of this book. In the immediate aftermath of Arthur's death, two other things happened. Ferdinand and Isabella sent an ambassador to Henry to demand Catherine's return as soon as possible, together with the 100,000 *scudi* (about £35,000) which had formed the first instalment of her marriage portion, and for good measure control of the lands which had been assigned for her dower, amounting to one-third of the revenues of Wales, Cornwall and Chester. However, to apply the carrot as well as the stick, and more reflective of their real purpose, was the instruction to negotiate a new marriage for Catherine to Arthur's brother, the 12-year-old Henry, and to come to terms over the dower and marriage portion.[23] It was recognized that this would require a papal dispensation because it was within the prohibited degrees of consanguinity, but the treaty itself was quickly drafted in September 1502, and formally ratified a year later. A copy of this treaty is also now held in the National Archives (E30/694).

The second development was the creation of Henry as Prince of Wales on 18 February 1504. Unlike Arthur, Henry did not take up residence at Ludlow, perhaps because of its unhealthy reputation, and his functioning as Prince seems to have been entirely formal. The council had managed to discharge its functions (after a fashion) in the 21 months since Arthur's death, and it is not at all clear that this new appointment made very much difference. Henry surrendered the lands of the Duchy of York, which he had held hitherto, and received instead the full patrimony of the heir to the throne. However, this was all more apparent than real because the issues from these lands continued to be paid into the King's coffers for his own use.[24] The new Prince's establishment, like Arthur's before it, was a charge on the treasury of the Chamber. The King did not neglect Wales, but his policies required no input from his son.

Soon after Henry's creation as Prince, the King began to use his prerogative of dispensation to modify the penalties provided by the anti-Welsh statutes going back to 1401. These had prohibited Welshmen from owning property in England or the English boroughs of Wales, and had forbidden them to bear arms. No Englishman was to be convicted at the suit of a Welshman, except in an English court, and Welshmen were barred from a whole range of offices. Most of these statutes had been confirmed as recently as 1447, and Henry did not attempt to repeal them—possibly sensing that raising such an issue in parliament might have the opposite of the desired effect. Instead he dispensed certain communities in North Wales from these penalties. Seven such dispensations were granted in all, starting immediately after the creation of the young Henry as Prince. On 28 October 1504 the inhabitants of the Principality Counties of Caernarfon and Merioneth were allowed to acquire lands and tenements within England, to become burgesses, and to hold their lands in Wales by English law, notwithstanding the statutes.[25]

Over the next three years similar privileges were granted to the inhabitants of the Lordships of Bromefield and Yale, Chirk, Denbigh, Cynmeirch and the County of Anglesey. The restriction on the conviction of Englishmen before Welsh courts was lifted, and in June 1508 all these privileges were extended to the Lordship of Ruthin. Although the statutes in question were not to be repealed until 1624, they effectively became dead letters in respect of North Wales by the end of Henry VII's reign.[26] Why this liberal policy was not extended to the south of the Principality or to the southern Lordships we do not know.

Perhaps in that rather more anglicized region other ways had already been found of circumventing the strict letter of the law. Henry remained keenly aware of the debt of gratitude that he owed to his subjects in Wales, and exempted a number of his individual servants from the restrictions on holding English lands and offices well before he began to grant these more general charters.[27] However, he never seems to have found it necessary to revisit the Principality, nor did the Prince of Wales do so after 1502. Insofar as he was motivated by Welsh sentiment, Henry confined himself to these dispensations and, in respect of government, in general stuck close to Yorkist precedent.

Henry, Prince of Wales was physically much more conspicuous than his brother had been. Born in June 1491, the third child of his parents, he was created Duke of York in October 1494. In the same year he had been named as the King's Lieutenant in Ireland, a position that he continued to hold until his accession in 1509, but he never visited the Lordship and his role there, as in Wales, was purely symbolic. He had inherited the magnificent physique of his maternal grandfather (Edward IV), and that was already apparent by the time that he had reached the age of 14. After 1502 he was the heir to the throne, and for that reason the King seems to have curbed his natural athleticism. Field sports could be dangerous, and too much hung upon Henry's life. He was encouraged to play tennis, to run at the ring and to shoot with the longbow, and professional coaches were employed to teach him, but the much more perilous exercise of jousting was forbidden, just as his later successors were to be forbidden to risk themselves in war.[28] From the skill and enthusiasm with which he began to tilt immediately after his accession, it may be suspected that this ban was more notable in the breach than the observance, but he certainly never jousted in public before 1509.

Similarly, his political training remained strictly theoretical. He read Caesar and Polybius assiduously, but took part in no campaign, and as far as we know did not even control the patronage that in theory belonged to his offices in Wales and Ireland. He was later described with some exaggeration as having been kept from the world like a young girl—under the influence of his tutor John Skelton—when he could have been establishing his credentials for government.[29] He was virtually confined to the schoolroom, although the boisterous companionship of other boys such as Charles Brandon and Edward Neville must have offered some compensation. The reason for this relative seclusion is obscure, but as the King's health began to fail after 1507, he may have been more than a little apprehensive of his magnificent son—a sentiment that Henry IV might well have appreciated. Obsessed with his own control, the king wanted no challenge, even by implication. The Prince's time would come, and it would not do him any harm to wait.

A similar attitude can be seen in the King's attitude to his son's marriage. As we have seen, a treaty for his union with Catherine had been quickly signed, and the necessary papal dispensation was obtained in the following year. However, it appears that the driving force behind this negotiation on the Spanish side had been Isabella rather than Ferdinand, and with her death on 26 November 1504 the political landscape changed. She had been Queen of Castile in her own right, and her heir was not her husband, but their daughter Juana. Juana, however, was away in the Low Countries, married to Philip, son of the Emperor Maximilian, and the mother of his sons. Ferdinand tried to use this circumstance to create a position for himself in Castile, and a party among the nobility there supported him.[30] However, if he succeeded in obstructing the succession of Philip and Juana, the next heir was not himself, but Catherine, unwed and eligible, but in England. Marriage or no marriage, Ferdinand went off the whole idea of bringing his daughter home.

At the same time, it seemed to Henry that England's interests would be better served by allying with Philip and Juana rather than the much-diminished Ferdinand. When Prince Henry reached the age of 14 (the canonical age for cohabitation by boys) in 1505, his father caused him to repudiate the agreement on the ground that he had not been consulted, and in 1506 the King signed the *Magnus Intercursus* with Philip.[31] What the Prince's real attitude to the now somewhat forlorn Catherine may have been, we do not know—but from the speed with which he picked her up in 1509 we may guess that he found her attractive. The political wheel, however, had not come to rest, because before the end of 1506 Philip was dead and Juana (it was conveniently alleged) had become deranged. With Catherine still safely stuck in England, this enabled Ferdinand to re-establish himself in Castile, where he remained—notionally as regent for his daughter, but effectively King—until his own death in 1516.

The dowager Princess of Wales meanwhile sustained herself in exile as best she could. In spite of theoretically holding her dower lands in Wales and Chester, she seems to have been permanently short of money and emotionally starved of companionship.[32] She took refuge in her religious observances, and in the consequent conviction that it was the will of God that she should marry Prince Henry. Whether this was simple piety, or based on surreptitious signals from him, we do not know. In 1507 Ferdinand formally accredited her as his ambassador in England. This was an unprecedented appointment for a woman, and gave her for about two years much needed status and resources.[33] Her father was an exceptionally clever politician, and chose this unusual way to harness both her enthusiasm and her undoubted intelligence. The fact that she soon became bogged down in the negotiations for a marriage between Henry VII's youngest daughter, Mary (then aged 11) and Ferdinand's grandson Charles (aged 7), and had to ask for support, was more a reflection of the deviousness of both monarchs than of any lack of ability on her part. As a result of these duties her command of the English language improved dramatically.

Henry died on 21 April 1509, at the relatively normal age of 52, and the wraps were suddenly and dramatically taken off the Prince of Wales. He in turn immediately announced that he would marry his sister-in-law, alleging his father's deathbed injunction, and all the lingering doubts about the validity of the dispensation and about financial arrangements, were suddenly swept aside. Catherine's pious conviction was dramatically vindicated, to the obvious astonishment of all the allegedly well-informed observers — including her own father. In due course this vindication was to be of crucial importance. They were crowned together on Midsummer's Day, like characters in a fairy tale, and for the time being seemed extremely happy with each other. While Henry VIII went about the business of asserting himself, confirming his council, and seeking a pretext for war with France, Catherine went about the equally serious matter of providing him with children.

Unfortunately, that proved to be a fruitless quest. She conceived promptly, within three months of their marriage, but the child that she bore on May 1510 was a stillborn girl.[34] In itself that was no more than a minor setback, but worse was to follow. With admirable persistence, Catherine was pregnant again within weeks, and their second child, born in February 1511, was alive, and a boy. The sound of rejoicing was deafening, but premature. Young Henry was immediately referred to as

Prince of Wales, although there was no time for his creation. Within a month he was dead, and a shadow fell between the happy couple. Henry probably took a mistress, but that was almost expected and Queens were inured to such developments.[35] In 1513 she became pregnant again, but this time miscarried, and there were rumours of divorce, reinforced by the fact that the King was seriously disenchanted with his father-in-law. Ferdinand had persuaded Henry to send an expeditionary force to Gascony, ostensibly with the aim of recovering that province for England, but had then left it high and dry while he seized Navarre, after which he had signed a separate peace with Louis XII, leaving the King of England to retrieve his army and nurse his sense of grievance.

However, there was no divorce, nor any serious talk of it, and Henry and Catherine persevered. At length in February 1516 they were rewarded with a child who lived and thrived. Unfortunately it was a girl, who was named Mary, and although her birth was celebrated with feasts, the planned tournament was cancelled and the vital question of the succession remained unresolved.[36] At first the King put a brave face on it, speaking hopefully of the boys who 'by God's Grace' would follow, but when Catherine miscarried again in 1519, he began to despair. Nor was his attitude towards his wife improved by the fact that his mistress, Elizabeth Blount, bore him a healthy son at almost exactly the same time.[37] This demonstrated to his way of thinking that his lack of a legitimate heir was all Catherine's fault. She was 35, her looks were fading and she was beginning to run to fat. She may well have passed the menopause at about this time, because she did not conceive again, and by 1525 it was clear that she would not, and could not, provide the King with the son which he so desperately needed.

It was in this context that Henry created his illegitimate son Duke of Richmond (a royal title that his grandfather had held as Earl) and appointed him Lieutenant of the North. At the same time his nine-year-old daughter, Mary, was sent to Ludlow with a magnificent household and a new council. An intriguing memorandum, dating from 18 August 1525, reveals the amount of elegant fabric allocated to the various attendants who were to establish her new home.

The names of all the ladies and gentlewomen who are to accompany the Princess into Wales with the quantity of the black velvet allowed to each.

Lady Salisbury; Lady Katherine Grey; Mrs Katherine Montague; Mrs Elizabeth Poole; Mrs Constance Poole; Mrs Anne Knevett; Mrs Dannet; Mrs Baker; Mrs Cecill Dabridgecourt; Mrs Frances Elmer; Mrs Anne Rede; Mrs Marie Wyncter; Mrs Peter; Mrs Anne Dannet; and Mrs Anne Darrell. Mrs Parker and Mrs Geynes are to have black damask. [Memorandum in the margin of the delivery of the velvet to each of the ladies by Mr. Leg, J. Scutte, Mr. Wheeler and Ric. Hage. Signed by Wolsey][38]

She was not created Princess of Wales because Henry was keeping his options on the succession open, but she was treated in every way as though she were, and was sometimes even referred to in that way.[39] Her household was presided over by the same Margaret Pole who had headed Catherine's establishment nearly a quarter of a century earlier. She was long since widowed and since 1513 had been Countess of Salisbury in her own right.

We have a fair amount of information about the Princess's years in the Marches, including a reasonably informative itinerary.[40] She was undoubtedly the focus of much demonstrative loyalty, and was of course recognized as the King's heir, but was too young to play any effective part in the administration that she nominally headed. In fact her tutor, Richard Featherstone, seems to have kept her assiduously at her books. It should be emphasized that Mary was at this point still the heir to the throne, and although not given the same education as would have been accorded to a boy, she was taught to the highest standard and out of the latest guides and texts. She was a bright child, and already fluent in Latin and French before she returned from the Marches.

If she had the company of any children of her own age, however, it has escaped the record. It is possible that some of those masquerading as ladies and gentlewomen of her Privy Chamber may in fact have been young female companions, but boys of her own age would have been strictly excluded. Her mother (and her Lady Governess) had very strict views about the corrupting nature of male company, and the instructions given to the latter in July 1525 about the Princess's moral and academic education were clear.

That is to say at due times to serve God, from whom all grace and goodness proceedeth. Semblably at seasons convenient to use

1 This illuminated manuscript of the fourteenth century shows Edward I creating his son, Edward of Caernarvon, Prince of Wales. The ceremony, which took place at the Lincoln parliament on 7 February 1301, features as part of the Latin chronicle *Flores Historiarum*.

2 The elaborate tomb of Edward the Black Prince in Canterbury Cathedral. Edward was Prince of Wales for 33 years and held magnificent court in Bordeaux, but he died aged 45 without ever acceding to the throne.

3 (*Right*) Henry IV's address at the creation of his son as Prince of Wales on 15 October 1399 was recorded in the contemporary Charter roll. It provided a valuable precedent for Prince Edward's ceremony in 1911, and this twentieth-century typescript formed part of the preparations. (TNA PC8/706).

4 (*Below*) The daily expenses of the household of Henry, Prince of Wales are listed on this parchment roll. His early years in the position were dominated by conflict in Wales, which proved a severe strain on his resources. (TNA E 101/406/2)

5 (*Opposite*) A rare depiction of Edward of Middleham, son of Richard III and Prince of Wales from 1483 to 1484. The Prince holds a sceptre and is portrayed standing upon his father's badge of the white boar, while the Royal Arms of England are set above.

CREATION BY HEN.IV. OF HIS SON AS PRINCE OF WALES, DUKE OF
CORNWALL, AND EARL OF CHESTER — CHARTER,R. C. V.129.

Henry, by the Grace of God, &c., say to all, &c. greeting. Know ye that of our special grace and of our certain knowledge and with the counsel and assent of the Prelates, Dukes, Earls, Barons, and Commonalties of our Realm of England in our instant Parliament being assembled at Westminster, we have made and created Henry, our very dear eldest son, Prince of Wales, Duke of Cornwall, and Earl of Chester, and have given and granted, and by our charter confirmed, to him the said Principality, Dukedom, and Earldom, and invested him with the same Principality, Dukedom, and Earldom so that being preferred he may preside there, and presiding may rule and defend the said parts by a coronet on his head and a gold ring on his finger and a gold staff according to the custom; to have and to hold of us to him and his heirs Kings of England for ever. Wherefore we will and firmly command for us and our heirs that the aforesaid Henry, our son, shall have and hold of us the Principality, Dukedom, and Earldom aforesaid, to him and his heirs Kings of England for ever as it aforesaid. These being witnesses: (&c.) ...

Given by our hand at Westminster, the 15th day of October.

By the King himself.

(R.C. third Report, p. 195.).

England

Ireland

Walys

by the grace of god kynge
of yreloud by veray mary
... dethlynde yn the ladde
fro kynge harre the secod
inheytyo In hys realme fil
... of hys lawes specyally
omyo and cherisshynge tho
... ycte myndynge he gat gret
... hettys wysely and sore and

The noble and myghty pryce · edward pryce of walys duke also
of comwale And corle of chestyr son & eyre to the moost hye &
excelent pryce · kynge Rychard the thyrd and hys moost noble
lady and wyfe · Quene Anne enheryto to bothe Royall possessios
he was borne yn the castell of myddlam in the northcuntre

6 (*Left*) This stained glass window in Great Malvern Priory shows Arthur, eldest son of Henry VII, at prayer. He was a popular Prince of Wales and his wedding to Catherine of Aragon saw widespread rejoicing, but he was to die in Ludlow in 1502, aged only 15.

7 (*Below*) The treaty between Henry VII and Ferdinand and Isabella of Spain for the marriage of Arthur, Prince of Wales, with their youngest daughter Catherine, 8 March 1493. (TNA E30/615)

8 The mighty seal of Ferdinand and Isabella attached to the marriage treaty. (TNA E30/615)

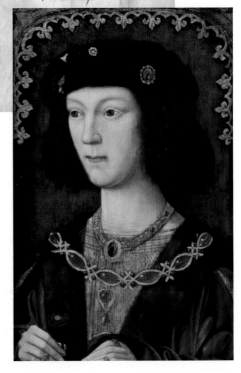

9 (*Above*) In 1533 a notarial exemplification (upper part) of the 1503 marriage treaty between Henry, Prince of Wales, and Catherine (lower part) was undertaken. The lawyers sought legal grounds to enable Henry VIII to put aside his Queen. (E30/695)

10 Henry succeeded his brother as Prince of Wales in 1504. This portrait, dating from *c.*1509, shows him as a beardless youth holding the Tudor rose.

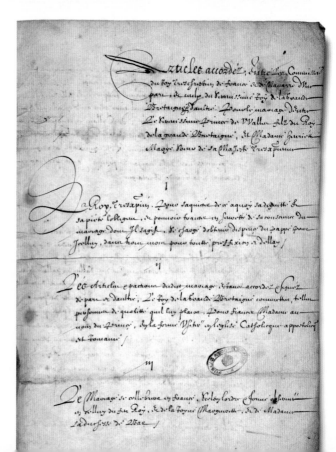

11 (*Above left*) Henry, Prince of Wales and Robert Devereux, 3rd Earl of Essex on the hunting field in a painting by Robert Peake the Elder. Henry relished physical activities and sports, and was often depicted bearing a sword.

12 (*Above right*) Prince Charles, Henry's younger brother, in a painting by Daniel Mytens from the early 1620s. A dignified and abstemious young man, he was very different in temperament and physique to his brother.

13 The treaty between England and France for the marriage of Charles, Prince of Wales, and Henrietta Maria, sister of the French King. The wedding took place in May 1625 after Charles's lengthy courtship of the Infanta Maria had failed. (TNA SP 108 544)

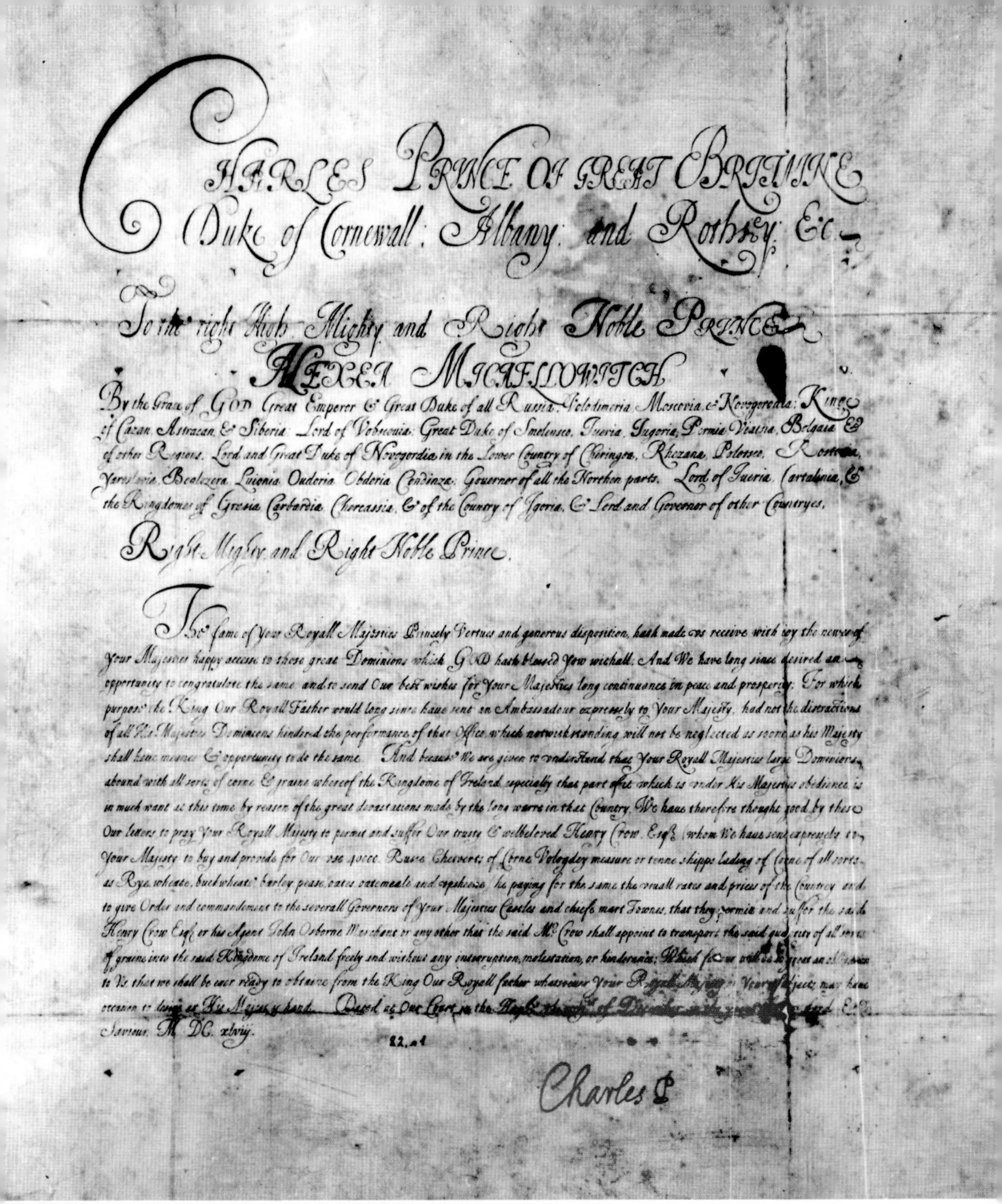

CHARLES PRINCE OF GREAT BRITTAINE
Duke of Cornewall: Albany: and Rothsey: &c.

To the right High Mighty and Right Noble PRINCE
ALEXEI MICHAELLOWITCH

By the Grace of GOD Great Emperor & Great Duke of all Russia: Volodimeria Moscovia & Novogrodia: King of Cazan Astracan & Siberia: Lord of Vobscovia: Great Duke of Smolensco, Tveria, Jugoria, Permia Viatka, Bolgaria & of other Regions. Lord and Great Duke of Novogordia in the Lower Country of Cheringra, Rhezana, Polotsco, Rostova, Yeroslavia, Beolezera, Livonia, Ouderia, Obderia, Condinza: Governer of all the Northen parts. Lord of Iueria, Cartalinia, & the Kingdomes of Grusia Carbardia, Cheracassia, & of the Country of Igoria, & Lord and Governer of other Countryes,

Right Mighty and Right Noble Prince.

The fame of Your Royall Majesties Princely Vertues and generous disposition, hath made us receive with joy the newes of Your Majesties happy accesse to those great Dominions which GOD hath blessed You withall. And We have long since desired an opportunity to congratulate the same, and to send Our best wishes for Your Majesties long continuance in peace and prosperity: For which purpose the King Our Royall Father would long since have sent an Ambassadour expressely to Your Majesty, had not the distractions of all His Majesties Dominions hindered the performance of that Office, which notwithstanding will not be neglected as soone as his Majesty shall have meanes & opportunity to do the same. And because We are given to understand that Your Royall Majesties large Dominions abound with all sorts of corne & graine whereof the Kingdome of Ireland, especially that part of it which is under His Majesties obedience, is in much want at this time by reason of the great devastations made by the long warre in that Country, We have therefore thought good by these Our letters to pray Your Royall Majesty to permit and suffer Our trusty & welbeloved Henry Crow Esq. (whom We have sent expressely to Your Majesty) to buy and provide for Our use 40000 Russe Chetverts of Corne Vologdey measure or tonne shipps lading of Corne of all sorts, as Rye, wheate, buckwheate, barley, pease, oates, oatemeale and ... he paying for the same the usuall rates and prices of the Country, and to give Order and commandement to the severall Governors of Your Majesties Castles and chiefe mart Townes, that they permit and suffer the said Henry Crow Esq. or his Agent John Osborne Merchant or any other that the said Mr Crow shall appoint to transport the said quantity of all sorts of graine into the said Kingdome of Ireland freely and without any interruption, molestation, or hinderance; Which favour will be so great an obligation to Us that we shall be ever ready to obtaine from the King Our Royall father whatsoever Your Royall Majesty or Your subjects may have occasion to desire at His Majesties hand. Dated at Our Court in the Hague ... of December in the yeare of Our Lord & Saviour, M. DC. xlviij.

22.a1

Charles P.

14 Never formally created Prince of Wales, the future Charles II fled England during the Civil War and spent years of exile at foreign courts. In this letter to the 'Great Emperor and Great Duke of all Russia', written from The Hague in 1648, Charles is described as the 'Prince of Great Britain, Duke of Cornwall, Albany and Rothesay'. (PRO 22/60/74)

15 A medal commemorating the birth of Prince James, son of James II and Mary of Modena, in 1688. The arrival of the young Prince, widely seen as a Catholic heir, prompted English notables to invite William of Orange, the husband of James's elder daughter Mary, to accept the throne.

16 Rumours and suspicion surrounded the unexpected birth of James's son. This original account of proceedings at an 'extraordinary council' on 22 October 1688 presents the official version of events. (PRO 30/53/11/38)

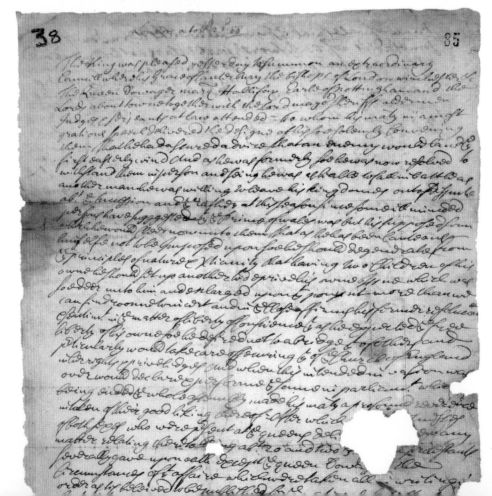

moderate exercise for taking open air in gardens, sweet and
wholesome places and walks which may be unto her health, solace and
comfort.… And likewise to pass her time most seasons at her virginals
or other instruments musical, so that the same be not too much and
without fatigation and weariness. To intend to her learning of Latin
tongue or French. At other seasons to draw [and to take great care of
her diet and personal hygiene.][41]

The reason given for her despatch was alleged to be the difficulty of
governing Wales without a Prince, 'forasmuch as by reason of the long
absence of any prince making continual residence either in the Principality of Wales or the Marches of the same … good order … hath greatly
been altered'.[42] Bishop John Voysey of Exeter presided over Mary's revamped council. The reason for this magnificent (and very expensive)
provision must be sought in Cardinal Wolsey's concern about the 'dark
corners of the land'. Wolsey had been the King's chief adviser since
about 1515, and Lord Chancellor since December of that year. The
domestic policy that he had persuaded the King to adopt was a continu-
ation of Henry VII's, keeping the provincial nobility on a tight leash
and increasing central control by the Crown. The activities of the Duke
of Buckingham in 1520–21 had warned him under both headings.
Buckingham had been far too keen on his own royal ancestry, and a
powerful man in what was still one of the least disciplined parts of the
Kingdom—Wales.[43] He had paid for his indiscretions with his head,
and that had sent a clear warning to other pretentious nobles, but it
had not cured the problem of Wales.

Since Henry's accession the council had continued in existence, but
it had become, in G.R. Elton's words, 'moribund'. Most of the Marcher
Lordships were by this time in the hands either of the Crown or of the
Crown's good servants, but the systems of control were dysfunctional,
and that included the council. Trying to enforce law and order was like
swimming in treacle, with the would-be enforcer bogged down in a
mire of customs, conventions and interests over which he had very little control.[44] Wolsey decided to work with the structures that were
there, and hoped by revitalizing the council to impose the discipline
that he believed had been there in Arthur's time, but that had subsequently been lost. He did not succeed. Voysey proved to be weak in
the face of the intransigence of some of the Welsh gentry, and in the

summer of 1529 Mary was withdrawn, thus weakening the symbolic relationship between the council and the Crown. In the autumn of that year the Cardinal fell from power, and the problem of Wales was left to his successor.

Mary's whole establishment during this tour of duty numbered over 300 persons, and cost in wages alone nearly £750 a year. The total cost was between £3,000 and £4,000 per annum. This was undoubtedly a factor in persuading the King to recall her, but the other was the increasing uncertainty of her position. Faced with the intractable problem of the succession, Henry had decided by 1529 against the possibility of legitimating his son Henry Fitzroy; the whole process was too uncertain, and too open to challenge. He therefore had either to settle for Mary, with all the unprecedented problems that would involve — or to repudiate Catherine and start again.[45] By the end of 1528 he had decided on the latter option, and in 1529 committed the catastrophic blunder of informing Catherine that they had never been married. Because the Queen was totally convinced that their marriage had been made in heaven, she was outraged and declined to 'go quietly' and take the veil. Had she done so, their marriage would have been ended without any doubt being cast on its original lawfulness, or on Mary's legitimacy. Because she refused to do so, however, she left Henry no option but to challenge the lawfulness of their original union, and with it Mary's legitimacy. By the autumn of 1529 he was therefore committed to a position that would make Mary a bastard, and therefore of doubtful use as either a royal representative or a counter in the diplomatic marriage stakes.[46]

However, in spite of proddings from Catherine's intended successor, Anne Boleyn, and her family, by 1530 he had actually done nothing. He still appeared with his wife in public, and a curious *ménage à trois* developed. That situation came to an end in 1531, but it was not until 1533 that Henry finally took the situation by the scruff of the neck. In January Anne was pregnant, and on 23 May the newly installed Archbishop of Canterbury, Thomas Cranmer, declared *in curia suo* that the King's marriage to Catherine was not, and never had been, valid. Ferdinand and Isabella's ratification of their daughter's marriage treaty to Henry, Prince of Wales, was scrutinized by lawyers who produced a notarial exemplification of the document, now held in the National Archives, in February 1533.[47] Cranmer's repudiation of the marriage was in direct defiance of a papal decree, and that necessitated in the following year a formal repudiation of all papal authority in England. Meanwhile Catherine was formally demoted from Queen to Princess Dowager of Wales, a designation that she furiously repudiated, and Mary from Princess to natural daughter. The King's efforts to impose this decision were more successful in the country at large than they were in respect of the two women—both of whom absolutely refused to answer to their new titles.[48] The result was both tragic and farcical, but it effectively ended any pretensions that Mary might have had to the position of Princess of Wales. Catherine died, still in denial, in January 1536, aged 51, but in July of that year Mary submitted. She was eventually restored to the succession—but only after the birth of Edward had appeared to make such a status academic.

Meanwhile the problem of governing Wales still awaited resolution. The King's mind had not changed. Firmer control needed to be applied, but Wolsey's method had failed, and the question remained how to achieve such a goal. As Thomas Cromwell moved from being a principal councillor to Secretary and Chief Minister between 1532 and 1534, he began to consider ways and means. Cromwell was a man unfettered by custom, and prepared to redefine the law to suit himself—or his master.[49] An effective Prince in the Marches was not an available option, and the council without a Prince was not working—or at least not working well enough. In 1534 he replaced John Voysey as President with the more effective Rowland Lee, and in the parliament of the same year put through an Act shifting the trial of murders and other felonies committed within the Marcher Lordships to the sessions of the nearest English shire.[50] At the same time the council was given a more formal structure as an equity court, with increased powers to hear complaints of an extrajudicial nature. Rowland Lee was quick to take advantage of these new powers, and began to conduct an energetic campaign against thefts and murders, packing off as many offenders as he could catch for trial in Shropshire or Gloucestershire.

All this, however, was mere tinkering, and in 1536 Cromwell came up with a radical solution, which was to prove definitive. All franchises within the realms of England and Wales had originally been granted by the Crown, although in many cases that had happened so long ago that the holders considered their rights to be prescriptive. Every so often a franchise escheated to the Crown—that is returned to the King by default of heirs—and rather more frequently franchises were redeemed by the attainder of the holders. In other words there was no doubt that the King remained the feudal overlord of all liberties, no matter how long their continuance. Feudal law did not, however, provide for the resumption of franchises as an act of policy, and it was that lack that the statutes of 1536 now supplied.

Parliament had recently expanded its competence in unprecedented ways. It had already abolished the greatest franchise of them all —the church—bringing ecclesiastical jurisdiction under the King's control.[51] Judged by all previous standards, such acts were *ultra vires*, but they were accepted, and that acceptance established a precedent that was never to be broken. The King had also legislated the order of the succession, not once but twice, and that had also never been done before.[52] The time was therefore ripe for a statute 'recontinuing ... certain Liberties and Franchises heretofore taken from the Crown', which abolished all such immunities and provided that the King's writ should run uniformly throughout the land. All courts hearing pleas of the Crown were from henceforth to be royal courts, and all distinctions of usage were abolished.

> Where divers of the most ancient prerogatives and authorities of justice appertaining to the Imperial Crown of this realm have been severed and taken from the same by sundry gifts of the king's most noble progenitours kings of this realm, to the great diminution and detriment of the royal estate, and to the hindrance and great decay of justice: for reformation whereof be it enacted ... that no person or persons, of what estate or degree soever they be, from the first day of July, which shall be in the year of our Lord God 1536, shall have any power or authority to pardon or remit any treasons, murders, manslaughters or felonies, or any outlawries for any such offences afore rehearsed, committed, perpetrated done or divulged, or hereafter to be committed, done or divulged by or against any person in any part of this realm, Wales or the marches of the same; but that the king's highness, his heirs and successors kings of this realm, shall have the whole and sole power and authority, thereof united and knit to the imperial Crown of this realm....[53]

The greatest franchise to be thus withdrawn was actually the Prince Bishopric of Durham, but other important liberties also disappeared, not least the Duchy of Lancaster.[54] Wales was dealt with separately. First the statute of 27 Henry VIII, cap. 5 laid down that all Justices of the Peace and Gaol Delivery in the existing counties of Chester, Flint, Anglesey, Caernarfon, Merioneth, Cardigan, Carmarthen, Pembroke and Glamorgan—in other words those parts of Wales already under direct royal control—should be appointed by the Lord Chancellor, and not by the Justiciar. This, it was alleged, would curb 'manifold robberies, murders … and trespasses', although in what way is not obvious since the Justiciars were equally operating in the King's name. Perhaps it was felt that the Chancellor was less amenable to local pressure— which would have been true.[55] This was then followed by a further Act, which simply abolished the multiple Lordships that had made up the Marches 'time out of mind'. They were replaced with the new shires of Denbigh, Montgomery, Radnor, Brecknock and Monmouth.

> Albeit the dominion principality and country of Wales justly and righteously is and ever hath been incorporated annexed united and subject to and under the Imperial Crown of this realm, as a very member and joint of the same, whereof the King's most royal majesty of mere droit, and very right, is very head, king, lord and ruler; yet notwithstanding, because that in the same country principality and dominion divers rights, usages, laws and customs be far discrepant from the laws and customs of this realm, and also because that the people of the same dominion have and do daily use a speech nothing like or consonant to the natural mother tongue used within this realm, some rude and ignorant people have made distinction and diversity … whereby great discord variance debate division murmur and sedition hath grown…. It is therefore enacted by authority aforesaid that divers of the lordships marcher shall be united, annexed, and joined to divers of the shires of England; and divers of the said lordships marcher shall be united, annexed and joined to divers of the shires of the said country or dominion of Wales.[56]

The old franchise officers simply disappeared. Each new shire, like the existing ones, was to be under the authority of a Sheriff, and provided with commissions of the peace and of Gaol Delivery. These were to operate on the English pattern, with Quarter Sessions feeding into judicial Assizes.[57] These statutes left some loose ends, and paid no attention whatsoever to the distinctiveness of Wales. The courts were to operate in English; all officials must speak that language. Welsh law was relegated to the Commote courts (equivalent of the courts baron in England), dealing with low-level civil disputes. A further statute in 1543 (34 & 35 Henry VIII, cap.26) went some way towards remedying these defects. The Assize circuits of Wales (except for Monmouthshire) were separated from the Courts at Westminster, and constituted into four Courts of Great Session, which operated independently. The new Sheriffs were also to account, not to Westminster but to existing Exchequers established long since at Caernarfon and Carmarthen, or to new Exchequers erected in Denbigh and Brecknock. Certain formal business was also routed to the Chanceries that existed alongside the Exchequers.[58] Moreover the Council in the Marches was now given statutory authority 'to hear and determine by their wisdoms and discretions such causes and matters as be or hereafter shall be assigned to them by the King's majesty, as heretofore hath been accustomed and used.'

The fiction of a Prince's council was thus finally abandoned in favour of a regional Equity Court, with jurisdiction not only over the whole of Wales as it was now constituted, but also over adjacent English shires, from Chester to Gloucester. Wales was now 'shire ground', and the only difference between English and Welsh counties was that the latter sent only one representative to the House of Commons, and their county towns the same. But Wales did not lose its identity. Its language continued to be the language of the market place, and was soon to be that of the church.[59] Its system of accountability remained distinctive, and above all it retained its own council—which continued to be called the Council in the Marches, although the Marches had now disappeared. Nevertheless by abolishing the Marcher Lordships and by making all justices appointable by the Lord Chancellor, the intractable problems of lawlessness were at last overcome.

After the accession of Henry VIII there were no Tudor Princes of Wales. Mary was a 'virtual Prince' from 1525 to 1529, but after her withdrawal there were no further attempts to govern Wales as a feudal dependency. The system set up for Edward of Caernarfon in 1301, and significantly modified by the creation of a specifically Welsh council for Edward of Westminster in 1471, was finally abandoned in the reforms of 1536–43. (These were not 'Acts of Union' as Wales had been part of the realm of England since 1284, but they were acts of unification, specifically bringing the law and its enforcement into line with

England.)[60] Why Henry's son, Edward, was never created Prince of Wales we do not know. It would have been desirable to make some gesture confirming his legitimacy and his status as heir, given the tangled state of the King's matrimonial affairs, but it was not done. Edward had been deemed Duke of Cornwall since his birth in 1537, but he received none of the revenues, his entire establishment remaining a charge on the Treasury of the Chamber—as Mary's had been earlier.[61] He never went anywhere near Wales at any stage of his life, and had absolutely no connection with his grandfather's land. Perhaps the King could not see the point of a purely ceremonial gesture, to which neither money nor work were attached. His creation was not omitted out of any consideration for his health because, apart from normal childhood ailments, Edward was famously robust as a child—contrary to what is sometimes believed.

Although it was getting more distant with each generation, Queen Elizabeth exploited her Welsh ancestry when it suited her, as her father and grandfather had done. 'From Cambria's soil, from Hector's seed, Sidanen [the silken one, i.e. Elizabeth] doth proceed,' wrote Lodowicke Lloyd in a helpful mood.[62]. She was able to build on the success of the 'Acts of Union', and the perception of her government as strong, stable and popular helped to gain the loyalty of the political nation (perhaps a quarter of the population, in Wales as elsewhere). A relaxed, pragmatic attitude to the Welsh language undoubtedly contributed to this process. Although by the terms of the statute of 1536 all proceedings in the royal courts were to be conducted in English, it was realized that many potential litigants did not speak it. So although the statute was observed in public proceedings, bi-lingual attorneys did most of the preparatory work in Welsh, a sensible compromise that worked. When a second judge was added to each of the Circuits of Great Session in 1576, it was even suggested that the new appointees should be competent in Welsh—although the suggestion does not seem to have been implemented.

The Council in the Marches continued to function effectively throughout Elizabeth's long reign, although not without problems and controversy. The most serious difficulty arose out of the fact that it held standing commissions of Oyer and Terminer. This entitled it to function as a court of Common Law, bringing its jurisdiction into conflict with that of the Western English circuits, and of the courts of Great

Session. The overlap caused endless confusion and some heated exchanges.[63] Under Elizabeth the council functioned most effectively as a local version of the court of Star Chamber in London. Its powers were the same as those of the London Council, and it was often more convenient for purely local disputes to be resolved at Ludlow or Shrewsbury. Between 1558 and 1603, the discipline of the Welsh people steadily improved, although it could be slow and frustrating work. However, it was a good sign that the Welsh were becoming more litigious. The Council in the Marches was flooded with disputes of all kinds, and the more important cases were increasingly taken to Westminster, particularly to the court of Star Chamber, thus strengthening connections with the centre of government.[64]

The problem of lawless violence did not go away entirely, and in one specific context actually increased. Parliamentary elections had been unknown in medieval Wales, because the country was not enfranchised, but now feuding gentry (who had once launched their retainers at each other indiscriminately) tended to focus on them. Small quarrels tended to end up in physical assaults, often involving those who were supposed to keep the peace. However, whereas compensation awarded by the traditional courts had often been disputed or ignored, now the penalties handed down by the Queen's courts could not be avoided.[65] In this process the Council in the Marches played an important part. When appealed to, it normally avoided conflicts with the courts of Great Session by handing the disputants over to the Common Law. So the council became a court of first instance, particularly useful when disputes involved those very gentry who might otherwise have considered them at Quarter Sessions. As Glanmor Williams observed, 'By its very existence the Council contributed enormously to order and good government in Wales.'[66] Only at the very end of the reign did the prerogative courts begin to become controversial, and those disputes did not at first touch the Council in the Marches. Chester was taken out of the council's jurisdiction after 1569, but otherwise it continued unchanged. Presidents and councillors came and went, but by 1600 the legal and political problems of Wales were largely things of the past.

The other significant thing that happened in Wales in the second half of the sixteenth century was the Reformation. There are no particular signs that the Henrician changes made much impact in the Principality;

the London Carthusians had no Welsh equivalents, and even the demise of *darvel gavan* seems to have provoked little indignation.[67] The Welsh gentry were no less keen than their English counterparts to lay their hands on former monastic property. When services began to be held in the vernacular, it was in Welsh, and that is one of the reasons why there were from the beginning enthusiastic Protestants in Wales—as there were not in Ireland.[68] There were, of course, recusants in Wales, and even a printing press on the Great Orme, but in that the country was no different from neighbouring parts of England. Apart from the language, by 1600 there were no meaningful distinctions to be drawn either politically or religiously, between the English and the Welsh— perhaps that is why the long-redundant penal statutes of the early fifteenth century were finally repealed (without protest) in 1624.

Elizabeth I, and more particularly William Cecil, her Secretary and chief adviser, made use of their Welsh ancestry when convenient to do so. Yet in general the connections between the Tudors and the land of their origin were not at all what their fifteenth-century ancestors would have anticipated. Instead of personal contacts through the sons of the royal house, after 1529 there was simply bureaucratic administration. This was partly genetic accident, but it was also partly calculated. Princes were great lords, and could be a nuisance, especially if they fell out with their sires. The Tudors had no desire to encourage either great lords or forms of devolved government, and were happy to take what advantage they could from their conspicuous lack of offspring.

CHAPTER IV

The Stuart Princes

Henry and Charles, the sons of James I, were the first Princes of Wales to have no traceable contact with the government of the country. As long as the Council in the Marches continued and there was a Prince of Wales, which roughly speaking means from 1610 to 1625, it was nominally his council, but in practice neither of them intervened in the Principality's government. The revenues, along with those of the Duchy of Cornwall and the Earldom of Chester, were received on their behalf, and by their own officers, but these were derived entirely from rents and other similar dues—not at all from the profits of jurisdiction, which went entirely to the Crown. For the Princes concerned —and for those who were to follow—allocation of these revenues was simply a re-arrangement that imposed some limitations upon the Prince's spending power.

James VI of Scotland had seemed in 1603 the best option for England, a country lacking a designated heir, never mind an established Prince of Wales. He was well connected and the father of two sons, which seemed to secure the future succession, and Henry indeed proved a successful Prince of Wales—a strong figurehead with ideas of his own. He died young, however, and his younger brother, Charles, unsuited by temperament to political compromise and expedient diplomacy, eventually inherited both title and throne. The Civil War almost cost Charles's eldest son, the future Charles II, his inheritance; never formally created Prince of Wales, he endured several years of exile in France before regaining the throne in 1660. Yet Charles II's failure to produce a legitimate heir saw the crown pass to another ill-suited brother, James II. In one of history's ironies, the birth of the next potential Prince of Wales, James Francis Edward, was no triumph for the self-defeating Stuarts. The sudden arrival of this Catholic Prince, surrounded in rumour and suspicion, rather proved the catalyst for the Glorious Revolution that finally swept the male Stuarts from power.

Rather surprisingly, the death of Elizabeth made little difference in Wales, perhaps an indication of how thin the association between the country and the Tudor dynasty had become by 1603. Whatever else he may have claimed, James had no pretensions to Welsh ancestry, and although his eldest son was already nine when he succeeded, it was to be another seven years before the King conferred the coronet upon him. James had been the heir to the English Crown since the execution of his mother, Mary Queen of Scots, in 1587. Although he had put on a respectable show of indignation over that event, he had in fact scarcely known her; they had been separated when he was about two, and their lives had radically diverged.[1] Whether Elizabeth ever explicitly acknowledged James as her heir is a matter of some doubt, but she had treated him since his mother's death as the only realistic candidate.[2] James was also in many ways a promising one. His grandfather had been King James V of Scotland, and his great-grandmother Margaret Tudor, Henry VIII's elder sister. He was male, Protestant and married, with a good clutch of children. The only obstacle in his way was the inconvenient fact that his mother (then an infant) had been ignored in Henry's last succession act of 1544 on the grounds that she had been born 'out of the realm'. As Elizabeth's own claim to the throne rested upon this same statute, it was inconceivable to repeal it while she was still alive. In practice, however, it could be constructively ignored—and that is what happened. In April 1601 Sir Robert Cecil, the Queen's Secretary, came to an understanding with James. He reserved his loyalty to Elizabeth for as long as she lived, but when she died, he undertook to bring James to the throne.[3]

Elizabeth died on 24 March 1603, and the proclamation of her successor that same morning provoked an 'undignified scramble' to be the first to bear the news north. As soon as the news reached him, James made haste to London, but his family did not immediately accompany him. This was partly by deliberate intention, because six-year-old Elizabeth and three-year-old Charles were comfortably settled and could not be readily moved, but it was also partly because the Queen, Anne of Denmark, was being difficult. The King had intended that his eldest son and heir, Henry, should accompany him, but Henry was at Stirling in the care of the Earl of Mar. Mar was with the King, but he had left careful instruction with his mother and younger brother regarding the Prince's journey. Anne arrived uninvited at Stirling, heavily pregnant, on 4 May, and demanded that Henry be handed over to her. Acting on the Earl's instructions, she was rebuffed.[4] The Queen then suffered a miscarriage and, taking advantage of her condition, refused to leave Stirling unless Henry was handed over to her. Mar returned post-haste to Scotland, but the Queen refused to move unless her requirement was met. This news was promptly conveyed to the King, who had many other things on his mind at that moment, and could have done without the distraction. He needed his son, and he needed his Queen, so a compromise was the only way out. Towards the end of May he relieved Mar of his responsibility for the Prince, transferring his custody to the Earl of Lennox. Then, acting on James's private instruction, Lennox handed on his responsibility to the Privy Council in Scotland, who then acceded to the Queen's demand.[5]

Anne and Henry left Stirling for Edinburgh on 27 May, and set off for England on 1 June. On their way south they were entertained by the Spencers at Althorp in Northamptonshire, where lavish celebrations were presented in their honour. For the time being Charles, not thought strong enough for the journey, remained in Scotland under the care of Lord and Lady Fyvie. It was not until the following year that he, too, travelled south. Both James and his family were unknown quantities in England. Although he was a man approaching 40, he had never been Prince of Wales, and nobody knew quite what ideas he might be harbouring. His *Basilikon Doron*, written as a statecraft manual for his son in 1598, was put on sale in London immediately after his accession, and raised more than a few eyebrows. What strange ideas was the boy being taught?

Henry and his mother were welcomed by the King at Windsor on 30 June, but for the time being no mention was made of the Principality. The boy was solemnly invested as a Knight of the Garter in a ceremony on 2 July, and everyone was suitably impressed, but it immediately became apparent that James was anxious to prise his son away from Anne. A special household was established for him, under Sir Thomas Chaloner as Governor, which numbered 141 persons by the end of the year. Henry was based at Oatlands in Surrey (a house now long since vanished), but led a peripatetic existence around other royal residences in the Home Counties.[6] This was partly to encourage demonstrations of loyal enthusiasm, and partly to keep the houses in use. There was no attempt to deny Anne access to her son, but the King was obviously determined that they should not live under the same roof for any length of time.

Henry's Scottish tutors remained in place, but their labours do not seem to have been particularly fruitful. A Venetian visitor to Oatlands as early as August 1603 described him as 'ceremonious beyond his years', and it is clear that the Prince preferred his sports to his books.[7] He rode and danced well, jousted and hunted with enthusiasm, and was generally as unlike his fragile younger brother as could be imagined. Physically Henry seems to have taken after his grandfather, Lord Darnley, although his father (who hated war games) was also a keen horseman and hunter. He quickly developed a taste for plays and masques, which were central to the entertainments of the Jacobean court, and was an early patron of Inigo Jones. Perhaps he was excited by the availability of such entertainments after a rather dour upbringing in Scotland, but Jones also seems to have been a favourite of his mother's. The Prince was a keen follower of the Twelfth Night celebrations, which he is known to have attended in 1604, 1605 and 1608, and may have done in other years.

James, aware of the interest that was developing in his heir, made use of him in various minor ways. For example he took an important place in the King and Queen's entry into the capital on 15 March 1604, and was initiated into the mystery of the London Company of Merchant Taylors at their Hall in July 1607. In 1605 he visited Oxford with the King, and was symbolically matriculated at Magdalen College.[8] There was no intention that he should actually go into residence, or follow the university curriculum, but his admission indicated James's continuing support for England's oldest university. It was at about this time, when he was 11 or 12, that Henry is alleged to have suggested that his younger brother should be trained for the Archbishopric of Canterbury, an idea not without a hint of sibling contempt for one who was already notoriously 'bookish'.

Henry, however, was not academic, possibly in reaction to his erudite father. Sir Charles Cornwallis, the Treasurer of his household, testified that 'he plied his book hard' for about two or three years, but other evidence suggests that 'princely sports' continued to take precedence. In October 1606 the French ambassador was impressed with Henry's ability to shoot with the longbow, to vault, run and ride, and concluded that he was 'not at all childlike'.[9] In the same year he apparently took part in a joust in honour of a visit by his uncle, Christian IV of

Denmark, which means that he must have been exceptionally well grown for his age—something confirmed by the numerous gifts of horses and suits of armour that he received. He aimed, in his own words, to be 'a soldier and a man of the world', perhaps to compensate for his father's famous preference for peaceful settlements.

In spite of everything that had been achieved, the new government still inherited problems in Wales. To some extent these were consequences of the council's success. Throughout Elizabeth's reign the Privy Council in London had kept a close eye on its 'daughter' in the Marches. By the same token it had consistently worked though the local council, giving it extensive responsibilities particularly over the enforcement of religious conformity and the mustering of troops. In the early years lawyers were the most numerous and active councillors, but by the time of the Spanish war county gentry had overtaken them both in numbers and activity. Only a handful of these were actually Welsh, but nearly all had extensive experience of March affairs.[10] Stability was aided by the fact that there were only two Presidents who between them spanned almost the entire reign: Sir Henry Sidney from 1559 to 1586, and the 2nd Earl of Pembroke from 1586 to 1601. Both were competent, and receptive of reforming ideas, but Sidney was handicapped by having to spend long periods on his other charge—in Ireland. Pembroke was also Lord Lieutenant of Wales, a natural but important extension of his powers in wartime, and as in England two or three of the more suitable gentlemen in each shire were appointed as his deputies. Unfortunately competition for these sought-after positions sometimes also added to the issues of local controversy.[11] Pembroke had to head off the possible threat in North Wales from the Earl of Essex. The Earl had extensive estates and an entrenched family position in Flint and Denbigh, so when his loyalty became suspect after the Irish fiasco, a careful eye had to be kept on his affinity in that area, although in the event nothing happened.[12]

Successfully established as a court of first instance, the council was overwhelmed with work—much of it trivial to the point of frivolity. As early as 1575 the council was being expected to deal with 1,200 cases a year, and was frequently sitting from six in the morning to six in the evening.[13] Tempers became frayed, and the Solicitor and the Attorney were regularly at each others' throats. The number of councillors was increased, but not sufficiently, and although suitability was supposed to be the main criterion for selection, patronage sometimes proved the stronger—several powerful noblemen had an interest in the government of Wales. Nor was the council's jurisdiction altogether unchallenged. Well as it was regarded within Wales, it was much resented in the English border shires. By the 1590s there was a chorus of resentment from the gentlemen of Shropshire and Hereford as well as those of Gloucestershire and Worcestershire, and this resentment was echoed by the Assize judges working the western circuits from Westminster over the council's perceived interference with their work.[14] It was this dissatisfaction, which grew steadily during James's reign, rather than any malfunctioning within Wales itself that led to the eventual demise of the council (along with the other prerogative courts) in 1642.

In spite of these dysfunctional aspects of the Council in the Marches, the Acts of Unification had in one respect been an unqualified success. Long before the end of Elizabeth's reign the shire had become accepted as the natural unit of government, in Wales no less than in England. The core of local government was now provided throughout the country by the Commission of the Peace, the popularity of which was reflected in an inexorable tendency to expand.[15] Accusations that men 'of mean credit' were being appointed were inevitable and need not be taken too seriously. In spite of this friction, the commissions on the whole did their jobs, both administrative and judicial, well, and when they did not they were called up short either by the council or by the courts of Great Session.[16] These courts, like the shires themselves, were successful, sitting twice in each year in each county. Their remit was wide and they gained a reputation for both impartiality and incorruptibility—in a world where justice tended to serve the most powerful kindred. Inevitably their workload also steadily increased. Between them the Council in the Marches and the Courts of Great Session had largely 'civilized' Wales by 1600, although it was to be some years before the unruly reputation of that country finally disappeared.

By 1608 the young Prince Henry was beginning to make some impact on public affairs. He developed an enthusiasm for ships and the navy later shared by other Stuart Princes—and Kings. When Phineas Pett built the *Prince Royal* in 1610, he named it for Henry, in return for the protection that the Prince had given the royal shipwright from the (well-founded) charges of corruption that he had faced two years earlier.[17] Henry was a warm supporter of Sir Walter Raleigh, and backed

—to the best of his ability—those who were anxious to renew the war against Spain. In fact, by the time that he was about 15 he could well have become an embarrassment to his father. His household, now based at court, had expanded to nearly 500, and was noted not only as godly and learned, but also as military. When artists represented the Prince of Wales, they nearly always chose to show him armed. His education may not have made him particularly erudite, but it had certainly made him a strong Protestant and a patron of learned preachers—it is even reported that he kept 'swear boxes' at his various residences!

The Prince also built up friendships with a number of young noblemen, including William Cecil, later the 2nd Earl of Salisbury. William's father, the Lord Treasurer, seems to have encouraged this relationship, no doubt with a politician's eye on the future.[18] Given his emerging political and religious convictions, Henry could easily have been a focus for opposition to his father's government in the same way as the eighteenth-century Princes were to become, but his influence remained little more than embryonic. He was warmly attached to his sister, Elizabeth, and to the best of his ability promoted the negotiations for her marriage to Frederick of the Palatinate, which took place in 1610 and at which he acted as bridesman. However, proposals for his own marriage were less enthusiastically received, largely because they came from Catholics. A Spanish match had been mooted as long ago as 1603, as part of then ongoing peace negotiations, and the idea was revived in 1605, after the peace was in place. The Prince apparently expressed the strongest opposition even then to 'marrying outside his faith', and the proposals came to nothing.[19] When a match with a daughter of the Duke of Savoy was mooted in 1610, it received the same treatment. He is alleged to have had a brief adolescent affair with Lady Frances Howard, but this may have been no more than a rumour designed to establish his orthodox sexual orientation, in view of his reluctance to contemplate marriage.

With a political role thus beginning to emerge, it was appropriate that the Prince's position should be further recognized, and in June 1610 he was formally established as Prince of Wales and Earl of Chester.

Wednesday [14 February 1610]. After the Lords came into the House, the Lord Treasurer, Robert Cecil, Earl of Salisbury, made a speech which was summarily and in effect as followeth: 'My

Lords, it is his majesty's pleasure that I should deliver unto your Lordships the cause of convening of this present session of parliament. First,
to relieve his majesty's necessity; secondly to create his eldest son, the
Prince Henry, Prince of Wales and Earl of Chester, as for Duke of
Cornwall he hath by birth … [or rather from his father's accession]….
The necessity of the Prince his creation is not tied unto the parliament,
for the king both for the time and place, or whether it shall be or no,
hath in his own power. But out of his indulgence, being a father, is
now pleased to give him that honour, who as he come beneath none
we could either hear or read of, so he passeth any. Although outward
contingencies are not to be built upon, yet omens to be avoided, for all
the princes which have been created Princes of Wales [which were 11
since the conquest] only three which were created out of parliament
[were] unhappy, and the rest most fortunate….[20]

The actual ceremony was devised by Cecil himself, there not having
been such an event for over a century, and the historian William Camden was engaged to research the precedents.[21] Camden was also asked,
significantly, to examine certain legal aspects of the relationship
between the Prince of Wales and the parliament—and of the preroga-
tives of the ancient princes *vis-à-vis* the King. Nothing seems to have
come of these investigations, but the event was surrounded by hints of
political importance. In the first place it was delayed until the Mayor
and Aldermen agreed to loan the King £100,000; secondly the ceremony was held in the old Court of Requests at Westminster Hall, the
very centre of administrative power; and thirdly the whole parliament
and many noble guests were present—so that the whole event was
likened to a coronation. The sword, ring and coronet were bestowed,
according to the tradition of Henry of Monmouth; there was a water
pageant, and 25 Knights of the Bath, personally selected by the Prince,
were dubbed.[22] Appropriately, there were theatrical performances, the
Prince jousted, and the celebrations went on for months, concluding
with a performance of *Oberon* devised by Ben Jonson and Inigo Jones
on 1 January 1611. Henry was officially ensconced at St James's Palace,
and the revenues of the Principality and the Earldom were handed
over to him, giving him a total income of some £15,000 a year. His
role as a patron of the arts, sciences and seafarers briefly flourished, and
no praises seemed too extravagant for this most promising young man.

Durae peragunt perusa sorores
Nec sua retro filia revolvunt.

If your end be, as I do assure myself, to encourage hope as well as to acknowledge merit, then I doubt not but by casting your eyes upwards you will easily discern with what grace and glory that bright star appears in the eye of Europe, which must continue light and glory in this kingdom after the setting of our cheerful sun…. But since … our steps [are] measured and our lives so limited as this worthy son is to succeed his father in all likelihood though I hope in mellow years, let us in the meantime keep in mind that this sweet blossom must come forward, spread an knit according to the measure of the silver-dropping dew that must distill from the beauty of your well affected minds….[23]

Alas for hope and expectation! In the autumn of 1612 Henry caught typhoid and, despite desperate attempts to save him, died at St James's Palace on 6 November, at the age of 18. His loss was deeply felt, not only by his parents and his siblings but also by the whole country. England, it was felt, had lost its 'new Renaissance'.

The Prince was interred in Westminster Abbey amid a universal chorus of grief, and the mantle of expectation descended uneasily upon the shoulders of his 12-year-old brother, Charles. Charles had been born at Dunfermline on 19 November 1600, and baptized at Holyrood on 23 December. He remained in Scotland until the summer of 1604, and when he came south he was placed in the care of Sir Robert and Lady Carey.[24] A small establishment was set up to care for him, but it would be an exaggeration to describe it as a household. Whereas Henry had been physically precocious, Charles was backward, 'both in his going and in his speaking', as it was expressed. He suffered from weak ankles, probably the result of rickets, and was slow to walk, although he seems to have grown out of this condition quite rapidly; neither as an adolescent nor as an adult did he suffer from any noticeable disability. It was otherwise with his speech impediment, the source of which is not obvious and which James is alleged to have wanted to correct by means of drastic surgery. As a child and a young man he showed great determination in overcoming this handicap, and learned to express himself lucidly, if hesitantly. It left him, however, with a life-long stammer that made him a reluctant communicator, particularly to any with whom he was not totally at ease. This could explain some, at least, of his subsequent behaviour.[25] Charles was never at ease with those not well known to him, and frequently seemed aloof.

There was, nevertheless, nothing at all wrong with his intellect, and even at the age of four he was described as being 'far better as yet with his mind than with his body and feet'. The Scottish minister Thomas Murray, subsequently Provost of Eton, was placed in charge of his education, and had the highest opinion both of his diligence and his attainment. When he was about eight, Murray declared that he could 'manage a point of controversy with the best student divines'—an exaggeration, no doubt, but a telling one. At the age of nine the Prince chose for himself the motto 'if you would conquer all things, submit yourself to reason', which was probably a piece of childish pretentiousness. (He might have done better in later life if he had interpreted 'reason' more pragmatically.) At the age of 12 Charles lost both the siblings to whom he was devoted—his brother Henry by death and his sister Elizabeth to a distant marriage. He was chief mourner at the former's funeral, it being the custom that parents should not attend, and the effect of this upon a sensitive disposition can only be imagined.

Charles was now Duke of Cornwall and of Rothesay, and sole heir to the Crown of England, Scotland and Ireland.[26] As such he was carefully guarded, if not cosseted, and it is probably just as well that he showed neither taste nor aptitude for the kind of rough play in which his brother had indulged, and for which he had been so much admired. Instead he seems to have imbibed a steady diet of strict Calvinist theology, which must have been somewhat at odds with the artistic and musical tastes which were already becoming noticeable, to say nothing of the High Church principles for which he later became famous. At the age of 13 he was confirmed in the Church of England, a necessary rite for anyone in his position, but one that Henry seems not to have undergone. Charles's loyalty to the Anglican church was later to prove far stronger than his Calvinist education, but both militated against that crypto-Catholicism of which he allowed himself to be suspected after he had come to the throne.[27] Although James had written the *Basilikon Doron* in 1598 as a statecraft manual and guide for his elder son, how much Henry benefited from it is difficult to say. The indications are that he would have chosen his own political philosophy if he had lived a few more years. Charles proved more biddable, and by about 1614 his father was applying himself seriously to his instruction.

'The best tutor in Christendom', as Francis Bacon somewhat syco-phantically put it. The King obviously thought that his pupil was shaping up well. On 3 November 1616, when Charles was a few days short of his 16th birthday, James created him Prince of Wales and Earl of Chester, conferring on him at the same time the revenues of those two palatinates.[28] The ceremony was lavish enough, but nobody this time thought of comparing it to a coronation—perhaps that issue had become sensitive.

When James visited Scotland in 1617, Charles for the first time took his seat on the Privy Council, and when the King returned he con-firmed him as a regular member. This was a gesture of confidence that Henry had never enjoyed, although he may have been on the cusp of it when death overtook him. He had been 18 at that time—the same age that Charles reached in 1618. There had been no adult Prince of Wales since Henry of Monmouth, so the precedent for this promotion was remote. However, by this time the Prince was recognized as something of an authority on maritime affairs (a taste that he did share with his brother), and when the Admiralty was put into commission following the enquiries of 1618, he was named as a commissioner.[29] He also took the seat to which he was now entitled in the House of Lords, becom-ing effectively the leader on his father's behalf by 1624.

Meanwhile, relations between James and his Queen, which had had their rocky moments before, had again cooled considerably. This may have been due partly to the King's increasing proclivity for male favour-ites. He acquired a new one in 1615 in the person of George Villiers, the accomplished but impoverished younger son of a gentry family. Anne seems to have been seriously put out by this relationship, and when she died in 1619 she left her personal estate to her son rather than to her husband.[30] This was no consolation to Charles, who had been close to his mother, but it led to a quarrel with James that had to be mediated by the Marquis of Buckingham (as Villiers had then become), equally a friend of both. Charles was chief mourner at his mother's funeral and, thanks to Buckingham's dexterity, no lasting estrange-ment from his father resulted. The Prince of Wales had initially been deeply suspicious of this intruder, who seemed to be taking his dead brother's place, but Villiers had managed to charm away his suspicions.

Instead international politics supervened. In 1618 war had broken out in Germany, and James's son-in-law, the Elector Frederick, had very ill-advisedly accepted the Crown of Bohemia from the rebel Czechs. In 1620 he was defeated and driven out, not merely from Bohemia but also from the Palatinate by the Emperor Ferdinand II.[31] James had already formed an ambitious plan to end the war by signing a treaty with Spain (the power behind the Emperor) involving a marriage between Charles and the Infanta Maria, daughter of Philip III. With England thus linked by marriage to both sides, the King might have been able to mediate a peace. We can imagine what Henry would have thought of such a proposal, but Charles was more amenable. He was willing to do (almost) anything to help his sister, and had even offered £5,000 from his own resources to ameliorate her position. As the situation in Germany worsened, the Anglo–Spanish negotiations struggled. With the 12-year truce in the Netherlands due to expire in 1621, it was even suggested at one point that Charles should lead an English army to annex the northern provinces. Such a bizarre suggestion got nowhere, and it soon became apparent that although Charles might be agreeable to the marriage there was powerful opposition to the idea in both countries.[32] The House of Commons expressed itself forcefully on the subject, and the Spanish church—and more importantly the Infanta herself—were also implacably hostile. Nevertheless Spain's resources were beginning to feel the strain of the war, and the English kept up their pressure for a withdrawal from the Palatinate. In 1621 Lord Digby, James's chief negotiator, extracted the promise of a ceasefire, but this was ignored by the forces on the ground. Finally, with the fall of Heidelberg in 1622, the whole of the Palatinate was overrun and there was serious talk in England of sending an army to recover it —an army for which parliament might even have been willing to pay. [33]

Spain was now in the driving seat, but was financially exhausted and unwilling to face an all-out conflict with England. Lord Digby (now Earl of Bristol) was therefore able to return to Spain with some prospect of success. Charles began to take lessons in Spanish, and to learn the stately dances of Iberia. Whether he really wanted to marry Maria or simply saw this as the best way of helping his beleaguered sister is not clear, but by the beginning of 1623 his sense of adventure was thoroughly engaged, and he persuaded his father to allow him to go a-wooing in person. Accompanied by the Marquis of Buckingham, and disguised by a paper-thin alias (as Jack and Tom Smith), he set off in February on what was supposed to be a quest of knight errantry.[34]

Journey of the prince and Buckingham from Newhall to Tilbury, where they crossed over to Gravesend, thence to Rochester, Canterbury and Dover whence they sailed; their fair riding coats and false beards, of which one fell off at Gravesend, causing suspicion, and messengers were sent after them.... They were stayed at Canterbury by the mayor on a notice sent him from Sir Lewis Lewkenor, who attended the ambassador [of Spain]. They got away, but were stayed again at Dover, where they gave some secret satisfaction. The Council knew nothing of their journey till Wednesday, when it was in everybody's mouth, but few believed it at first. The king sent to the council to say it was the doing of the Prince, who wants to try whether he is fairly dealt with, and not of Buckingham, and that they were not told because secrecy was the life of the business; they are ordered to stay, by proclamation or otherwise, the amazement of the people, who say it is done that the Prince may be married at a mass. It is thought a dangerous and unexampled experiment....[35]

The Prince was courteously but somewhat distantly received at the court of Philip IV, and allowed only a fleeting glimpse of the woman supposed to be the subject of his passionate quest. The Count-Duke of Olivares, Philip's powerful Chief Minister, decided to demand the full emancipation of English Catholics as the price of a deal, and that neither Charles nor Bristol was empowered to concede. In spite of being enormously impressed with the splendour and formality of the Spanish court, which created an enduring ambition in him, the Prince became increasingly frustrated. Accustomed to a more relaxed atmosphere, his movements were restricted by rigid protocol and he began to feel like a prisoner in the Escorial, while his negotiation was going nowhere. At the same time his own behaviour, and that of Buckingham, began to cause increasing offence, causing the Earl of Bristol to grumble that they had set back Anglo–Spanish relations by years. The Prince's passion (if it had ever existed) became thoroughly chilled, and he and Buckingham returned to England on 7 October in a distinctly edgy frame of mind.[36] In theory Charles remained committed to the marriage, but when his gifts and token were returned, and full rights continued to be demanded for the English recusants, the negotiations ground to a halt. The 'voyage of the knights of adventure' had ended in fiasco, but the results for Charles were entirely positive. His refusal to yield to Spanish pressure over the recusants had made him popular, and he had gained immensely in self-confidence. More equivocally, perhaps, his friendship with Buckingham had become warm and close, and Buckingham had fallen out seriously with the Earl of Bristol.

The Duke of Buckingham is willing to meet the desire of the Earl of Bristol for a reconciliation, but cannot mediate for him with the King and the Prince until his answers are satisfactory, and he makes a confession that he did harm by allowing the marriage to proceed in general terms, without coming to particulars; that in the treaty for the restitution of the Palatinate, he had not compassed the person of the Prince Palatine; that he had advised the education of the eldest Palatine Prince in the Emperor's court, and his change of religion; and had urged the stay of the Prince of Wales at the Spanish Court. If he will thus confess, and throw himself upon his majesty's mercy for his errors of judgement, the Duke will endeavour to have him restored to favour.[37]

Charles at this point is an interesting young man. Described as 'dignified in manner and active in habits', he was particularly noted for his excellent horsemanship and his impeccable morals. Refined and abstemious, he seems to have been trying to distance himself as far as possible from the rackety image of his father's court. Where Henry had appealed to the godly and the military to establish his identity, Charles seems to have relied on restraint, coolness and dignity. It was an interesting role reversal from the last time that an adult prince had confronted his father in the early fifteenth century (p.61). Both politically and personally, his relationship with James fluctuated. In 1621 he had tried (unsuccessfully) to rescue Francis Bacon from impeachment on behalf of his father. When Charles returned from Spain, however, he found himself heading a popular movement of resentment against the 'Spanish Match'. This role did not altogether suit him, because it required a rather more charismatic identity than Charles could establish, and the King seems to have regarded his son's unexpected popularity with some alarm.

James's foreign policy was now in tatters, and in 1624 he took the unprecedented step of turning to parliament for advice. Disillusioned with all things Spanish, Charles took the lead in the House of Lords in demanding a 'patriotic coalition' against Spain—in other words, war.[38] To that course James remained adamantly opposed, and another quarrel between the Prince of Wales and his father briefly ensued. The Count of Mansfeld, a mercenary soldier, was funded to conduct a kind of surrogate war to regain the Palatinate (of which Frederick had been formally deprived in 1623), but he took the money and achieved precisely nothing. Meanwhile the Duke (as he now was) of Buckingham was urging an entirely different strategy—that of alliance with France. This appealed to the King as a means of bringing pressure to bear on Philip IV without resort to war, and it appealed to Charles because of his friendship with Buckingham. In November 1624 an agreement was signed with the government of Louis XIII, which redeployed the Prince as a bridegroom for the King's young sister, Henrietta Maria.[39] The price of this success was the suspension (but not the repeal) of the penal laws against Catholics, and this was sufficient reason for the House of Commons to object to the match. However, by Christmas 1624 it was a *fait accompli*, and Charles eventually married his young French bride in May 1625.

By that time he was no longer Prince of Wales. James I had died on 27 March, urging his son to defend the church and to be loyal to his friendship with Buckingham—both of which things he was to do at infinite cost to himself. The old King was buried with fitting ceremony in the tomb of King Henry VII at Westminster Abbey. There was an ironic appropriateness about this symbolism, because both men had founded new dynasties, and both had lost a cherished son on the threshold of adulthood. In other ways they had differed dramatically, but each had been succeeded by his 'spare' rather than his intended heir. However, whereas Henry VII would have rejoiced (although in some bewilderment) at the exploits of his successor, James VI and I would have only cause to grieve.

Charles's reign was to be a succession of celebrated disasters, which there is neither space nor need to explore here. At first his loyalty to Buckingham helped to embroil him in two unnecessary wars, first with Spain and then with France, both of which ended in expensive humiliation, and contributed to strained relations with his wife—not surprising when her husband was at war with her brother. Buckingham's assassination in 1628, deeply felt by the King, helped to end the wars and brought Charles closer to Henrietta, who in turn was learning to curb her Catholic enthusiasm with discretion.[40] In 1629 she bore him a son who lived only a few days, and on 29 May 1630 gave birth to a Prince who was named for his father, and was to grow up to be Charles II. His arrival was greeted with suitable rejoicing, as soon as it became clear that he was whole and healthy, and great relief by his parents. The new heir was the first Prince to be born in England since Edward in 1537. At four months he was described as 'so fat and tall that he is already taken for a year old', but he was never created Prince of Wales and his father's personal government was already running into difficulties.

The revenues of the Principality had returned to the Crown on Charles I's accession, and at first the change of regime had little effect in Wales. The only noticeable development of the first 30 years or so of the seventeenth century was the steadily increasing unpopularity of the Council in the Marches. By about 1630 it was being regarded as an underhand way of avoiding the 'real justice' handed down by the Courts of Great Session, and its machinery was becoming clogged up with trivial and unnecessary suits, expressive of the innumerable petty feuds plaguing the region.[41] During the King's personal government, between 1630 and 1641, it also began to acquire a more sinister reputation as an instrument of oppression—a perception ironically shared by all the prerogative courts. Institutions designed to enable the King to apply his equity directly, using royal justice to emancipate his subjects from the tyrannies of local elites, now began to be seen as enforcers of an irresponsible absolutism. The prerogative was not controlled by parliament, and was getting radically out of step with the will of the political nation.[42] When the Long Parliament got into its stride, in 1642, all the prerogative courts were abolished by statute, including the Council in the Marches.[43] The shires that had been under its jurisdiction now had no option but to resort to the Common Law, or to legislation for the redress of their grievances.

Parliament made no effort to woo the Welsh-speaking community, as it did in England, with pamphlets and newsletters, but the early royalist enthusiasm was not sustained. Even as early as the battle of Edgehill on 23 October 1642, the Welsh distinguished themselves chiefly by running away, and the value of the regiments raised in Wales earlier in the year began to be seriously doubted. Long-standing local feuds reignited under the labels of 'royalist' and 'parliamentarian', as they had two centuries earlier under York and Lancaster.[44] More importantly, many able-bodied men, and many gentlemen, simply 'sat still' while the fighting was far off and they felt themselves disengaged from the issues. The King's headquarters were briefly at Shrewsbury in October 1642, but he soon moved off to Oxford and the zeal of his followers in the Principality waned. Lord Herbert of Raglan did manage to raise another 1,500 men for the King in 1643 by using his local influence, but the large numbers of the previous year were no longer forthcoming. On 5 February 1644 Prince Rupert, a soldier with no local knowledge or connections, was made President of Wales and Captain General of Cheshire, Lancashire, Worcestershire and Shropshire. But these grand-sounding titles meant very little, and Rupert never seems to have engaged with Wales or its problems. Indeed he lost control of the whole of mid-Wales when Sir Thomas Myddleton won the battle of Montgomery on 15 September 1644.[45] By this time the King had been heavily defeated at Marston Moor, and the whole royalist war effort was in disarray. After a second, and decisive, defeat at Naseby in the summer of 1645, Charles retreated for a while into South Wales, but it was no longer the safe refuge that it might once have been, and he returned to Oxford. After a series of further defeats, and the loss of Bristol, in May 1646 the King gave up the struggle and surrendered to the Scots at Newark.[46]

The role of Wales in the Civil War had eventually been neither glorious nor decisive, and its men had mostly been defeated and killed in battles far away. So it is not surprising that the second Civil War was a damp squib. Evidence captured at Naseby had demonstrated that the King was negotiating with the Catholic powers, and particularly the French, to come to his assistance. When this became known, his defence of the faith began to look like a sham, and those in Wales who had supported him for that cause drew back. There was a small-scale rising in Glamorgan, which was defeated at St Fagans on 8 May 1648, and punitive measures were taken against towns such as Wrexham and Oswestry that were thought to have become disaffected.[47] Suspicions of Welsh attitudes were strong in London, and the medium-term consequences of the wars were regime change, economic disruption and much suffering. Even the Welsh drovers were for a time denied access to the markets in England upon which their livelihoods depended.

From 1648 to 1653 the Rump Parliament—that part of the House of Commons that was left when the army had finished expelling its royalist and Presbyterian opponents—ran a radically deflated Wales. The

House of Lords and the monarchy disappeared in 1649, and at county level the sheriffs and justices of the peace were replaced by county committees. These consisted, in Wales as in England, of such members of the traditional establishment as were willing to work with the republican government, supplemented by lesser gentry, merchants and freeholders—in short anyone who could put forward a plausible case for 'substance'.[48] The great majority of the old elite withheld their services, even if they had not been active royalists, and the committees were always struggling to establish any kind of credibility. In spite of Oliver Cromwell's genuine desire to create a stable regime, in practice the army maintained these committees by force, and executed anyone who publicly criticized the Rump, a fate that befell Christopher Love, a Presbyterian minister in Wales, on 22 August 1652.[49]

Having got rid of the Rump Parliament in April 1653, Cromwell then assumed a quasi-monarchical executive authority as Lord Protector, and attempted to give his position substance with a new constitution. Parliament was resurrected, and this time all the Welsh shires were given two seats, while Cardiff and Haverford West were also enfranchised with one member each.[50] However, the representative character of these members was not improved by the removal of the old 40-shilling franchise qualification, and its replacement with a £200 property base. This meant that only the well-to-do could vote and the democratic element that resided among the old freeholders disappeared. In every county power was now in the hands of the 'well affected', those who were personally loyal to Cromwell and had often made a killing either out of the army or out of its supply contracts.[51]

Troubled by evidence of a royalist conspiracy, in 1655 Cromwell superimposed regional military governors on the existing committee structure, and Wales was placed under the control of Major-General James Berry. Berry was an honest man, who did his best. However, he had to contend with a sullen tide of resentment, made worse by the work of the bitterly disliked committees of sequestration, who were particularly busy where royalist sentiment had been strong, as it had in most of Wales. After about a year, Berry was withdrawn and three new supervisory committees were established: one for North Wales, one for South Wales and one for Monmouthshire.[52] There was no improvement in the political climate and those who had profited from the regime, such as Philip Jones of Glamorgan, were held in hatred and contempt. The bards mocked republican ideals in the safe medium of Welsh.

> Putting the head where the rump should be
> And putting the tail in the front, may be,
> Chopping and changing perpetually,
> Making great mock of each noble degree....[53]

By the time the Protector's magic wand was removed by his death in 1658, it had become clear that the Great Revolution had resulted in no acceptable form of government whatsoever. Although this was not very obvious in Wales, Cromwell had been socially quite conservative, and would dearly have liked to work with the traditional elites if they had been willing to accept him. However, that was not to be, and the more like a King he became, the less justification there was for his existence. He remained to the end a military dictator, and when his son Richard lost the confidence of the army, there was no longer any justification for continuing the republican regime.

Wales played no significant part in the events of 1659–60, which led to the King's return, but Charles II's accession had an immediate impact upon the country. Back came the Commissions of the Peace, with something very like their traditional membership, and erstwhile committee men either faded into the background or ran for cover. Back came the sheriffs, and the traditional manner of appointing them. Back also came the Council in the Marches.[54] Alone among the prerogative courts that had been abolished in 1642, the council was restored. Why this should have been so is not very clear, but Charles clearly felt that there was a case for treating Wales as different, perhaps because of its distinctive language and kinship structures, but perhaps also because the Courts of Great Session had retained their separate existence throughout the troubles.

Charles himself had no particular connection with Wales. Although he had been born in 1630, long before political crises overcame his father, he had never been created Prince. He was often referred to by that title, and some historians since have used it, because that was the traditional designation of the heir to the throne, but it was never formalized. When the Countess of Oxford had been appointed his governess in 1631, and when his household was created a few years later and Dr Brian Duppa appointed as his tutor, he was referred to in that way.[55] At the age of eight this household was located at Richmond, and he was provided with several classmates in the form of the young children of the late Duke of Buckingham, but even at that early age it was clear that (unlike his father) he had no appetite for scholarship. He had a lively curiosity and was an enthusiastic sportsman, but very limited intellectually. Temperamentally he was more like his maternal grandfather, Henry of Navarre, than either of his own parents.

Before the war broke out that was to change his life, the 11-year-old Prince was used by Charles I in a last-minute attempt to save the Earl of Strafford from execution. On 11 May 1641 he was sent, dressed in robes of state, with a formal message to the Lord Keeper of the Great Seal, Sir Richard Lane. If this was a deliberate attempt at pathos it did not work, but it must have made a deep impression upon the child. When Henrietta Maria went to France in 1642, young Charles remained with his father. 'The Prince', as Clarendon later observed, 'should never be far from him'. So close was he, in fact that both he and his brother James, then aged nine, witnessed the battle of Edgehill from close enough to have been within cannon rage. Fortunately the parliamentarians did not know he was there. When the King was on the brink of total defeat in 1646, he sent his son down to Cornwall, of which he had been the titular Duke since birth, and from where, on 4 March, he retreated to the Scilly Isles. On 17 April the Prince went to Jersey, where he enjoyed the exposed and somewhat precarious lifestyle of the isolated royal adolescent, and from there in June, after his father's surrender to the Scots, he retreated to France.

There he joined his mother at St-Germain, and his somewhat fragmented education was resumed. After Charles I's execution in January 1649 (an event of which he learned in traumatic detail), he was recognized all over Europe as King of England—but such recognition brought him no material assistance. In 1650, the Prince went to Scotland where a party received him as Charles II, but he never secured his position and his incursion into England came to a disastrous end in 1651 at the battle of Worcester, after which he was again a fugitive and an exile until 1660. Charles was undoubtedly recognized as Duke of Cornwall for as long as it mattered, but the titles of Chester and Wales were attributed by sheer convention, as had happened to Mary a century before.[56] In a letter to the 'Great Emperor and Great Duke of all Russia', Alexei Mikhailovich, Charles is significantly described as

Prince of Great Britain, Duke of Cornwall, Albany and Rothesay. Dated 16 December 1648 and signed by the Prince himself, it was dispatched from The Hague, where Charles had gone to take nominal command of a Parliamentary fleet broken away to the royalist cause. The letter itself, now in the National Archives, petitions for 'all sorte of corne and graine' to relieve want in 'the Kingdome of Ireland, specially that part of it which is under His Majesty's obedience.' Whether the grain ever arrived is unknown, but such strategic manoeuvrings were clearly part of the Prince's role during his years of exile.[57]

Charles II was married in May 1662 to Catherine of Braganza, who brought with her the enormous dowry of £300,000, plus the island of Bombay and the port of Tangier. Notoriously, however, the couple had no legitimate offspring. Charles's brother James, who succeeded him in 1685, remained Duke of York until his accession. James had first married Anne Hyde, the daughter of the Earl of Clarendon, in 1660. She had presented him with two daughters, Mary and Anne, but had died in 1671. He then married Mary of Modena in 1673, and over the next 10 years she had borne him five children, none of whom had survived infancy. James was a Catholic convert, and that provoked the bitter conflict known as the Exclusion crisis, when an alliance of opposition politicians had sought to bar him from the throne.[58] In spite of the bitter passions aroused by the so-called Popish Plot, Charles had outmanoeuvred and defeated the exclusionists, so that when he died James succeeded in apparent peace.

It soon became apparent, however, that religious divisions ran deep. In the decade or so after the restoration, Protestant dissenters had caused the most anxiety, because of their associations with the republican regime. Quakers refused the oath of allegiance—because they rejected all oaths—and by the summer of 1660 the gaols had been full of them. But after 1670 that mood began to pass, and the Catholics resumed their position as the principal threat to an Englishman's (or a Welshman's) liberties and faith. If James had been content to keep his religion a private matter, the general acquiescence with which he had been greeted in 1685 might have turned into a warmer loyalty, but he was extraordinarily clumsy. Catholics were thrust forward into key positions in politics, the army and the administration. Even the High Church party, which had opposed the exclusionists, was alienated, and men began to look hopefully towards the Protestant daughters of

James's first marriage.[59] The King was now 55, and it looked as though the succession would pass to Mary and her husband, William of Orange, by the due course of nature.

Then, on 10 June 1688, with anti-Catholic feeling simmering strongly, Mary of Modena gave birth to a son who showed every indication of surviving. Interested parties were immediately sceptical. The infant was supposed to have been smuggled into the palace in a warming pan, and so on, and popular pamphlets were quick to exploit the drama. So universal were these rumours that the government felt constrained to publish the *Depositions made in Council, 22nd October 1688 concerning the birth of the Prince of Wales*, which testified to the authenticity of Mary's motherhood, and the official account of proceedings at this 'extraordinary council' on 22 October is held in the National Archives.[60] Young James was never created Prince, or Earl of Chester, but it seems to have been assumed that he was entitled to those dignities from birth—as he was with the Duchy of Cornwall.

Events then moved swiftly and dramatically. William, invited by a powerful coalition of Lords, landed at Torbay on 5 November and entered Exeter four days later. At the same time the former Marquis of Worcester, now Duke of Beaufort, was commissioned to raise 10,000 men for King James in Wales. This was to include a special 'Prince of Wales' regiment to be raised in the south by Colonel Thomas Carne of Glamorgan.[61] Wild rumours flew through the Principality: the papists had burned Bangor, Protestants and Catholics were fighting openly in the streets of Welshpool. On 17 November King James left London, ostensibly to confront his enemies in the West Country, and Prince James was sent to Portsmouth under the care of the King's half-brother, James Fitzjames, Duke of Berwick. However, on 23 November the King suddenly and inexplicably lost his nerve, and instead of fighting, fled to France. His son returned to London, and on 9 December took ship with his mother and went to Calais. The ex-royal family was warmly welcomed by Louis XIV, who never ceased to recognize James II as King of England, and given the château of St-Germain-en-Laye as a residence.[62] Meanwhile the ex-King's forces in England and Wales, bereft of both a leader and a cause, did nothing. Their officers accepted William, for lack of any real alternative, and they were shortly after disbanded, while the politicians worked out a new settlement of the Crown.

The effects of the so-called 'Glorious Revolution' were nationwide.

In Wales, as in England, there was a reshuffling of local power elites as the Catholics and their Tory allies beat a discreet retreat, and were replaced with Whigs and former Exclusionists. On 13 February 1689 the Crown was settled jointly on William and Mary for life, and upon their heirs, if any.[63] William and Mary had been married since 1677, and their union had so far been childless, but Mary was only 27 so there was still hope. In the same parliament the Council in the Marches was finally abolished, along with the Exchequers and Chanceries of Caernarfon and Carmarthen, which had long since become moribund. As ordinary parliamentary taxation had been extended to Wales as long ago as 1543, the only distinctive feature remaining in the Principality's government was the Courts of Great Session, which preserved their autonomy down to 1830. Mary died childless in 1694, and William did not remarry. The question of the succession was therefore resurrected. By the terms of the revolutionary settlement the next heir was Mary's 35-year-old sister, Anne.

> II. And be it further enacted by the authority aforesaid that if any person or persons shall from and after the said first of May [1696], maliciously, by writing, printing, preaching, teaching or advised speaking either publish or declare that his present majesty is not the lawful and rightful king of these Realms, or that the late King James or the pretended Prince of Wales hath any right or title to the Crown of these Realms, or that any person or persons hath or have any right or title to the same otherwise than according to an Act of parliament made in the first year of the reign of his present majesty and the late queen, entitled, An Act Declaring the Rights and Liberties of the subject and settling the Succession of the Crown, such persons being thereof lawfully convicted, shall incur the danger of Praemunire mentioned in the Statute of Praemunire made in the sixteenth year of the reign of King Richard the Second....[64]

Anne was married to George of Denmark, but her innumerable pregnancies had resulted in only one child who lived beyond infancy, William, Duke of Gloucester. It was William's death in July 1700 that focused political minds, resulting in the Act of Settlement of the following year.[65] This statute laid down that after Anne, the Crown should pass to the descendents of Elizabeth, Countess Palatine, the daughter of King James I. In March 1702 William III died, and parliament re-inforced the Act of Settlement with an oath of abjuration, specifically aimed against any revival of the claims of the exiled James Stuart, the son of James II (who had died in 1701). At the same time the 14-year-old Prince was attainted, thus forfeiting both his recognized title to Cornwall and his unrecognized titles to Chester and Wales. Although he lived until 1766, and rebellions were raised in his name in both 1715 and 1745, James Stuart had no further connection with Wales; and since he had gone into exile at the age of a few weeks, it could be argued that he never had.

There was no created Prince between Charles I's accession in 1625 and the elevation of George I's son, also George, in 1714, and during that time all that was left of the distinctiveness of Welsh government was drained away. By 1714 only the Courts of Great Session and the language remained. Yet under William and Mary both England and Wales became more stable. Daniel Defoe, visiting Wales for pleasure in 1710, records the hospitality that he encountered on this 'heavy journey', a far cry from the experiences of English travellers barely two centuries before: 'we generally found their provisions very good and cheap, and very good accommodation in the inns, and that the Welsh gentlemen were very civil, hospitable and kind, the people very obliging and conversable, and especially to strangers'.[66]

Meanwhile, the Crown revenues had been transformed by the intro-duction of a Civil List. This was basically an updated version of the Earl of Salisbury's Great Contract of 1610, whereby all the traditional income of the monarch was diverted to the public purse and replaced with a parliamentary allocation. This had been under consideration since 1691, and was eventually realized in 1698, when the list was set at £700,000 a year. At the same time, all the public expenditure for which the King had hitherto been responsible (such as the armed forces) was transferred to the State. The issue was not without contro-versy, and several MPs protested.

> We have provided for the navy, we have provided for the army, and now at the latter end of a session, here is a new reckoning brought us; we must provide likewise for the civil list.... Certainly such pensions, whatever they may have been formerly, are much too grand in the present want and calamities which reign everywhere, and

it is a general scandal that a government so sick at heart as ours should
look so well in the face.... Mr. Speaker, let us save the king what we
can, and then let us proceed to give him what we are able....[67]

The days of the Stuart Princes were over. In this very different political
climate, future Princes of Wales could take nothing for granted—not
even their finances. By the time of William's death, only the Household and the Privy Purse of the traditional royal expenditure remained
to the King. The effect of this upon the next Prince of Wales, son of
Elector George of Hanover, remained to be negotiated.

CHAPTER V

The Princes of Leicester House

In front of Blenheim Palace in Oxfordshire, there stands a statue of Queen Anne. It makes this plain and rather dumpy little woman—the last of the Protestant Stuarts—appear positively regal, but that is not the point. She had married Prince George of Denmark in 1683, but despite indefatigable pregnancies only one child had survived beyond infancy. This boy, William, Duke of Gloucester never became Prince of Wales; he died in July 1700 at the age of 11, two years before his mother acceded to the throne. Anne had been 37 at the time of her accession, so a successful birth was not out of the question, but it was never likely, and it did not happen. Her death 12 years later proved a momentous event, the announcement of which passed into folklore. It had, of course, been anticipated, and as early as 1701, while William III was still alive, an Act of Settlement ruled on the future order of succession. Anne was the hereditary heir, if the Catholic and exiled James Stuart was excluded, but if she were to die without children the next heir was the Electress Sophia—'the most excellent Princess Sophia, Electress and Dowager Duchess of Hanover' (as she was termed), daughter of Elizabeth 'the winter Queen' and granddaughter of James I. Sophia was over 70 in 1701, and had been a widow for many years. She died shortly before Queen Anne, leaving a son named George, upon whom the throne was to devolve in 1714.

George I was a thoroughgoing German. When he succeeded he was already 54 years old and had been Elector of Hanover for the past 16 years. So unwelcome was the thought of his accession to some Tories that Viscount Bolingbroke attempted to persuade James Stuart to abandon his Catholicism, completely without success. Moreover, the French supported James, and they were never popular allies in England. The Privy Council worked fast and hard to secure a peaceful transition. The ports were closed and the garrisons at the Tower and Edinburgh Castle were strengthened, but none of these precautions were needed.

George was certainly well set in his ways, showing neither the desire nor the aptitude to learn the language of his new realm. His priorities remained Hanoverian, but he was well briefed on the politics of Great Britain, and not least on the lingering Jacobite threat. In accordance with the Regency Act of 1707, the new King immediately appointed 18 Lords Justice to assist the main officers of state in conducting the government until his arrival, when he would confirm appointments or make new ones. He knew about the English party system, and was anxious to avoid falling into the clutches of either the Whigs (whom he distrusted) or the High Tories, who would be unsympathetic towards his German priorities.[1] The Whigs, however, were divided, and less threatening than they seemed. So although the ministry that he established was largely of that persuasion, his continued reliance on his Hanoverian advisers at court gave them less power than they might have wished.

George put the Treasury into commission, and thereby signalled that he wished to be his own chief minister. Lord Halifax, a Whig who had served William III, came back to head the Treasury Commission, while the Earl of Nottingham, a moderate Tory, became Lord President of the Council.[2] In accordance with precedent, the old parliament was dissolved at the end of 1714, and assiduous efforts were made to secure a Whig majority in the subsequent elections—interference that was resented, but that achieved the desired result. Immediately thereafter several of the Tory leaders, including Oxford and Bolingbroke, were impeached for their intrigues with James Stuart and fled to France. These moves undoubtedly contributed to the Jacobite risings later in the year, and for a while seemed dangerous, particularly in Scotland.[3] When the risings were suppressed, and George had been recognized in Scotland as well as in England, the Tories were left tainted by the association, and the long period of Whig ascendancy had begun.

The King had disposed of his wife in 1694. The younger Sophia had been rash enough to embark on an affair with Count Königsmarck, as a result of which she had been exiled to Ahlden and imprisoned, and he had been murdered. This meant that there was no Queen, and although, as one observer put it, George arrived 'with a fat duchess on either arm', neither of these mistresses could fulfil that role. Known respectively in the unkind circles of the court as 'the Maypole' and 'the Elephant', each was to acquire clients of her own and wield some influence in the land. However, George's son had also accompanied him from Germany, landing with him on 18 September. Aged 31, the younger George was just as German in origin and upbringing as his parent. His youth had been disrupted by the disgrace of his mother, to whom he was much attached, so that he had been brought up largely by his grandparents, and it may have been for that reason that he was much more English in his orientation than his father, even before he ever set foot in the country.

In spite of being kept out of England by Anne for personal reasons, Prince George spoke fluent English, and had been created Duke of Cambridge in recognition of his reversionary right to the throne in November 1706.[4] He had served as a cavalry commander on the allied side at the battle of Oudenaarde in 1708, at which he had displayed conspicuous bravery. He had thus been a colleague of the Duke of Marlborough and was well regarded in England, even before his arrival. On 22 August 1705 George had married Caroline, daughter of Johann Friedrich, the Margrave of Brandenburg-Ansbach, and their eldest son, Frederick Lewis, was born in 1707. Although German was the first language of both his parents, Frederick seems to have been brought up bilingual, and most of his political future was to be in England. Within a few days of his arrival, on 22 September 1714, George was created Prince of Wales—a gesture that should have indicated a good relationship with his father, but in fact seems to have owed more to the elder George's need to consolidate his grip on English royal traditions.[5]

Relations between the two seem to have been strained even before their arrival. This derived possibly from George I's awareness that his son attached less importance to Hanover than he did, but also from the King's dislike of Caroline, or any 'clever women'. As soon as he was convinced that his position in England was secure, the King decided to visit his German lands, leaving his son as 'Guardian of the Realm' in his absence. However, this was more by precedent than by choice, and he gave the Prince of Wales only very limited powers. He could not, for example, fill any office without the King's consent. The Prince had already taken his seat in the House of Lords, and was attending council meetings, but he had been given no share in the government nor, before his Guardianship, any official responsibilities.[6] Consequently, when George I left England at the end of July 1716, conditions for a split in the ministry were ripe. The King had taken some of his English advisers with him, and their priority, obviously, lay in supporting their master. Yet those who had remained behind were, in the circumstances, bound to be committed to the Prince. A crisis of choice loomed—court or country? Britain or Hanover? Almost from the time of its signature in 1713, the Treaty of Utrecht had bred resentments to which the German principality was uniquely exposed. George I protected it by entering into an alliance with France in November 1716 to defend the treaty, and this turned the international situation in Britain's favour, leading first to the Triple Alliance (with the Dutch) and then the Quadruple (with the Emperor). The effectiveness of this Alliance depended largely on the English fleet, but it brought stability of a kind to the European scene.[7]

That was more than could be said for domestic politics. The King was deeply suspicious of his son's popularity, measuring it as an isolationist reaction against his European involvements, and had forbidden him to summon parliament in his absence. He was also fed insubstantial rumours that the Prince was intriguing with Walpole and Townshend, although in fact he had little liking for either. When George I returned in January 1717 and faced parliament, he found the Commons in an ugly mood. The Country Party were hostile to his alliance with France, and their leaders were now confused by the politics of the court. Prince George quarrelled openly with his father almost as soon as the latter was back in the country. The ostensible cause was a disagreement over the christening of the Prince's second son, George William, for whom the King tried to insist that his Lord Chamberlain stood as godfather, but the real reason was the cold way in which the King shrugged his son aside as soon as he was back in direct control. As a result of this quarrel, which involved Thomas Pelham, the Duke of Newcastle and led to formal complaints on both sides, the young George was excluded from the court of St James and deprived of his royal guards.

The King's disproportionate reaction soon backfired, because by the end of 1717 there were two courts—one at St James and the other at Leicester House, and what has been dubbed the 'reversionary interest' was gaining political support.[8] The King retaliated by making it clear that any one who frequented Leicester House would not be welcome at his own establishment, and the Prince ordered his followers in the House of Commons to withdraw their support from the ministry.

In April Charles, Viscount Townshend was dismissed, and Robert Walpole resigned. Both transferred their allegiance to Leicester House. The Tories began to recover from their electoral defeat of 1715, and the scandal of the royal family's split began to encourage Jacobite intrigues. The King was becoming paranoid, and the Prince began to fear disinheritance. In January 1718 George even began to consult the judges in order to secure control over the education of his grandchildren — a bid for domestic absolutism that was deemed to have sinister political implications and that immediately led to a period of bitterness and confusion. One of the reasons for the King's fear of his son was that he was well aware of the attractions of Leicester House, a court that was more cultured and more literate than his own, and that was recruiting some of the best political wits of the age — notably Walpole at this point. The latter was particularly close to Caroline, a relationship that could have spelled danger for both of them.

By 1718 Walpole in the Commons and Townshend in the Lords were making life as difficult as possible for their former colleagues, rallying and leading the Tory peers and squires on issues where they had previously opposed them. The impeachment of the Earl of Oxford (mooted two years before), over which Walpole had changed sides, could easily have exposed his duplicity, but he succeeded in avoiding this, and both he and the Earl survived.[9] More effective in derailing him was defeat over the Occasional Conformity Act, another issue on which he had changed sides. This was repealed in spite of Walpole's strenuous efforts, and his opposition consensus began to break up under his feet. The Duke of Argyll, a prominent member of Leicester House, returned to the court as Steward of the Household, and an unsuccessful Jacobite invasion in 1719 rallied the gentlemen of England to the ministry.

By the summer of 1719 Leicester House was sufficiently subdued for the King to pay another visit to Hanover. When he returned in the autumn a whole range of measures, broadly intended to strengthen the King's positions, were introduced into parliament. There was suspicion of this 'creeping absolutism', and they ran into immediate difficulties, so that Leicester House revived. What really brought an end to the feud, however, was not parliamentary victory or defeat, but the rise and rise of the South Sea Company, upon which the plausibility of so much of the government's programme rested. In the early days of the quarrel, in 1715, Prince George had been the Governor of the company, but as its operations and pretensions expanded, the King replaced him in 1718. By 1719 the company was proposing to take over the National Debt, which then stood at £31,000,000, and its progress seemed unstoppable.[10] Awed by this apparently irresistible momentum, the Prince and his followers sued for pardon, and on 23 April the King and his son were formally reconciled. Robert Walpole did much of the intercessory legwork and Lady Cowper (who may well have been an eyewitness) later recorded the event.

> The Prince ... saw the King in his closet. The Prince made him a short compliment, saying it had been a great grief to him to have been in his displeasure so long...and that he hope the rest of his life would be such as the King would never have cause to complain of. The King could not speak to be heard but by broken sentences....[11]

Townshend and Walpole were received at court, and shortly again entered the ministry. By the end of June the South Sea Company stock stood at a record high, and George felt able to pay another visit to Hanover.[12]

When he returned, the vaunted South Sea Company was on the brink of collapse. Rivalry with the Bank of England and the bankruptcy of the Sword Blade Company brought about a crisis of confidence, and the whole credit system was shaken by the panic. The King, his ministers and his court were directly in the line of fire, but critics were to some extent restrained by the thought that the discredit of the dynasty might open the way to the Jacobites, who had no commitment even to honour the National Debt. The Prince of Wales, who if he had remained aloof a little longer might have escaped unscathed, was as compromised as the rest. By December 1720 parliament was on the warpath. Walpole produced an ingenious but abortive scheme for a transfer of stock, which did a little to restore confidence, but by the beginning of 1721 it was obvious that heads must roll. The prevailing feeling was that a monstrous fraud had been perpetrated, and an Act of Parliament confiscated the property of the directors of the company, forbidding them to leave the country.[13] The Chancellor of the Exchequer ended up in the Tower, and Lord Stanhope died of an apoplectic fit. Only Walpole's parliamentary skills saved the ministry from complete collapse, and the King from disastrous discredit. At the same time this was an entirely English crisis. The Hanoverians were not involved, and their influence at court began to decline.

George was not at all grateful—he hated Walpole—but he knew that he needed him. He had checked the Country Party when it had threatened to bring down the Court, and he would check the court party if it threatened to ignore the Country. The Prince of Wales had lost a major investment, because he had been a director of one of the South Sea Company's subsidiaries, so he did not escape the storm, but for the time being he retreated from the political fray. After the reconciliation with his father, and more especially after the South Sea collapse, he behaved with markedly greater discretion. This was partly because he had taken as his political adviser Sir Spencer Compton, the Speaker of the House of Commons and a close ally of Walpole.[14] He maintained friendly contacts with the Tories, not least to discourage them from further intrigues with the Jacobites, but made no attempt to interfere with the processes of government. By August 1723 a sense of calm had descended on the administration. 'We are now in a state of tranquillity and satisfaction beyond what I have ever known', Walpole was able to write to Townshend.

This tranquillity was preserved in spite of, rather than because of, what was happening at court. George I still hankered after European schemes, in spite of the opposition that they always aroused, and in that he was encouraged by Lord Carteret, one of his Secretaries of State, who had been busy ingratiating himself at court while Walpole concentrated on the City and parliament. Townshend, however, countermined him by making friends with the King's formidable mistress, Ehrengard Melusine von der Schulenburg, now the Duchess of Kendal. She proved more than a match for Carteret, and managed to maintain tranquil relations between the administration and the court in spite of the King's restless ambitions.[15] George travelled backwards and forwards to Hanover, but in spite of their reconciliation allowed the Prince of Wales very little scope during his absences. By 1725 Walpole's management of the political machinery was well nigh complete. Never had the resources of government been more efficiently deployed, and the King had finally abandoned his attitude of dislike, if not entirely of suspicion. Walpole's acceptability at court strengthened his position in parliament, and his control of parliament made him more acceptable at the palace. With this consensus the Prince of Wales did not attempt to interfere. His father was now 65 years old and, although not obviously in failing health, his time was likely to be short. The Prince had no obvious leverage, and saw no point in being difficult for the sake of it, so he settled down to wait.

He did not, in the event, have to wait very long. George I had left for Germany at the beginning of June 1727, but he was taken ill and died at Osnabrück on the 11th of the month. The news reached Walpole first, and he immediately went to the Prince of Wales and told him (in his bedchamber if the story is to be believed) that he was now King. Many expectations had waited upon the accession of George II, and most of all the belief that Walpole would be ousted. The new King had frequently expressed his dislike of the 'four governors' as he called them—Robert and Horatio Walpole, the Duke of Newcastle and Lord Townshend. As office holders and their opponents alike crowded to Leicester House to pay their respects, Walpole was rather brusquely referred to Sir Spencer Compton for instructions.[16] Compton, however, was no match for the experienced minister, even if he had wanted to be, and very shortly found himself consulting Walpole over the content of the new King's first address to his council—which would be a sort of declaration of intent. The two men had worked together during Walpole's days at Leicester House, and it was not long before Compton became convinced that only Walpole could deliver the control of the Commons, which would be essential to the King's programme.

Meanwhile, popular enthusiasm for the new king was swift to abate. His admiration of Hanover became increasingly apparent, and as John, Lord Hervey was to write from his position as Vice Chamberlain of the Household

Hanover had so completed the conquest of his affections, that there was nothing English ever commended in his presence that he did not always show, or pretend to show, was surpassed by something of the same kind in Germany. No English or even French cook could dress a dinner, no English confectioner set out a dessert; no English player could act; or English jockey ride, nor were any English horses fit to be drove or fit to be ridden. No Englishman knew how to come into a room, nor any Englishwoman how to dress herself, nor were there any diversions in England, public or private, nor any man or woman in England whose conversation was to be borne—the one, as he said, talking of nothing but their dull politics, and the others of nothing but their ugly clothes. Whereas in Hanover all these things were in the utmost of perfection....[17]

Significantly, Queen Caroline had no opinion of Sir Spencer. Apart from anything else he paid far too much attention to the King's mistress, Henrietta Howard, but it is by no means certain that he was being stupid, or naïve, in this situation. In effect he endangered his own position at court in order to ensure continuity in government, and Walpole soon delivered in one matter of the greatest importance to the King. He persuaded parliament to raise the Civil List allowance from the £700,000 provided in the original act of 1698 to £800,000, with an additional £100,000 jointure for the Queen.[18] Compton was raised to the peerage as Lord Wilmington, and Walpole and Newcastle settled down to manage the election that followed the demise of the Crown. Newcastle had an unrivalled patronage of borough seats and between them they secured a working majority. When the new House met for the first time in January 1728, it elected Walpole's candidate, Arthur Onslow, as its Speaker.

By this time the opposition was both divided and demoralized. The high hopes of June had been dashed, and too many of their apparently principled leaders had turned out to be little better than place-seekers. However, by 1729 Leicester House had a new occupant, and the familiar wheels began to turn once more. Frederick Lewis had been born in Hanover on 31 January 1707, when according to the Act of Settlement he was fourth in line to the throne. His early life had been spent in Germany, where in 1713 his grandfather the Elector appointed Johann Friedrich Grote as his governor and tutor.[19] When most of his kindred moved to England in 1714, the young Frederick remained behind 'to represent the family'. While his father was created Prince of Wales, and began to enjoy the social and political life of London, Frederick acted as the ceremonial head of the Hanoverian court.

Prince George, however, was not unmindful of his son's English prospects. The boy was carefully taught English—rather oddly by a French Protestant tutor—and he began to make friends with some of the English lords who visited the Electorate with his grandfather, most notably Lords Carteret and Townshend. In 1716 he was created a Knight of the Garter, and although this was done in Hanover it further strengthened his ties with England. He also began to be known as the Duke of Gloucester, although it would appear that the title was never officially conferred.[20] The dukedom had been vacant since 1700, and the revenues remained vested in the Crown. After 1720, when George I passed the age of 60, it began to be suggested that it was high time for his grandson to be summoned to England. The English clergy, worried perhaps about his continued immersion in Lutheran doctrine, were particularly insistent. It did not happen, perhaps because the King was reluctant to resurrect Leicester House during a period of comparative tranquillity, or perhaps because relations between Prince George and his now adolescent son were already uneasy. Nevertheless his contacts with England remained close, and it was an English surgeon, Charles Maitland, who inoculated the boy against smallpox in 1723, in what was then a pioneering operation.[21]

In the same year and after an interval of 16 years, Caroline produced a second son. In 1726 both royal brothers were officially enrolled in the English nobility, Frederick as Duke of Edinburgh and William as Duke of Cumberland. By this time Frederick was 19, and there began to be talk of his marriage, but all plans were cancelled when his grandfather died in June 1727. Still Frederick did not come to England, and he played no part in George's London obsequies. Instead he remained in Hanover and led the mourning for the Elector there, along with his great-uncle, Ernest Augustus. Then in August 1728 Ernest Augustus also died, leaving the young Duke of Edinburgh as the only Prince of the Electoral house in Germany. He immediately began to display a political independence that disrupted relations with Prussia and proved immensely offensive—not to say insulting—to his father, who was not only the new King of England, but also Elector.

By this time George had concluded that he had better have his way-ward son where he could see him, and where he could do less harm, in London. He was summoned to England at short notice on 4 December 1728, and created Prince of Wales on the 8 January following.[22] It seems to have been the King's intention to regularize and control his son's political activity. On 21 January Prince Frederick took his seat in the House of Lords, and shortly after he became Chancellor of Trinity College, Dublin. The King also intended to keep him on a tight rein financially, no doubt to curb any temptations to develop an independent patronage network. He was granted £24,000 a year out of the

Civil List, and in addition received £9,000 from the revenues of the Duchy of Cornwall, which had been granted with the Principality.[23] For the time being no application was made for a separate parliamentary grant, and the £100,000 worth of debt that he had incurred in Hanover was absorbed by the Crown. By 1729 his independence was real, but very circumscribed, and when George II went to Hanover in May of that year, he named the Queen as regent instead of his son. There could be no more eloquent testimony to the strained relations between the two men.

Meanwhile Frederick, now aged 23, was sowing his wild oats. In some respects this was innocuous enough. He patronized William Kent, the architect and landscape designer, and commissioned from him a river barge that still exists in the National Maritime Museum. He began to build an art collection, and patronized Philip Mercier the painter, then at the height of his powers. He became friends with John, Lord Hervey and in a different sense with Diana Spencer, daughter of the Earl of Sunderland. There were rumours of marriage, but instead he transferred his affections to Anne Vane, the daughter of Lord Barnard, who bore him an illegitimate son in 1732. (This led to the ending of his friendship with Lord Hervey, whose mistress she had previously been.[24]) Anne was installed in fashionable Soho Square, which must have been some consolation for her discovery that the Prince was a most unsatisfactory lover.

In the same year Frederick added to his authority in Cornwall by becoming Lord Warden of the Stannaries, and absorbed the significant fees into his income. In 1733 he acquired Carlton House in London at a cost of £6,000, and promptly set about embellishing the nine-acre garden with some 15,000 trees. His restless energy was also beginning to find an outlet in specific opposition to the court. He took on new and younger political advisers, notably George Bubb Dodington, and began to flirt with the Tory opposition. None of this was very serious as yet, and for the time being he kept a foot in the palace door. In 1734 he formally asked his father to find a wife for him. Perhaps this was a gesture of reconciliation, or perhaps he could think of no other way to rid himself of Anne Vane. In any case the King selected the 17-year-old Princess Augusta of Saxe-Gotha, and she and the 29-year-old Prince were married in April 1736 in the Chapel Royal at St James's. Anne Vane promptly went back to Lord Hervey, but both she and her son by Frederick were dead by the end of the year.[25]

Frederick's marriage forced an issue over money. When his father had been created Prince of Wales he was already married and a father, so parliament had made a Civil List allocation of £100,000. As a bachelor, Frederick had received £24,000. Now he asked for the full £100,000, which had actually been provided in the Civil List of 1727, with a confidence undoubtedly boosted by a triumphant wedding and the flattering addresses that had been tabled in parliament. However, the King refused his request. Walpole managed to manipulate parliament into granting what George was prepared to concede, which was £50,000.[26] Frederick had hoped, by wooing various of the opposition leaders, to gather a majority for his full allowance, and he was bitterly disappointed. His resentment festered, and at the end of July 1737, he forced the issue. With Augusta heavily pregnant and about to go into labour, Frederick suddenly moved her from Hampton Court, where the King was also resident, to St James's Palace. Apparently the reason for this bizarre behaviour was his unwillingness to allow any child of his to be born under the King's roof—although St James's was equally 'the King's roof', and why he did not return to Leicester House remains a mystery. However, the insult to his father was deliberate, and was taken by the King and the Queen in that spirit.

The inconvenience of this gesture to Augusta was also considerable. St James's Palace was unprepared, and the beds were damp, although there were female servants available to help with her labour, which was almost immediate. As soon as the child was safely delivered, Frederick and Augusta were ordered to leave St James's, and George refused to see his son. In a furious letter to Frederick the King berated his heir's unsatisfactory conduct, deplored his lack of consideration for Augusta and expelled him and his family from St James's forthwith.

This extravagant and undutiful Behaviour in so essential a Point, as the Birth of an Heir to my Crown, is such an Evidence of Your premeditated defiance of Me & such a Contempt of my authority, & of the natural Right belonging to your Parents as cannot be escaped by the pretended Innocence of your Intentions, nor palliated or disguised by specious Words only. But the whole Tenor of your Conduct for a considerable time has been so entirely void of all real Duty to Me, that I have long had reason to be highly offended with you.[27]

Instead he announced formally that 'whoever goes to pay their court to their Royal Highnesses the Prince and Princess of Wales will not be admitted to His Majesty's presence', and conveyed the same message to foreign ambassadors.[28] The stand-off of 20 years earlier had been recreated, and there were two rival courts, one wherever the King happened to be and the other at Leicester House or Kew. Opposition leaders, and particularly the young, sought places in the Prince's household. George Lyttleton became his Private Secretary and William Pitt, who had lost a commission in the Dragoon Guards for political reasons, became a Groom of his Bedchamber. The Prince had been cheered in September 1737 when he left St James's, and the King was advised to effect a reconciliation for the sake of his own popularity—advice that he refused. By the summer of 1738 Leicester House was the acknowledged headquarters of the Country Party.

By this time the Prince's establishment was also large, and growing rapidly. In 1736 he had 40 servants with salaries in excess of £100 a year, compared to the 44 that his father had had in 1717; by 1747 the number had grown to 64, and had reached 71 by 1751. The salaries were comparable to those paid by the King—the Groom of the Stool was paid £1,200 a year—and all this on a budget (at first) of no more than £59,000 a year.[29] Unsurprisingly one of Frederick's first objectives was to get his allowance raised, and this would mean getting rid of Walpole. By March 1738 he was shadowing the parliamentary opposition, now being led in the Commons by William Pitt, and heading the criticism of the political corruption upon which Walpole appeared to be surviving. This was a popular position to adopt, and he became known as 'the people's Prince'. The Country Party was mostly (but not exclusively) Tory, and Viscount Bolingbroke's *Idea of a Patriot King* was largely aimed at the Prince of Wales.

By 1739, when he voted in the Lords for the first time, Frederick was playing the patriotic card for all it was worth. He supported the idea of war with Spain, less out of conviction than because it was a popular option; he patronized belligerent performances at Covent Garden, and 'Rule Britannia' was dedicated to him. In order to maintain this posture, he stretched his resources, and many years later the son of one of his leading supporters estimated that his late father had spent £20,000 in support of the Prince at this stage.[30] He rented Norfolk House, which was bigger than either Leicester House or Carlton

House, and also took up the lease of Cliveden in Buckinghamshire. Excluded from the court, he set out to make Bath a fashionable alternative, and very largely succeeded, although there too he rented rather than built appropriate premises.

By 1740 some 3 peers and 11 MPs were on his payroll, and the latter figure had risen to 15 by the time the next election came around in 1741. Although the Duke of Newcastle remained loyal to Walpole, by the time that the new parliament met in December 1741 it was clear that Duchy influence in Cornwall, combined with the patronage of the Duke of Argyll in Scotland, had brought in some 20 new opposition MPs, and that Walpole's control of the Commons hung by a thread. The long serving minister might still have survived if the King had not taken fright at the thought that the war that he had been seeking might lead to the invasion of Hanover. He backed off from supporting Austria against France, and instead signed a treaty with the latter in order to protect the Electorate.[31] The patriotic lobby was furious and Walpole only narrowly survived a vote to have the King's correspondence laid before the House.

It was to be his last service to the Crown. He had not particularly approved of the King's sensitivities over Hanover, but, as the longest serving minister, he had done his duty. However, Walpole's whole position had been based on his unique aptitude for bridge-building and coalition-forming, and as the Court Party and the Country Party drew further apart over this issue, he found that maintaining a foot in both camps had eventually left him chronically unstable. In January 1742 he was defeated on a number of issues in the Commons. None of these was a vote of confidence, but he felt (rightly) that they were signals that his control had evaporated, and on 2 February he resigned.[32] The King adjourned parliament for a fortnight while he sorted out a new ministry.

Those optimists who believed that Walpole's fall would solve all problems were speedily disillusioned. In fact it would be several years before George II found a satisfactory answer to the questions that his departure posed. But one person who had good cause to be satisfied was the Prince of Wales. Within a few months Sir William Pulteney, later the Earl of Bath, had negotiated a reconciliation between the Prince and his father, and the Earl of Wilmington, the new First Lord of the Treasury had steered a measure through parliament that gave Frederick the full £100,000 a year that he had been campaigning for.

Walpole may not have been a particular bone of contention between the two, but his departure had certainly increased the fluidity of the political situation, and that in turn had opened the way for a deal to be done. They combined (for a little while) in support of a coalition ministry, and the King agreed to the new allowance—although not without a reluctance which boded ill for the duration of the peace. Part of the trouble was caused by the fact that Walpole's fall had been a personal rather than a party issue. There was no question of the Whigs going out of office and being replaced by the Tories. Instead the 'King's friends' as they called themselves, reorganized under new leaders. They were the party of government, a loose but immensely powerful organization, which could equally be seen as the party of office-holding. Those who stood against them, who in fact were mostly country squires and as law abiding as any, could easily be represented as subversive—as enemies of the good order of the Hanoverian state.[33] Just as the Court Party was an alliance of individuals with different interests but a common aim, so Leicester House consisted partly of Tories, but more prominently of disaffected Whigs—those who were temporarily out of favour and looking for whatever patronage they could find. Leicester House was consequently a necessary counterpoise in the complex balance of mid-eighteenth century politics, and did not go away even when the Prince and the King were on relatively good terms.

Irrespective of their personal feelings, the dynamic of this situation pulled the two men apart, and when the Prince tried for a while to maintain his loyalties to both sides, he got no thanks for his pains. Within a year of the ostensible reconciliation, it was being said, 'He [the Prince] has neither power, influence nor credit.... His interfering for anyone is the sure way of ruining his interest—undone with his own party, neglected by the court'.[34] This was an exaggeration, but on many of the main issues of the day the Prince had every right to feel marginalized. During the Jacobite crisis of 1745 he was sidelined and given no chance to demonstrate his undoubted loyalty. Formal requests were complemented by informal pleas, such as the anonymous note received by the Duke of Newcastle on 25 September 1745: 'May it please your Grace, To consider whether or no it will be convenient for the Prince of Wales to come down to York to animate us by His Presence under our calamitous circumstances.'[35] Nor was this an exaggeration to those contemplating the Scottish assault. Another letter to the

Duke, written the following day, 26 September 1745, noted that 400 weapons had been received and delivered to the inhabitants of Carlisle. It continues in bleaker vein: 'No doubt Your Grace knows the condition of Our Garrison. We have 20 Cannon and four Gunners, two Companys of Invalids with three officers. This extreme nakedness makes me greatly fear the bad consequences. 'Tis pity such loyal subjects should want commanders. But what may lay in my power to encourage the Citizens shall not be wanting.'[36] The suggestion that Frederick might visit York was not acted upon, and he was reduced to 'staging a mock siege of Carlisle castle' for the benefit of his dinner guests.

Some Tories may have sympathized with the Young Pretender, but such an accusation could never be levied against George's heir. Frederick wanted to go and fight in the war of the Austrian Succession, but in that case all precedent was against him, and his request was refused. To his chagrin his younger brother, the Duke of Cumberland, was allowed to go instead. And yet he continued to discharge a necessary political function, because without Leicester House the 'respectable' opposition would have had nowhere to go and might well have been driven into subversion. It may well have been George II's ambition to run what we would now call a 'one-party' state, but that was never an option in the eighteenth century, and by making sure that the Tories had a focus of patronage—and of hope—Frederick contributed significantly to the stability of England.[37]

The Prince of Wales was also, of course, dynastically important. His eldest child had been a daughter, Princess Augusta, but Prince George had followed in 1738 (born in a house in St James's Square rented from the Duke of Norfolk) and Edward, William and Henry had been added to the family over the following years. In all nine children survived infancy, and it was upon Frederick and his sons that the future of the dynasty depended, however much George II may have disliked the fact. The Prince also drew to himself a talented group of young men who began to promote him as the constitutional future. He would be the monarch who, in the best British tradition, would promote political harmony based upon a peaceful alternation of government and opposition, in place of the confused internal strife of Hanoverian Whiggery. As early as 1749 Frederick's aides were already planning speeches and ceremonies to accompany his accession, although whether even such a momentous event would have succeeded in installing a

Tory ministry remained to be seen.[38] Among their plans was a determination to get the President of the Privy Council to call it immediately after the King's death was announced, 'that there may be no time for cabal', and to summon both Houses of Parliament at the earliest opportunity.

There is certainly reason to doubt the feasibility, if not the honesty, of these schemes. The 'Carlton House declaration' of 4 June 1747, adopted as a Tory manifesto in the following February, guaranteed the Civil List at £800,000, but also proposed a £300 property qualification for MPs, presumably with the intention of excluding the smaller place holders. Aware of the controversial nature of this proposal, the manifesto was accompanied by plans to gerrymander parliament in the best Whig tradition, and that alienated important people such as William Pitt.[39] At the same time, it was pointedly intended to make more extensive and imaginative use of the members of the royal family, including (for example) the deployment of Frederick's youngest brother, Prince Henry, to the West Indies. Some progress was made in securing parliamentary recognition for these intentions while the King was in Germany in 1750, but the fact remained that the Tories and the opposition Whigs, who formed the two wings of Leicester House, both disliked and distrusted each other, and that placed the reality of the whole programme in doubt.

At the same time, Frederick had other projects in hand, apart from plotting the downfall of the Whig administration. In addition to maintaining his interest in art, literature and above all the theatre, he also established what later became the Royal Botanic Gardens at Kew.[40] In these respects he was something of a paradox, his admiration for Swift and Pope, his patronage of Italian opera and his collection of Van Dycks and Rubens sitting uneasily beside a typical Hanoverian zest for late-night gambling and bull-baiting sessions. He patronized Handel, collected fine silver and was excellent at children's games. Altogether he was far more versatile and talented than is generally recognized, or than was common in his family.

However, all these worthy causes, political and otherwise, were brought to an abrupt end by the Prince's sudden death at Leicester House on 20 March 1751. He had been complaining of a pain in his side for about two weeks, but the end when it came was very sudden, probably from the bursting of an undiagnosed abscess on his lung. He was buried with proper ceremony at Westminster Abbey on 17 April and interred with the traditional demonstrations of grief: 'the White Staff Officers are to break their Staves, and to throw them into the vault.'[41] Nevertheless, it appears that the King was less grief-stricken at the loss of his oldest son than relieved at the disappearance of the main focus of opposition to his policies. Frederick's affinity immediately collapsed because his widow, the Princess Dowager, made haste to submit to George II in the interests of her son, the future George III, who was 13 years old, and entirely dependent upon his grandfather's will.[42] This submission was justified by the Regency Act passed later in the same year. The Queen had died in 1737, and the Princess Dowager was named as regent for her son, in the event of the King dying before he achieved his majority. The Duke of Cumberland was named as President of the Regency Council in such an eventuality; he was mortally offended at not being offered the regency, so his relations with his sister-in-law became worse than they had been at any time during Frederick's life. However, such an arrangement remained hypothetical, and was not eventually needed. Frederick's death had changed the whole political scene, and it remained to be discovered how the pieces would fit together again. Meanwhile the former Prince of Wales became the subject of one of the briefest and most heartless epitaphs ever penned: 'Here lies Fred / who was alive and is dead'. It is only fair to add that his patriotic friends found more generous things to say, and there were also many laments and effusions.

His eldest son, the young Prince George, was created Prince of Wales on 10 April 1751. This was in accordance with precedent, as the only previous occasion upon which a Prince of Wales had died in his father's lifetime leaving a son of his own had been in 1376, and on that occasion also Richard had been newly created (p.44). The normal rules of inheritance did not apply to the Principality, the Earldom or the Duchy of Cornwall, because George was recognized as Duke of Edinburgh from the moment of his father's death.[43] The Earldom of Chester travelled with the Principality, but the Duchy was separate and he was not so created. Presumably the King was only too happy to keep the revenues!

When George was born in 1738, he became the first male of the royal house born in England since the future James II in 1633 (except the Old Pretender, who was immediately disinherited). Rumours of his backwardness as a child were probably exaggerated, or invented altogether, by malicious court gossip. Both his parents spoke German as their first language, and George seems to have been brought up bilingually in German and English. He was fluent in speaking, reading and writing both languages by the time that he was eight. We do not know much of his early relations with his father, but his mother's affections seem to have focused mainly on his younger brother, Edward, which may explain the fact that he grew up to be rather reserved and taciturn, a characteristic that might easily have been interpreted a 'backwardness'.[44]

In 1749, aged 11, he had been created a Knight of the Garter, and George Lewis Scott was appointed as his tutor, a safe but not very stimulating choice; and the assistants, who ministered to his special needs (such as French), did not succeed in rectifying that deficiency. The sons of some of his father's familiars shared his lessons, but competition was not encouraged, and George grew up to be a rather shy youth of no more than average ability. Later in life he became a great bibliophile, and developed a keen appreciation of music, but neither of these traits can be traced back to his schooldays.[45] Of course he was still under the regiment of Scott and his team when his father died, and there is no sign that his circumstances immediately changed, except that he was given a modest establishment of his own, and based officially at Savile House, next door to Leicester House, which remained his mother's residence. It may be that whatever intellectual curiosity the Prince of Wales possessed was killed off by regular 12-hour days in the classroom, where his regime included not only Latin, Greek, Geometry and Arithmetic, but also the reading of Joseph Addison's political papers—enough to stifle any youthful exuberance. Apart from riding and dancing, his only known relaxation was provided by a variety of pets, of which the most unusual was a female quagga (a kind of primitive donkey from South Africa). Of this creature George Edwards wrote in his *Gleanings of Natural History* (1758) 'The noise it made was much different from that of an ass, resembling more the confused barking of a mastiff dog'. It was apparently an intractable beast, but the Prince was fond of it, and at least it prepared him to inherit the royal menagerie, which is more than can be said for his predecessors.

Not long before George II's death, Earl Waldegrave, an unenthusiastic governor of the Prince, gave a cool assessment of his charge.

The Prince of Wales is entering into his twenty-first year, and it would be unfair to decide upon his character in the early stages of life, when there is so much time for improvement. His parts, although not excellent will be found very tolerable if they are properly exercised. He is strictly honest, but wants that frank and open behaviour which makes honest people appear amiable.... His religion is free from all hypocrisy, but is not of the most charitable sort; he has rather too much attention to the sins of his neighbour. He has spirit, but not of the active sort; and does not want resolution, but it is mixed with too much obstinacy ... he is uncommonly indolent, and has strong prejudices.[46]

In spite of (or perhaps because of) these perceived imperfections, interest in the heir apparent was intense. He was seen as more focused on England than either his grandfather or his great-grandfather, and there was eager speculation about the potential of a youthful King. He had become the heir at the age of 13, and his later tutors and mentors were more politically engaged than they might otherwise have been. Lord Harcourt, for example, who assumed the management of his household, was a zealous Whig, while Scott (who was most notable as a gifted mathematician) had been recommended by Bolingbroke. Frederick, whose demise may have been less unexpected to himself than it was to his friends, left a testament for his son, in which he urged him first and foremost to be a good Englishman. The Prince of Wales had become thoroughly familiar with the problems posed by the 'Hanoverian connection', and although he had been born to it, his son had not. He urged George to separate them, advice not taken until eventually enforced by circumstances in 1837.

His other equally well-intentioned but equally doomed advice was to eradicate the parties, which Frederick believed from close experience had bedevilled English politics since his grandfather's accession. This did not necessarily involve the elimination of opposition, but Frederick seems to have believed that the mere existence of party labels encouraged politicians to find grounds for differences that might not otherwise have existed. He seems to have had an old-fashioned constitutionalist vision, where opposition would focus on particular issues rather than on programmes, and would consequently be constantly dissolving and reforming. Perhaps he thought that the resulting instability would work in favour of the Crown's authority, as the central fixed point around which all politics would revolve. It may have been some misunderstanding of Frederick's testament that led to a row in the Dowager Princess's household in 1752, when the Prince's Governor, Lord Harcourt and his Preceptor, Thomas Hayter, Bishop of Norwich, accused Scott and one of his assistants of teaching the boy Jacobite principles.[47] It is hard to imagine what this could have meant, except some kind of absolutist doctrine, which could easily be misconstrued from what Frederick had said about parties, or from a reading of Bolingbroke's *Patriot King*, which was enjoined by Scott. Interestingly, both the King and the Princess Dowager came down on the tutor's side, and both Harcourt and Hayter lost their positions for entertaining what the committee of investigation described as malicious fabrications. It is interesting to see how easily, a century after the Civil War and more than half a century after the Revolutionary Settlement, such fears about 'royal absolutism' could be exploited.

Politically, the 1750s were dominated by the Seven Years War, which had much to do with changing ministries, and with the rise of Pitt, but little to do with the Prince of Wales. He achieved his majority in 1756, the first year of the main conflict, but for the time being made no impact. As was appropriate he was given his own Civil List allocation and his own establishment, but he preferred for the time being to stay with his mother, whose influence over him remained very strong.[48] The most significant change which took place was that Lord Waldegrave's duties as his Governor came to an end, on the Prince's personal insistence in a somewhat adolescent tantrum. He was replaced as Head of the Prince's establishment by Lord Bute, undoubtedly George's own choice. In spite of being a didactic, humourless man, Bute had been close to Frederick, whom he had first met during a rainstorm at Egham races. He was appointed a Lord of the Bedchamber, and had been asked by Augusta to stay on after Frederick's death. He had thus had ample chance to get to know the young Prince, and became his close friend, as well as his chief adviser. It was under his guidance that the first signs of George's version of 'patriot kingship' began to emerge. The Prince was particularly impressed by the classically themed play *Agis*, which was being performed at Drury Lane. 'I cannot praise enough', he wrote to Bute, 'the noble generous sentiments which run through the whole play'.

However, it was one thing to express such sentiments, and another to do anything about them. The Prince was probably just finding his feet, but he began to find himself being accused of indolence, and these charges distressed him. He encouraged reports that he had strenuously defended the constitution against a military coup, allegedly plotted by the Duke of Cumberland, but since both the plot itself and the Duke's involvement remained in the realm of conjecture, little can be made of this, beyond the fact that he did not like his uncle.[49] Meanwhile, the Prince had moved eventually to Leicester House and the 'reversionary interest' began to reappear. Formal relations between Leicester House and the court remained correct, even polite. There may have been little warmth, but on the other hand there was nothing of the overt hostility that had characterized the last years of Walpole's ministry. In fact it was soon 'business as usual', because no sooner had Pitt come to terms with Bute in 1758 than he fell out with the Prince over the war in Germany. By 1760 Pitt was the 'blackest of hearts', a true snake in the grass—a difficult and embarrassing position for Bute, whose relations with both parties continued to be cordial.[50] Meanwhile the latter's influence over the Prince continued to be so great that he even persuaded him to undertake further studies—of modern history and politics, of agriculture and economics, all highly relevant to his future role. 'I am young and inexperienced', George is alleged to have said, 'and want advice. I trust in your friendship which will assist me in all difficulties'. In short, Lord Bute had become a surrogate father to the young man, who even sought his advice when he fell passionately in love with the beautiful Sarah Lennox. Bute strongly advised him to restrain himself, which on this occasion he did.

By 1759 young George's marriage was under active consideration, and that revealed an unexpected aspect of his 'patriotic' stance. He disliked the petty German courts, which had supplied a steady stream of brides for English Princes (and were to continue to do so), and when Caroline of Brunswick was proposed to him, he turned her down. His reluctance does not appear to be due to any exceptional innocence, or even to sexual inexperience. As early as 1754 he had become involved with one Hannah Lightfoot, the daughter of a Quaker tradesman from Wapping. How he might have met her is an interesting question, but she seems at first to have been reluctant to become George's mistress (in contrast to the court dames who would have died for the privilege). Perhaps that was part of her attraction. Rumours that some form of 'marriage' ceremony took place between George and Hannah have existed for centuries, and documents in the National Archives, including a 'certificate' dated 27 May 1759 and apparently witnessed by William Pitt, appear to indicate this.[51] However, it was never officially acknowledged, and according to (her) family tradition Hannah was married off to a Mr Axford, although several of her subsequent children were allegedly fathered by the Prince. Whether, or how, he provided for these offspring is not clear, and Hannah lived her later life in obscurity, but George's sense of responsibility was strong, and he probably did so. That remains his secret.

Two years after rejecting Caroline, and weighed down with the responsibilities of monarchy, George was persuaded to think again and accepted (without enthusiasm) the plain but sensible Charlotte of Mecklenburg. They were married at St James's on 8 September 1761, and crowned together at Westminster on the 22nd.[52] In their case, the love came later, but it was to be one of the most successful and dynastically fruitful of all the Hanoverian unions, producing 15 children over the space of some 20 years.

Meanwhile, George II had died of a heart attack on 25 October 1760 at the age of 77, and the new era that many had been anticipating finally dawned. Partly because he was young—and far more handsome than his putative rival, the (no longer) 'Bonnie Prince Charlie'—and partly because of the ideas that he had been encouraged to adopt, the new King was an idealist. He would sweep away the corruptions of party and interest, which had determined so much of the pattern of recent politics, and replace them with men of goodwill who would realize his concept of a non-partisan government. His falling out with Pitt would, if anything, make that process easier. At the same time the 'Leicester House interest' was also looking for a clean sweep, but to install themselves in power, not to make way for political innocents. The King started his reign by lecturing his Privy Council on the evils of 'this bloody and expensive war', and issuing a proclamation 'for the encouragement of piety and virtue'. He would not, he declared, allow Treasury money to be spent on the forthcoming elections, leaving professional politicians, of whatever colour, deprived of their *milch* cow and at the mercy of a genuine expression of popular opinion.[53]

This royal manifesto quickly emerged as wildly over-optimistic. A ministry with a working majority (which it was likely to retain) could be adjusted, but it could not be abandoned, either for a Tory or a non-partisan alternative. Nor could a war, which had a good deal of popular momentum behind it, simply be abandoned. Bute entered the ministry and Pitt (eventually) resigned. The departure of Pitt opened the way for a 'King's party', but it bore little resemblance to the incorrupt, idealized team of George III's imagination. In fact it bore a suspicious resemblance to the old Leicester House set, and on that basis—much to George's disappointment—the old political wheels kept on turning.[54] Ministries would change, and particular interests would come and go; policies would be negotiated and abandoned, both at home and abroad. But of the kind of revolutionary change that the new King had yearned for, there was no sign.

Only in one important respect was there a real change. There was now no reversionary interest and the King was newly married. It would be many years before another Prince of Wales could emerge with enough experience and resources to provide a haven for alternative ministers. That had briefly been the situation following Frederick's death, but after about five years Leicester House had been re-created. George may have been naïve, but he had the structure and the resources, and although he may not have clearly understood the implications, he offered some kind of a base for the aspiring. Now that was gone, and could not, in the nature of things, return for about 20 years. In the meantime, alternative ways would have to be found to keep the fires of political opposition burning. It might have seemed that the disappearance of Leicester House had left the King's friends with a clear run, but politics is never that simple and it soon transpired that those friends were as divided by policy and interest as ever the old Whigs and Tories had been. So much was this so that they soon lost all coherence as a political grouping, and George III was left to manage a political system remarkably like the one he had inherited.

CHAPTER VI

The Prince Regent

Beau Brummell's famous query, 'Alvanley, who's your fat friend?'—
uttered at a select 'Dandy Ball' of July 1813—captured a view of the
Prince Regent that has stood the test of time. Of all the Princes of
Wales, including his grandfather and great-grandfather, he has perhaps
remained the most notorious. Politically abrasive, extravagant and
debauched, his vices have perpetually outweighed his virtues, and the
caricatures of contemporary cartoons have cast a long (and wide)
shadow. Yet he was a sensitive and discriminating patron of the arts,
leaving us the Royal Pavilion in Brighton and giving his name to an
architectural style famed for its elegance and charm. He was a woman-
izer whose marriage was a disaster, and who died without a legitimate
heir. Coming to the throne when he was already probably past redemption in the public mind, his short reign saw the nadir of the British
monarchy. 'Prinny' has since stood as an ominous warning to all his
successors.

Prince George, later to be George IV, was conceived with great
promptness and born at St James's Palace on 12 August 1762. He was
eventually to be the oldest of 15 siblings.[1] It was a very public advent,
into a palace crammed with dignitaries and officials, in marked contrast to the somewhat furtive arrival of the last heir born to a reigning
King—Prince James in 1688. In spite of having been first reported as a
girl, he was soon perceived to be 'a large and pretty boy', and was displayed to an admiring public on 'Drawing Room Days' at St James's,
'between one o'clock and three'. He was recognized from his birth as
Duke of Cornwall and Rothesay, Earl of Carrick and Baron Renfrew,
and was created Prince of Wales and Earl of Chester on 17 August—even
before he had been baptized. The Archbishop of Canterbury performed
the latter rite in the Queen's Drawing Room on 8 September, when
he was named George Augustus Frederick. In the usual manner, an
establishment was created for him within the royal household. It was

headed by Lady Charlotte Finch as Royal Governess, and consisted almost entirely of women, including an Assistant Governess and several nurses. Owing to the royal fecundity this establishment, with a steady turnover of personnel, was to remain in existence for many years. When he was taken out to enjoy the air in Hyde Park, admiring crowds followed him; no Prince of Wales before him had endured such an exposed infancy, but he came to no harm.[2]

As the child grew up, and his family increased, the King struggled with problems both foreign and domestic. The exuberant idealism that George III had displayed as a youth obstinately refused to defer to the realities of the political world after his accession, and he found himself in a constant state of frustration and distress. In 1765, and already the father of three sons, the King suffered some kind of nervous collapse. This would now be described as 'stress related', and can be seen as a precursor of the mental illness that he was later to suffer, but at the time it was not so diagnosed, and George made a rapid recovery. The experience did, however, prompt him to some serious thought on the subject of the succession. He was only 27, but mortality was uncertain —what was to happen if he were to die before his eldest son achieved his majority—an event which was 15 years off, even by the most optimistic calculation? After all, his own father had died in his 40s. He drew up a proposal for a regency government, but stopped short of naming an actual regent, reserving to himself the right to nominate any member of the royal family normally resident in England.[3] This was to make some rash assumptions about the circumstances of his departing, and in reality said nothing which was not obvious, but it is indicative of a depressive streak in George's mentality which was to become more evident over the years. The fact that he had little confidence in his siblings was also reflected in the Royal Marriages Act of 1772.

Meanwhile, at the age of two and a half, the prince was sufficiently 'forward' as to be able to make a brief statement in the process of making a charitable donation, and at four could respond with precocious gravity to anxious enquiries about his health. The latter were occasioned by the fact that he, too, had been inoculated against smallpox, a process that involved being confined to bed for a few days, although it was by now a routine matter.[4] He continued to be 'shown off' a good deal in public, attending the theatre to see children's plays, and being taken to military reviews, and even to the races at Ascot. At the age of three and a half he was made a Knight of the Garter, and his precocity was made much of in the King's 'public relations'. By the age of five he could read and write, and had mastered the rudiments of English grammar, and at the age of six began a rigorous educational regime involving a range of subjects and commencing every morning at seven o'clock. Altogether he was considered a very promising child—healthy, vigorous and intelligent.

However, George III was also a great believer in peace and regularity for the upbringing of children, and himself preferred Bower Lodge at Kew or Richmond Lodge to the exposure of St James's or Buckingham House in central London. Both Richmond Palace and Windsor Castle were in a state of decay, and the King did not like Hampton Court, so he spent a lot of time at Richmond Lodge, and it was there that his children underwent their earliest education.[5] In 1771 the King's mother died, and the White House at Kew, which had been her residence, became vacant. The King and Queen moved in, but so rapidly was the royal family expanding that even that commodious building soon became overcrowded, and at the age of 11 Prince George, along with his next brother, Prince Frederick, were moved next door to the Dutch House (now known as Kew Palace). Here they were settled with their tutors, under the nominal control of Robert d'Arcy, the Earl of Holderness, by this time their Governor. Holderness was a dull, punctilious man, but he was also a valetudinarian and most of the detailed control of his charges was exercised by Leonard Smelt (as Sub-Governor) or Bishop William Markham of Chester (Preceptor).

Smelt and Markham were of an age (both were 52 on appointment) and of complementary talents. Smelt was a soldier—an engineer—of an outgoing and friendly disposition. Markham was a scholar and a former Headmaster of Westminster, deeply learned but inclined to be pompous. They ran a tough regime—tougher, in all probability than either of them would have chosen—on the strict orders of the King.[6] It appears that, as his children began to grow up, George became increasingly critical as a father. He loved them as babies, but distrusted the onset of puberty. The Princes enjoyed a wide ranging and rigorous education, and were for the most part very well taught, but they were deprived of the company of other children of similar age, and were constantly bombarded, on their father's orders, with moral precepts and exhortations. In spite of the fact that George was intelligent, and far more accomplished than most of Europe's young Princes, being competent in several modern languages and in Latin, both boys lacked outside stimulation. They had few amusements, apart from the occasional concert, and were regularly beaten for their notional misdemeanours.[7] Their mentors became increasingly uneasy at this unfeeling treatment, and in 1776 were replaced by men of sterner mettle. Their new Preceptor, Dr Richard Hurd, Bishop of Coventry and Lichfield, was described as 'stiff, cold and correct'. Soon after his appointment he drew up a 'plan of study' that shows him to have been by no means an unenlightened teacher, but his grinding intensity soon became a sore trial on the Prince's spirits. By the time that he was 16, the younger George was a talented, versatile youth. He was likeable, well mannered, good-looking and generally attractive, and Hurd described him as 'a very promising pupil'. George seemed to please everyone with whom he came into contact—except his father, who had lost faith in his dutiful protestations.

It is impossible for me to express the feelings of my heart and the sentiment of gratitude with which I was filled upon receiving your Majesty's most gracious and affectionate letter. I flatter myself that by the pains I shall take in imbibing your Majesty's admirable principles of virtue and religion, and in following your excellent advice of looking up at all times to our great Creator, you shall not find all the care and trouble you have been at in my education misspent, but that on the contrary, you will find me hereafter not only worthy of your affection as a child, but of your esteem as a friend. It shall always be the principal object of my life to deserve your Majesty's expressions of tenderness and affection, and to do all in my power to contribute to the happiness you receive from the most excellent of women.[8]

Although pleased with his son's accomplishments, George III found him untruthful, duplicitous and wanting in religious sincerity. The inevitable had happened, and the King's anxious intolerance of the slightest backsliding had recoiled spectacularly. In spite of all his superficial charm, the Prince had turned into a rebellious adolescent with a taste for self-indulgence and bad company. These little weaknesses had been surreptitiously encouraged by two of the King's younger brothers, the Dukes of Gloucester and Cumberland, neither of whom shared

George III's rigid sexual morality.[9] Indeed it was their scandalous marriages and affairs that had prompted the Royal Marriage Act, which made it virtually impossible for any member of the royal family to marry anyone who was not a Protestant Prince or Princess.

No descendant of the body of his late majesty King George the second, male or female (other than the issue of princesses who have married, or may hereafter marry, into foreign families) shall be capable of contracting matrimony without the previous consent of his Majesty, his heirs or successors, signified under the Great Seal and declared in Council ... and that every marriage or matrimonial contract, of any such descendant, without such consent first had and obtained, shall be null and void to all intents and purposes whatsoever. Provided always, and be it enacted by the authority aforesaid, That in case any such descendant ... being above the age of twenty five, shall persist in his or her resolution to contract a marriage disapproved of or dissented from, by the king, his heirs or successors; that then such descendant, upon giving notice to the king's Privy Council ... may at any time from the expiration of twelve calendar months after such notice given to the Privy Council as is aforesaid, contract such a marriage.[10]

It was, allegedly, the Duchess of Cumberland who encouraged the Prince's philandering, which was soon to become notorious. Exactly when this began in earnest is a matter of some uncertainty. He is alleged to have seduced one of the Queen's maids of honour when he was 16, but his first traceable infatuation began in the spring of 1779, when at the age of 17 he fell passionately in love with Mary Hamilton, a granddaughter of the Duke of Hamilton, and one of his sister's ladies-in-waiting. He wrote to her extravagant letters of devotion, and begged for a lock of her hair. Mary, however, was 23, and cautious. She responded to his impetuosity with much talk of her honour, and by December of the same year his ardour had cooled, although this probably had less to do with Mary's scruples than with the advent of Mary Robinson.

Mary was an attractive actress of Irish origin, married for convenience to an articled clerk in London called Thomas Robinson. In the autumn of 1779 she was taking London by storm, and on 3 December 1779 she appeared as Perdita in *A Winter's Tale* at Drury Lane. The Prince (who had to obtain permission to go and see the play) was immediately smitten. He bombarded her with amorous messages and eventually persuaded her to visit him. Mrs Robinson was soon induced to leave the stage and her philandering husband to become the Prince's mistress. He called himself 'Florizel' and the affair between the adolescent Prince and the beautiful actress became the talk of London. It burned out after a few months, when another dashing young lady came on the scene, but Mary was not going to go quietly. George had made her lavish promises, and even given her a bond for £20,000, payable when he came of age. She had also retained some of his more indiscreet letters. It eventually cost the King £5,000 and an annuity of £500 to buy her off, leaving his Majesty deeply chagrined that his low opinion of his first-born had been so strikingly vindicated. The Prince's 18th birthday was inevitably greeted by an acerbic blast from his outraged sire, 'your love of dissipation has for some months been with enough ill nature trumpeted in the public papers'. In spite of all the King's efforts, the monarchy's moral probity was being called into question.

It is therefore not surprising that when George was given his own establishment in 1780 he was required to reside with his parents in Buckingham House (to which they had eventually moved in 1775). The King's intention was to subject him to the most rigorous supervision, to prevent any new Mary Robinsons from appearing on the scene, but of course it did not work. In spite of being placed under a virtual curfew, and required to accompany the King on his morning rides and to church on Sundays, young George soon developed all the delinquent's skills in evading his mentors. By the summer of 1781 he had been seen 'riding like a madman' in Hyde Park, getting involved in drunken brawls at Vauxhall and Ranelagh, and seducing more than one gullible or susceptible damsel.[11] Much to his distress his brother Frederick had been sent to Hanover the previous year to improve his German and develop diplomatic skills. Although Frederick was no innocent either, the King now enlisted his help in trying to restrain the Prince of Wales, believing that the liking and mutual respect that existed between them would persuade George to listen to brotherly admonition. Frederick reacted sensibly, urging his brother above all things to be careful of his health, and to keep on good terms with his parents. George ignored him, and his dissipations became wilder and more noticeable. Not surprisingly, he was taken ill, and for a few weeks the sickbed curbed has activities. His physician, Sir Richard Jebb, was alarmed, but within a fortnight the Prince had shaken off his ailment, and resumed his 'wild ways'.

Emotional storms seem to have dominated the Prince's life as he approached 20, and raise doubts about his mental stability. In the spring he met Countess von Hardenberg, the wife of a hopeful Hanoverian diplomat who had come to London to improve his career prospects. Madame von Hardenberg was a tricky and experienced customer and, when she allowed George to have his way with her, began to talk of 'running away together'.[12] Desperately torn, the Prince tried to run away himself, but the King would not hear of him leaving the country. In a state bordering on distraction, he confided his trouble to his mother, and was so overwrought that he passed out dramatically. The Queen, moved by his plight but not really very sympathetic to his self-induced nightmare, persuaded the King to pack the Von Hardenbergs back to Germany, where the Countess first tried her hand with Prince Frederick and then quarrelled with him bitterly.

George's affairs with women were a nuisance and an embarrassment, but it was the men with whom he was keeping company that caused most anxiety at Buckingham House. Anthony St Leger was merely racy and entertaining, but Charles James Fox was a serious politician, with a formidable intellect and equally formidable charm. He sensed a revival of Leicester House, and when Lord North's Tory ministry resigned over the American debacle in 1782, the King was forced to hold his nose and invite the Whig, Lord Rockingham, to form a government. He did so, and Fox became one of the Secretaries of State, rising to be Foreign Secretary in the coalition government that followed Rockingham in 1783.[13] Not only was Fox a Whig—and a damned clever one—but he was also a true soulmate of the Prince when it came to dissipation. He regularly drank at White's club into the small hours, even on days of important parliamentary debates, and is alleged to have lost £11,000 at a sitting while gambling there. His extravagance was legendary, and on another occasion he is supposed to have won no less than £32,000—a fortune of many millions by modern computation. He picked up more than one of the Prince's discarded mistresses (including Mary Robinson) and eventually married one of them in 1795.[14]

In March 1782, at the time of Lord North's resignation, that and the situation in America combined to drive the King into such a state of depression that he contemplated abdication. At the end of the month he even drew up an instrument to that effect, expressing his intention to retire to Hanover, and leaving the Crown of Great Britain to his 'dearly beloved son' Prince George. No doubt the last expression was what we now call 'political correctness' because no one could have been less dearly beloved at that time.[15] It did not matter because the King was dissuaded and the document remained private, but it is eloquent testimony to his state of mind. It is also likely that he perceived, in the intimacy of his son with Fox, the beginning of a new round of that classic Hanoverian confrontation between monarch and heir that had so afflicted relations between his own father and his grandfather in the days of his youth.

In 1783 Prince George reached the age of 21 and moved his estab-lishment out of Buckingham House to Carlton House, no doubt as a symbol of the political attitude that he intended to adopt. Fox, equally mindful of the importance of the alliance, and no doubt aware of the scale of the Prince's debts, in September 1783 moved in the House of Commons that George be given a full Civil List allowance of £100,000. The King was outraged by such effrontery. The Prince's previous allow-ance had been £27,000, plus £12,000 from the Duchy of Cornwall, which he could now receive direct having achieved his majority. This, his father conceded, might not now be enough, but £100,000 was out of the question! 'A shameful squandering of public money', he called it 'to gratify the passions of an ill advised young man'. Eventually a negotiated compromise was reached, along the lines of the previous generation. The Prince could have £50,000 a year, plus the income from the Duchy, and a £60,000 capital grant to pay off some (at least) of his debts, and this was accepted without goodwill on either side. The King wrote 'I cannot conclude without mentioning that his own good sense must convince him how little reason I have to approve of any part of his conduct for the last three years; that his neglect of every religious duty is notorious; his want of common civility to the Queen and me no less so, besides his total disobedience of every injunction which I have given'.[16]

Prince George celebrated his rather equivocal victory by instituting an immense (and immensely expensive) programme of refurbishment at Carlton House, turning it into an exhibition piece of architecture, domestic furnishing and artistic good taste.[17] He had been given the house on the understanding that he would be responsible for its maintenance—but this was not quite what the King had had in mind! A magnificent Corinthian portico was installed, along with an Italian marble temple, water cascades and elegant lawns. Inside a Chinese salon hung with yellow silk anticipated the Royal Pavilion in Brighton.

The Prince's engagement with politics, on the other hand, made little progress. In November 1783 at the opening of parliament he had taken his seat in the House of Lords, while Fox fired the *Morning Chronicle* with enthusiasm for a speech on the recently concluded treaties with France, Spain and the United States—in other words the end of the American War of Independence. Fox's days in office, however, were numbered. Early in December the Duke of Portland's government fell over a defeat on the Government of India bill, and on the 19th, with ill-concealed glee, the King sent for the younger William Pitt (then aged 24) and asked him to form an administration. In the general election that followed, Fox was duly returned for Westminster, and one of his most demonstrative (and provocative) supporters was the Prince of Wales, who celebrated his electoral victory with a display of the buff and blue colours of the Whigs in Carlton House gardens, where the King could not fail to notice it. However, that had not been quite the role that George had envisaged for himself in national politics. Although only three years younger than the incoming Prime Minister, he remained, in the words of the Bishop of Llandaff 'a man occupied with trifles, because he [has] no opportunity of displaying his talents in the conduct of great concerns'. His father, on the other hand, might well have asked—what talents?

Meanwhile, his activities at Carlton House had piled up an enormous burden of debt, some £270,000—a situation that alienated him still further from the puritanical King, although not from his mother, who this time was sympathetic. George was anxious to economise by living abroad, but although this would effectively have deflated his political ambitions, the King would not hear of it. Instead he reluctantly authorized some means of dealing with his mountainous debts. The Prince, however, had another reason for wishing to go abroad, and one that he did not disclose, even to his brother Frederick. In March 1784 Maria Fitzherbert had arrived in London for the season, and since George was now of age and at liberty to attend its functions, they soon met. She was a personable and wealthy widow, about six years his senior, and George was soon in love again—this time, it would appear, genuinely. She resisted his advances, and he began to think seriously of marriage as the only feasible route to gratification. Unfortunately there were three excellent reasons against this. In the first place she was a commoner, and thus unsuitable by tradition; in the second place she was a Roman Catholic, and the law forbade such a union; and in the third place by the Royal Marriages Act he needed the King's consent.[18]

To escape his attentions, Mrs Fitzherbert proposed to return abroad, and in desperation George staged an attempted suicide, and effectively blackmailed her into accepting his ring. Confused, and uncertain what to do next, she then withdrew to France and for months the Prince bombarded her with pleading letters, and sought with increasing desperation to follow her. He did not succeed, but after about a year, Maria Fitzherbert returned, having fallen out with a number of her French servants. George renewed his pressure, and this time found her less reluctant. He had some difficulty in finding a Church of England minister who would be venal enough, or ambitious enough, to conduct a clandestine marriage ceremony, but eventually ran to earth Robert Butt, one time vicar of Twickenham but now a prisoner for debt. In return for his discharge, Butt agree to perform the ceremony, and on 15 December 1785 they were married in Mrs Fitzherbert's drawing room in London. The circumstances involved the greatest secrecy, and afterwards the couple left for a surreptitious honeymoon at Ormeley Lodge, near Richmond.[19]

Maria's ambiguous status was soon the talk of London. A few realized that a morganatic marriage had taken place, many more guessed it, and as many speculated. The lady did not move into Carlton House, but rented another house nearby. Contrary to popular belief, Fox was not privy to the Prince's secret, but the political alliance between them was renewed and strengthened. Although he had no specific information, the King was deeply suspicious, and began to press his son to marry a foreign Princess, pressure that George turned aside by vowing that he would never marry at all, and that the Crown should descend to the sons of his brother Frederick.[20] In 1786, again overwhelmed with debt and in a melodramatic frame of mind (which came naturally to him), he closed Carlton House, dismissed many of his staff and withdrew with Mrs Fitzherbert to Brighton. Fox applauded this cost-cutting exercise, but advised that the economy might be wasted if he did not set up a trust fund for the repayment of his debts. Into that fund he would need to transfer at least £35,000 of his annual allowance, because otherwise his creditors would denounce his economies as a sham.

There was method in all this seeming madness, not least his diplomatic withdrawal to Sussex. It was all intended to shame his father into giving him the £100,000 that the Prince thought he deserved—and it did not work. It was eventually parliament rather than the Crown that came to the rescue, but not before a high profile row in which Fox had denied that any marriage existed, and George fell out spectacularly with Maria Fitzherbert. Fox had in fact been informed by Mrs Fitzherbert's family, but indulged in this duplicity because he did not want to raise what could easily have become a constitutional issue. However, emotions that were quickly aroused were quickly appeased, and in May 1787 there was a general reconciliation. This included the King, who professed himself gratified that the press reports of his son's behaviour indicated 'a more sober' attitude and better company. His affability, at least, was gaining some reward. Parliament agreed that George should have another £10,000 a year out of the Civil List. This was way short of what he wanted, but he was also offered a one-off grant of £161,000 towards paying off his debts, and a further £60,000 towards the completion of Carlton House.[21] The Prince returned to Brighton with Maria in a remarkably contented frame of mind, and his good humour survived for the remainder of the year.

One reason for this was that he was lavishing much care and attention (and money) on building the Royal Pavilion in Brighton. The first version of this remarkable construction was a long, low Graeco-Roman house faced with cream-coloured tiles, its centre piece a domed rotunda encircled by six ionic columns bearing classical statues. The finest architects and interior decorators were employed, including Henry Holland who had worked on Carlton House, but the design inspiration came from the Prince himself.[22] He had been visiting the town since 1783, and had at first leased Grove House, but it was the building of the Pavilion and its occupation by his entourage that gave the pleasures of the seaside their first great fashionable exposure. The Prince's good humour was further improved by the return of his brother Frederick from Hanover. They had been apart for six years, and Frederick had never met Mrs Fitzherbert.

Then in October 1788, the King complained of feeling unwell. As the month progressed he became rapidly worse—intermittently in pain but, more worryingly, constantly loquacious and erratic in his behaviour. By the middle of November the doctors confessed themselves baffled, and his death was being widely rumoured. This, it soon transpired, was overly pessimistic, but his reason was certainly too far impaired to enable him to discharge his duties. At dinner on 5 November he physically attacked the Prince, who was deeply shocked, and the Queen had to be moved into a separate bedroom for her own safety. Reluctantly, Pitt faced up to the fact that there would have to be a regency, and that the regent would have to be the Prince of Wales.

This was controversial. Not only was Pitt aware that the Prince disliked him and would probably seek to use his powers to have him replaced, but George also appeared to have returned to a life of dissipation in London after his contented spell at Brighton. The cartoonists and satirists made hay, and the old King was suddenly remarkably popular. From his taste for bucolic simplicity and his interest in agriculture, he became know affectionately as 'farmer George'.[23] Fox claimed in the Commons that the Prince's right to the regency was inalienable, but parliament insisted that constitutionally the office was in its own gift. Eventually, at the beginning of February 1789 a regency Act was passed, naming the Prince as regent, but restricting his powers—particularly over the grant of pensions and offices. Reluctantly, George took the position as offered. The Whigs, realizing that their hope of ousting Pitt would be doomed to disappointment, fell back on quarrelling among themselves. In fact the whole 'crisis' was a storm in a teacup, and more useful in demonstrating the unsuitability of the Whigs for government than anything else. The Prince continued to be seen as a dissipated fool, although his actual behaviour seems to have been rational and correct enough, and in any case within a month the King had recovered.

The whole episode had been beset with acrimony and confusion, caused in no little measure by the failure of the King's principle physicians, Drs Warren and Willis, to agree as to treatment, or even diagnosis, and to issue contradictory bulletins. At one stage the Prince and the Duke of York were denied access to their father, something that the Prince denounced as outrageous and constitutionally improper since his ministers were allowed to go in. At another point Prince

George was convinced that his father had recovered, a conviction that led to a blazing row with his mother, who seems (for reasons that are not now clear) to have been seriously distressed by the behaviour of both her sons. Having thus quarrelled bitterly with his mother during the crisis, George now found himself ignored by both his parents. His unpopularity was such that the Whigs, who continued to be the 'Leicester House' party, began to consider him as an electoral liability. He could not even get his candidate elected for Cambridge University, a sure sign that he was in the political wilderness! When he arrived at the thanksgiving service for his father's recovery in St Paul's Cathedral, the crowds booed him lustily.[24] He took refuge in horse racing, boxing and (as usual) the bottle. However, he avoided spectacular scrapes, and as his father's medical condition continued to improve, so his mood eventually mellowed. On 4 June 1791 he was permitted to attend the King's birthday celebrations, and on 12 August their reconciliation was demonstrated by the holding of a royal ball at Windsor in honour of his own anniversary. On both occasions George displayed (according to *The Times*) 'charming manners'.

His rehabilitation was also marked by being permitted to play at soldiers. On 26 January 1793 he was made Colonel-in-Chief of the 10th Light Dragoons, known as 'The Prince of Wales's Own', a commission backdated to 1782 to give him seniority. He was almost absurdly gratified by this gesture, declaring that his father had given him 'the greatest of all blessings', although it was made perfectly clear to him that there was no chance of his being involved in active service. This was a real issue, because the international situation was deteriorating, and later that same year Revolutionary France declared war. George accompanied the King to the Horse Guards to inspect the expeditionary force setting out for Holland, but that was as near as he got to the action. His time with the 10th Dragoons was spent (as might have been expected) in parades, parties and role-play. George took part in manoeuvres on the South Downs, and camped near Brighton in the most luxurious style. He celebrated his 31st birthday by giving a 'very superb entertainment' to the officers of the regiment. It was all highly unreal, but it did give him some insight into the realities of military marches, and some experience of a (very contrived) command.

Meanwhile, unable to adjust his lifestyle to his means, the Prince's debts again began to accumulate. His brother Frederick, the Duke of

York, had solved his financial problems by marrying the plain but sensible Frederika, daughter of the King of Prussia. They were married in Berlin in November 1791, and the Duke was able to add £18,000 a year to his allowance.[25] As he also received the revenues of the Bishopric of Osnabrück, his total income was by now £70,000 a year. It is not surprising that the Prince found such a prospect appealing. He had borrowed money all over the place that he was unable to repay, and his racing stable alone was costing £30,000 a year. He tried suspending work at Carlton House, and even closed it again for a while; he also reduced his racing establishment, but nothing came anywhere near to solving his problems. He, too, would have to get married. Fortunately this prospect was made more attractive by the fact that he had fallen out with Maria Fitzherbert. By the summer of 1794 they were living apart, and George had taken as his mistress Frances, Countess of Jersey. Deplorable as this no doubt was, it eased his situation in several ways. Then the Court of Privileges ruled that his brother Augustus's marriage to Lady Augusta Murray was null and void, which made it inevitable that his own union with Maria would be similarly treated, should it be challenged. In August 1794 George went to see his father and told him that he had severed all connection with Mrs Fitzherbert and was now prepared to enter a suitable marriage.[26]

The Prince, who made no pretence that he was marrying for love, seems to have adopted the 'blind dating' method and opted for Princess Caroline of Brunswick—almost the only candidate whom no one had thought to canvass. His mother, who knew something of the lady and her background, was appalled, but the King was satisfied, and that was what mattered. Caroline was 24, but gauche and boisterous in her demeanour—appallingly indiscreet as some claimed—and what was euphemistically described as 'loose' in her habits.[27] Altogether she needed a much firmer hand than the Prince was ever likely to offer her. She had, as Lord Malmesbury commented, no judgement, and needed the guidance of a sensible and steady man—which was not a description of George. Altogether she was not an ideal choice, but the Prince had now decided that he would have to do something about the succession himself, and was not disposed to be picky. He no doubt believed that he could continue to gratify his finer sensibilities elsewhere. Under Malmesbury's auspices the formalities of the marriage treaty, now held in the National Archives, were swiftly completed.

It is concluded and agreed, that the Marriage between His Royal Highness George Augustus Frederick, Prince of Wales and Her Highness Carolina Amelia Elizabeth, Princess of Brunswick and Lunenburg, shall be solemnized in Person in the Kingdom of Great Britain, according to the due Tenor of the laws of England and the Rites and Ceremonies of the English Church....[28]

Despite the elaborate language, the Prince no doubt believed that he could continue to gratify his finer sensibilities elsewhere.

They were married on 8 April 1795 in the Chapel Royal at St James's, the bridegroom having fortified himself with rather too many brandies in order to endure the experience. In spite of this unpromising start, the marriage was at first surprisingly successful. The couple were reported (and reported themselves) to be 'very happy', and Caroline became pregnant almost at once. This was probably her strong suit as a wife, and on 7 January 1796 she gave birth to a daughter. The sex of the child was a disappointment, but should have been a mere hiccup. Unfortunately in the nine months that it had taken to produce Princess Charlotte, their relationship had collapsed completely. This was not entirely the Prince's fault, although his continued partiality for Lady Jersey was certainly a factor. Caroline's eccentric behaviour irritated her husband beyond endurance. She wrote scurrilous letters about the Queen to Brunswick, and some of these missives were intercepted.[29] He took to avoiding her company as much as possible, and she became (understandably) lonely and frustrated. They tried to negotiate an *entente* to live apart, but the King would not hear of a formal separation because of the public nature of his position, and the public (not very well informed in this instance) sided enthusiastically with the Princess.

George was outraged at his wife's behaviour in the 1796 election, during which she openly applauded another Westminster victory for Fox—from whom he was at that time seriously estranged—and became almost hysterical in his denunciations. She had become, he thought 'the tool of the worst of parties at this moment, the democratik...'[30]—an ominous charge in the light of the fate of the French royal family. It is possible also that George was nothing like the stud that he liked to imagine himself to be, and that Caroline was fuelling his hatred by making this known to all and sundry. By the end of the year the couple were completely and notoriously estranged, and from 1799 Caroline lived at Montagu House in Blackheath. George's misery was compounded by the fact that his financial situation was again desperate. His income stood at £73,000 a year, but his debts had soared to £630,000. Pitt proposed that £38,000 a year of the income should be devoted to the liquidation of this massive burden, but so unpopular was the Prince by this time that he ran a considerable political risk in being so forbearing.

George was abused whenever he appeared in public, and there were even rumours that he would be excluded from the succession—although it seems that such reports were unfounded. Eventually it was agreed that his income should be increased to £113,000, with £65,000 of that sum being devoted to the repayment of debts.[31] He would thus have to manage on £48,000 a year at a time when other sources of possible funding were drying up—no one having much faith in him as an investment. The Prince was forced to economize, and to cut back his staff drastically, but he did not resort to closing any of his houses. After all, if he were to continue at Carlton House, his wife would have to live elsewhere—and be provided for. The only consolation that the Prince enjoyed in all this appalling mess was the news that Maria Fitzherbert was prepared to take him back. In 1796 there was an emotional exchange of letters, when each supposed the other to be dying, and there then followed a protracted negotiation in the course of which the Prince's siblings (but not, of course, his parents) were unanimous in urging her to acquiesce. Scrupulously, Maria referred her case to the church—which in this case meant Rome—and eventually secured a decision in favour of their reunion. Although they were not man and wife by the laws of England, they were so in the eyes of the church, and therefore not only might, but should be reunited.[32] With his domestic happiness in some measure restored, the Prince began to relax a little, and this, inevitably, meant further debt. No matter how hard he tried, he seemed to be incapable of living within his means, although Mrs Fitzherbert, who had means of her own, was by no means the burden on him that Caroline had become.

There was also, of course, still a war on. All his brothers served, with varying success and distinction, but George, for all his clamour, was not allowed to see active service. It would have needed only a moment's thought to have realized that this was strictly in accordance with precedent, but the Prince chose to regard it as a personal affront, and a slur on his courage and patriotism. To add insult to injury, both his younger brothers now outranked him in military terms. In December 1803 he allowed the correspondence in which his request had been rejected to be published in the *Morning Chronicle*, an indiscretion that led, indirectly, to a catastrophic falling out with his erstwhile favourite brother, Frederick, Duke of York.[33] In spite of his amiability and generosity (to say nothing of his intelligence), George seems to have been incapable of getting anything right. In 1797 the Irish Whigs had wanted him appointed Lord Lieutenant, but the King would not hear of it. His desire to command a regiment in the field had met with a similar response, and when in 1801 Pitt had been compelled to resign over Catholic Emancipation, Addington had immediately taken over with the King's approval—the Whigs not being given the slightest opportunity.

Then, in the middle of February 1801, the King became ill, with symptoms alarmingly similar to those of his collapse in 1789. A regency was again discussed, and it was made clear to the Prince that this would have to be in the same restricted form as before. He accepted, and began to make tentative plans, in consultation with the Duke of Devonshire and the Marquis of Buckingham, for a new administration.[34] The King had recovered by April, and no regency was eventually needed, but this time the Prince had made a favourable impression by the correctness of his behaviour—an accolade that he seldom earned, either in the past or in the future. The only problem was that he had fallen out with his mother again, suspecting her of falsifying the King's condition in order to stave off the regency that he clearly desired. In February 1804 the King was taken ill again, and the events of three years earlier repeated themselves. This time his bout lasted until June, spreading alarm and confusion throughout the political world, but again there was no regency. Instead the King and the Prince fell out again, because the former's behaviour continued to be erratic, and the latter became increasingly apprehensive of meeting him. The interview did not in fact take place until November, and then, very unexpectedly, it resulted in an emotional reconciliation. Unfortunately the King continued his regular visits to Blackheath to visit Caroline and Charlotte, and that, as was observed at the time, meant that the reconciliation was unlikely to last.[35]

There was no doubt that Caroline's behaviour left a lot to be desired. She was raucous and vulgar and kept bad company. Even the

King, who remained rather fond of her, could not deny this, and when Charlotte was eight, in 1804 he formed a plan to have her educated apart from her mother at Windsor Castle. The Prince agreed, but only on the condition that her mother's rights of access should be strictly limited. John Fisher, the Bishop of Exeter, was appointed as her tutor, because in due course she might well be the Queen. Relieved of direct responsibility for her daughter, the Princess's behaviour became yet more bizarre, and serious accusations began to be made about the goings-on at Montagu House. So grave did these stories become that they were brought to the attention of the cabinet, and in the summer of 1806 the King was reluctantly persuaded to appoint a Commission of Enquiry. On 29 May Lord Erskine, the Chancellor, Earl Spencer, one of the Principal Secretaries of State, and Lord Greville, First Commissioner of the Treasury and the Chief Justice were formally requested by the King to investigate the truth of 'certain written Declarations touching the Conduct of her Royal Highness the Princess of Wales'.[36]

The Commissioners heard all sorts of wild stories, some of them no doubt invented, and came to the conclusion that Caroline's behaviour had indeed been wild and, on occasion, adulterous, but they exonerated her from the charge of having borne an illegitimate child.[37] They concluded that she was a kind-hearted and generous woman, but incurably reckless. The Prince wanted an Act of parliament to dissolve his marriage, but it was pointed out that, through the fog of malice and accusation, charges had been brought, but not actually proved, and all that happened eventually was that the Princess found herself cut off from the royal family, neither the King nor the Queen now being willing to be tainted with such wantonness.

Meanwhile, the Prince had re-entered the political arena, and on the fall of the Addington government in 1804, in the words of one observer, he 'considered himself the head of the Whig party'.[38] When William Pitt died early in 1806 at the age of 46 he was succeeded by the so-called 'ministry of all the talents'—a sort of coalition headed by Lord Grenville, with Fox as Foreign Secretary. George's influence increased proportionately, although it never became as great as he would have wished. The downside of all this was that his estranged wife began to cultivate his political opponents, and contrived to get the whole issue of her status re-opened. The King somewhat wearily referred her complaint back to the Cabinet, which debated the issue long and confusedly before delivering the advice that she should be received again at court, although not without admonition as to her conduct. The government, however, declined to pay her debts, which by then amounted to some £49,000, referring that instead to her husband. Although still struggling with his own debts, the Prince eventually agreed to pay this off at £17,000 a year.[39] This was a generous gesture in the circumstances, but one for which he got no credit at all in the public estimation. When his brother the Duke of York became involved in an odious scandal in 1809, he found himself divided between family loyalty and political conviction, and equivocated. As a result his reputation plummeted still further, and as age and infirmity increasingly overtook the King in 1810, a less promising candidate for either the succession or the regency could hardly have been imagined.

1810 was to prove an eventful year. In January 1809 the English army in Spain had been forced to retreat to Corunna, and had lost its commander, Sir John Moore. This had been followed by the disastrous expedition to Walcheren, which had cost thousands of lives for nothing.[40] 1810 saw a recovery in military terms, with Wellesley's victory at Bussaco in September and the successful defence of Torres Vedras, but the King's second youngest, and much loved, daughter Amelia, died on 2 November, and the Duke of Cumberland became involved in an even more damaging scandal than that which had destroyed the Duke of York.[41] On top of all this, the 72-year-old King was showing distressing signs of lapsing into insanity again. By 3 November, shattered by the news of Amelia's death, he was confined to a straightjacket, but thereafter grew somewhat calmer, and the doctors were divided in their opinion as to when—or whether—he might be expected to recover. The Prince behaved with great correctness, and did not attempt to interfere in the politics of the situation, but he made it clear that he would not be willing to accept a regency on the same limited terms as before. After all, the country was deep in war, and needed unequivocal leadership. However, Spencer Perceval, the Prime Minister, remained adamant and the ministerial changes that would have accompanied a regency remained only under discussion.

By the end of January 1811 hopes were being entertained of George III's recovery, and it began to look as though the Prince's scruples would not matter. However, within a few days the nettle had been grasped. In the interests of political stability, the Prince would waive his right to alter the ministry. Charles James Fox had died in 1806, and there was no other Whig politician about whom he felt equally strong.[42] Although the move was seriously unpopular on the streets of London, and with radical politicians, on 5 February 1811 the Prince of Wales was sworn in as regent at Carlton House. At the age of 48, he at last had some real responsibility. Spencer Perceval was relieved, but the only people who seem to have been genuinely pleased were his royal brothers, who had rallied strongly to his support as January had gone on, and had thus tainted him still further in the eyes of the radicals, to whom they were all a bunch of scandalous wastrels.

The King did not recover, although he was to live for another nine years, and the second decade of the nineteenth century is known to history as 'The Regency'. The Prince looked considerably older than his real age—especially without his make-up. He was also very fat, a condition that prompted the famous query from Beau Brummell (with whom he had fallen out). Although the regency had been granted in the first instance for a year only, and no ministerial changes followed, the Prince decided to celebrate his advent with a great ball at Carlton House on 19 June, ostensibly in honour of the exiled survivors of the French royal family. It was a lavish affair, involving a dining table 200 feet long, and endless dishes in and out of season. The radicals had a field day. The guest list also laid down some important social markers. The Queen was not there, out of consideration for the sick King. Princess Caroline was not invited, and neither was Princess Charlotte, who at 15 was showing distressing symptoms of her mother's character. More significantly, Maria Fitzherbert was not there either. She had been definitely displaced in George's affections by Isabella, Marchioness of Hertford, and having been told 'you know, madam, you have no place', withdrew with dignity.[43] While remaining in her own eyes George's lawful wife, she had ample means of her own, and they never spoke again. However, the Prince regarded himself as formally separated, and made her an allowance of £6,000 a year (which he could ill afford).

Although George remained superficially as suave and charming as ever, especially to strangers, as the months went by he became increasingly worried and preoccupied. 'You know,' he said at one point, 'playing the King is no sinecure'.[44] In spite of the passage of years, his judgement seems to have been no better than before. Although he made no attempt to change the ministry, he was determined to protect his patronage in other ways, and insisted on reinstating his brother the Duke of York as Commander-in-Chief, despite the disgrace that had led to his retirement two years earlier. On the other hand he fell out publicly with the ultra-conservative Duke of Cumberland, and that did something to restore his image.[45]

Meanwhile the King became markedly worse. His illness was probably porphyria, but it left him completely incapacitated and sometimes ragingly insane. As the Duke of York reported to the Prince Regent in July 1811:

> I am this instant returned from Windsor, and am truly grieved to inform you that everything continues in the same melancholy way. His majesty was very irritable this morning, refused to put on his clothes when desired to get up, and continued to reject all food until two o'clock, when he told Dr. Heberden that if he offered any to him he would take it. In consequence his majesty tasted some jelly and drank a large draft of milk, and then asked for some hasty pudding. Dr. Willes, who I saw just before I got into my carriage, seems very much cut down and told me that if anything the king was a shade worse today. In short, appearances continue to be as bad as possible....[46]

Consequently there was no option but to extend the regency indefinitely when the 'probationary' year expired in February 1812. By this time the Whigs were thoroughly disillusioned with the Prince Regent's failure to act on their behalf, expressing 'a total lack of confidence in [his] steadfastness and good faith'. There were resignations from his household amid charges of ingratitude and perfidy. George retaliated, and there were furious quarrels.[47] On 11 May Spencer Perceval was assassinated, and this unprecedented event left the Prince Regent in a great state of agitation. Death threats had also been issued against him, and the memories of the revolutionary violence in France were still fresh. Lord Liverpool became Prime Minister and there was a shake up in the Cabinet that brought in Lord Castlereagh as Foreign Secretary. Within a matter of days the new government had succumbed to a vote of no confidence, but the Prince Regent knew what he wanted: a Tory ministry that would pursue the war to a successful conclusion and avoid the controversial topic of Catholic emancipation.

In a short space of time Lord Liverpool was back, although with a recast team, and he was to last for 15 years. In this crisis, George displayed at last the kind of resolute leadership that the populace had been demanding. He gave the country stability, but he got small thanks. His image became worse than ever, and the death threats continued. This was partly due to his continued extravagance, but the fact of the matter was that there were now two royal establishments to maintain, as well as numerous royal siblings to be supported, and a family on that scale did not come cheap. The Prince Regent's debts had risen again to £552,000, and his request for a £150,000 a year 'regency allowance' was turned down.[48] However the Queen and her unmarried daughters were finally given an adequate establishment of £196,000 a year, and thus ceased to be a burden on the Prince—to his great relief. Needless to say he was vilified in the *Examiner* (an opposition paper) as 'a libertine, over head and ears in debt and disgrace, a despiser of domestic ties'. The editor got two years in gaol for libel, but that was small consolation to the victim, who must have been wondering what on earth he could do to turn his reputation around.

He drank himself ill, and some thought that he would go mad in his turn. In spite of her irresponsible conduct, his estranged wife continued to be popular, and mobs gathered in London urging her to burn down Carlton House. Numerous satirical cartoons, often vitriolic in tone, championed the Princess's cause. Many are now held in the National Archives, their hostility still striking after almost two centuries. Lady Douglas, who had contributed allegations against the Princess to the 'Delicate Investigation', was depicted as 'A Venomous Viper Poisoning the R——l Mind' in 1813, while another of 1820, entitled 'How to get un-married—ay, there's the rub' portrays the unhappy couple still yoked by the relentless 'Matrimonial Knot'. The corpulent George struggles to free himself, exclaiming 'There is but little trouble in tying the Knot, but your quizzes of the cloth draw it so tight….' The Princess, stout but dignified, is supported by blind (and female) Justice, who declares 'Your exemplary conduct is worthy imitation … the world must approve your seeking refuge in the wholesome and protecting laws of your country.'[49]

Not surprisingly, the Prince Regent was anxious to get her out of the country, and even prepared to double her allowance (to £50,000) in order to achieve that. Finally, in 1814, having blotted her copybook with all respectable society, Caroline was persuaded to accept the offer and withdrew (loudly protesting) to Brunswick.[50] That left Charlotte, his loveable but troublesome daughter. Charlotte was a showy, rather coarse girl, and as strong-minded as her mother. A marriage was negotiated for her with Prince William of Orange, admittedly not an attractive prospect for any girl. She objected, gave way in June 1814, and then adamantly refused to go ahead when she discovered that she would be expected to live in Holland. For this defiance she was placed under restraint at Warwick House, and began to fear that she would be cut out of the succession.

However George was not a man to bear grudges, and he was genuinely fond of her. Before the end of the year they were reconciled, and he had paid her debts, which amounted to £20,000. Eventually she was persuaded to accept a union with Prince Leopold of Saxe-Coburg—a talented but impoverished young man, and they were married in May 1816.[51] Since Leopold was financially dependent on his wife, they settled at Claremont Park. They appear to have been extremely happy, and Charlotte quickly became pregnant. However, on 5 November 1817 she was delivered of a stillborn son, and herself died the following day. Both her father and her husband were devastated, but it was the former (characteristically) who indulged in the more extravagant professions of grief.

Public affairs did not offer much relief from all this private distress. Although the Prince enjoyed the victory celebrations in 1814, and happily conferred the Order of the Garter on the new King of France, Louis XVIII, the country at large was in a violently discontented frame of mind. Ever since the Corn Law riots of 1815 there had been intermittent outbreaks of violence, revolutionary gatherings and fierce threats against the established order.[52] By 1816 a national revolution seemed a distinct possibility because the yeomanry, the first line of defence against insurrection, were themselves becoming disaffected. In 1819 regular troops were used to disperse a mass protest rally at St Peter's Fields in Manchester—the so-called Peterloo massacre—and the following year a rather febrile conspiracy to murder the entire Cabinet was detected. There was no mass insurrection, and the Cato Street conspirators were executed on 1 May 1820, but the Prince got none of the credit for this survival. He was violently unpopular except among his own particular friends, and the monarchy was a liability rather than an asset to those charged with the preservation of public order.[53]

Nevertheless the regency was in its own way a period of achievement. George was interested in the Grand Strategy of the later phases of the war, rejoiced at the news of Napoleon's retreat from Moscow, and meticulously supported the Duke of Wellington from the Peninsular campaign onwards. He had carefully fended off those politicians who wanted a negotiated peace in 1811, and backed the soldiers' desire for a decisive victory in the field. In April 1814 he wrote to his mother that he felt confident that he had done his duty—and even ventured to hope that she might be proud of him. His own regiment, the 10th Light Dragoons, was in the thick of the action at Waterloo, and he fantasized about having been present at the battle himself. In fact, of course he saw no action, but he was the first Protestant Prince to be awarded the Order of the Golden Fleece, to say nothing of the honorary colonelcy of a Hungarian regiment! It was also the period of his most creative building projects, when his collaboration with John Nash reshaped several parts of London, when the Royal Pavilion in Brighton was completed, as was the strange Hindu fantasy of Sezincote, near Moreton-in-Marsh. The latter, conceived for a rich nabob, was nothing to do with the Prince, but Nash added the famous oriental dome in the summer of 1818. None of this made much impression on the political radicals at the time, but posterity owes George at least a nod of gratitude.

On 29 January 1820, King George III died. Queen Charlotte had predeceased him in 1818, and he was a very lonely, deranged figure by the time that he died. George mourned extravagantly for both his parents, and struggled to cope with his wayward siblings. The Duke of Cumberland was at length prevailed upon to retire to Germany in 1818, and that same year Edward, Duke of Kent married Prince Leopold's sister, Mary Louise Victoria. Although he died in 1820, it was Edward who guaranteed the succession by fathering Princess Victoria in 1819. Victoria grew into a handsome winning child of whom all her ill-assorted relations became extremely fond.[54] The search continued for a bride for William, the Duke of Clarence, who had eventually been persuaded to give up Dorothea Jordan (his version of Maria Fitzherbert) in 1811. In 1818 he was also settled with Princess Adelaide of Saxe-Meiningen. By the time that the old King died, most of the family's problems appeared to have been tidied away. Except of course for Caroline, who although out of sight (in a sense) was by no means out of mind.

After her withdrawal to Brunswick in 1814, the Princess's behaviour had become yet more extravagant and scandalous—so much so that her English servants steadily abandoned ship and were replaced with assorted Frenchmen and Italians, many of dubious reputation, most notably her Chamberlain and notorious lover Bartolomeo Pergami.[55] How much of this was sheer self-indulgence, and how much a calculated insult to her estranged husband (she was still styled 'Princess of Wales') we do not know, but George felt that he could not ignore it. An official English enquiry team trailed her from July to November 1818, and concluded that all the stories were more or less true. The Prince wanted a divorce, but to his chagrin found the Cabinet opposed. Suppose the court should rake up that old affair with Maria Fitzherbert?

So the affair stood when George IV succeeded to the throne, and something had to be done. He could offer to continue her allowance on the condition that she stayed abroad. The King lost a sharp tussle with his government over the Civil List, but the election that followed the demise of the Crown returned a Tory majority, so there was no chance of changing horses. Caroline thus became an obvious weapon for the Whig opposition, and although her more responsible political advisers urged caution, she announced her intention to return immediately in order to claim her rights as Queen.[56] Sweeping aside all objections, she returned to London in the summer of 1820, and took up residence at Brandenburg House in Hammersmith. The London crowds rallied round and cheered her to the echo—less because they liked or approved or her than because of her open defiance of the King. Put on his mettle, George quickly launched another enquiry in August, and when that reported on 6 November, immediately launched a Bill of Pains and Penalties in parliament. This was an extrajudicial procedure intended to secure a conviction without trial, rather like an Act of Attainder except not relating to treason. Attempts to reach an 'out of court' settlement having failed, when the Bill came to a vote in the House of Lords it passed by so slender a margin that the government advised against putting it to the Commons. To the King's bitter distress and disappointment, the measure was abandoned, and bonfires were lit at Brandenburg House.[57]

Public opinion, however, turned out to be an unreliable prop, and time was running out for the Queen. Rather surprisingly, as 1821 advanced the popular tide turned against her, and in favour of her beleaguered husband. Because she had neglected to pay the repair bills, Brandenburg House was falling apart, and she was forced to move to Cambridge House in South Audley Street. There she made the mistake of announcing that she would attend the coronation as Queen. Needless to say, no provision was made to accommodate her intention, and when she turned up at the abbey on 19 July 1821 she was refused admission. Instead of applauding her spirit, the bystanders jeered her, and she retired, shattered and humiliated. Her health was destroyed by this rebuff, and she died only three weeks later, on 7 August. She was buried, by her own wish, in Brunswick, but the English government paid the bill. There was a final defiant demonstration in her favour as the coffin was borne to Chelmsford for transmission to the continent, and then she was gone.[58]

George was on his way to Ireland when the news reached him, and even he did not pretend to grieve. He was always very popular in Ireland, and was noted to be in remarkably good spirits on this occasion. The trip was a resounding success—and he needed a success. In October he went to Hanover for a second coronation, and had a friendly meeting with Metternich. By 1823 his energies were beginning to flag, which was not surprising in a man who had 'consumed his royal person' so unsparingly and for so long. His latest companion was Lady Conyngham, but no one claimed that they were more than just friends. His wife had died insolvent, and George had personally honoured her bequests, particularly to her servants. He fell out with the Whigs over the increasing radicalism of the allies with which they were associating themselves, but his relations with the Tories were not much better, and by 1827 he was beginning to look increasingly impotent politically.[59] His opposition to Catholic Emancipation was notorious, and was reinforced by the return from Germany of the Duke of Cumberland in 1828, and yet when the Relief Act was presented for the royal assent on 10 April 1829, he accepted it without complaint.

Partly for this reason, his relations with his government improved in the last months of his life, and as his health steadily declined in the early months of 1830 a kind of peace descended upon his troubled life. He died after a long and complex illness on 26 June 1830, and was succeeded by his oldest surviving brother, William, Duke of Clarence, who took the title of William IV. Although he and his brothers had sired an unknown number of illegitimate children over a period of 30 years, Charlotte had been his only legitimate daughter, and the only child of the next generation still alive at the time of his death was the 11-year-old Princess Victoria, daughter of his brother Edward.

George had been an extravagant man in every way—in his tastes, in his emotions and in his habits. He loved women, food and wine, and frequently indulged in all three to excess. He was frequently ill, and in many ways he did remarkably well to survive to the age of 68. More than a little touched with the madness that undid his over-restrained and puritanical father, he could also be charming, witty and generous to a fault—the chief reason that his finances were always in such a mess. The Prince Regent's legacy, ensured by the architect John Nash, includes the Royal Pavilion in Brighton, as well as the remodelled Buckingham Palace and the development of the area of London that now takes in Regent Street and Regent's Park. He bequeathed the Royal Library to the British Museum, building a new wing to house it, and patronized many of the finest writers and intellects of the period. In many ways he was the last of the flamboyant monarchs and he paid the price in almost lifelong unpopularity. Although he never overstepped the bounds of constitutional propriety, that was not for want of trying, and his political no less than his romantic adventures were widely resented by a nation which had its own inflexible rules of propriety. By the time that his much less colourful brother died in 1837, it was obvious that the monarchy would have to re-invent itself in order to survive. Fortunately, Victoria was just the girl for the job.

CHAPTER VII

The Prince of Pleasure

Bertie, the longest serving Prince of Wales to date, was a survivor. In spite of the most unrealistic expectations entertained of him by both his parents, and the draconian regime to which he was subjected in consequence, Albert Edward emerged as a rather engaging figure. He had great gifts of tact and diplomacy that—together with a serious bout of typhoid—helped the monarchy to overcome a powerful republican movement in the early 1870s. Related to many of the crowned heads of Europe, Bertie's style of 'family diplomacy' was valued by successive governments, but he was popularly considered a cheerful hedonist, known to the public for his appearances at Cowes and Ascot. His diverse associates caused disquiet to many at court, but his influence brought a new flexibility and insouciance to the rigid society of Victorian times. When, after 60 years in waiting, Edward finally achieved the throne, he gave his name to a style of life and amusement that defined a flamboyant and colourful age.

The only daughter of the Prince Regent and Caroline, Charlotte, died in childbirth in 1817, by which time her parents were bitterly estranged.[1] Caroline died within weeks of her husband's coronation, without ever being recognized as Queen, and for the 10 years of George's reign there was therefore no Prince of Wales. George was succeeded in 1830 by his oldest surviving brother, William, Duke of Clarence, who had married at the age of 52, after a long and fruitful liaison with Dorothea Jordan. His wife, Adelaide of Saxe-Meiningen, bore William two daughters, but both had died in infancy, in 1819 and 1821. Consequently for the seven years of William's reign, from 1830 to 1837, there was no Prince of Wales either; William's heir was Victoria, daughter of his younger brother, Edward, Duke of Kent, who had died in 1820. Just 18 years old and unmarried when she acceded to the throne, Victoria sought to rescue the monarchy from the baleful influence of George III's sons, and the public took to her at once.[2] Because

Hanover followed the Salic Law (a practice that barred females from the throne), the 120-year association between the two monarchies then came to an end, with her uncle Ernest, Duke of Cumberland, succeeding to the German kingdom. Although Victoria had been the heir since her uncle William became King, she had never been created Princess of Wales. There was no precedent for a woman to hold that status — as remains the case to the present day.

Victoria was strongly attached to Lord Melbourne, the Prime Minister whom she inherited, and her household was consequently filled with ladies of the Whig (or Liberal) allegiance. 'She is surrounded by Whiglings, male and female', as the Duke of Wellington observed.[3] When Melbourne, whose position was weak, was defeated on a minor issue of confidence in 1839, the Queen refused to dissolve parliament and the Prime Minister survived, for the time being. His influence with Victoria was very great, and she referred to him in terms of endearment, but the question of her marriage was urgent, and on that issue he could say little. Before her accession the greatest influences upon her had been her Hanoverian governess, Baroness Lehzen, and her mother, Mary Louise Victoria — sister to that Leopold, now King of the Belgians, who had been briefly married to George IV's daughter Charlotte.[4] Although none of these counted for much in political or constitutional terms, when it came to marriage the situation was otherwise. It was this circle that put forward Albert of Saxe-Coburg, the son of another brother of the Duchess of Kent, as a candidate. Both were Protestants of compatible regiments and, although he and Victoria were first cousins, that was not considered to be an impediment. The couple were married in February 1840, and in November of the same year their first child was born, and named for her mother — Victoria. It was to be several years before the title of Prince Consort was bestowed, but for the next 20 years Albert was to be the most influential person in the Queen's life. Although a severe parent, he was in other respects a wise and cultivated man. Well suited to an emerging industrial power that had outgrown Regency excess, Albert was to carve out for himself a unique place in the affairs and affections of his adopted country.[5]

Within a couple of months of giving birth, Victoria was pregnant again, and by October of 1841 was fretful and depressed. She had survived two attempts upon her life, the economy was in the grip of recession, and when four successive budgets showed deficits, Peel was able to force a second vote of no confidence against Melbourne.[6] This time there could be no question of refusing a dissolution, and in the general election that ensued the Tories secured a comfortable majority of 90 or so. Melbourne finally resigned on 8 November 1841 and Peel was sworn in. For the next five years he was to lead an extremely strong government, but that was no consolation to the Queen. The very next day she went into labour, 'suffering severe pain', as her journal later admitted, this being before the days of painkillers, or even of chloroform. However, supported by Albert she survived the ordeal and before the end of the day was delivered of a healthy boy.

So Albert Edward, as Victoria insisted upon calling him, was born at Buckingham Palace on 9 November 1841. He was styled Duke of Cornwall and of Saxony from his birth, and about a month later was created Prince of Wales and Earl of Chester.[7] In accordance with the custom established in the previous century, he received the revenues of Cornwall at once, although they were to be administered for him until he came of age. There was great rejoicing in the country at large, and some respite from the economic misery. 'God save the Prince of Wales', the crowds shouted, relieved that the monarchy was now safe for the future. They loved their young Queen, but she was an anomaly, and they were not to know that longevity was eventually to give her an iconic status.

Victoria's spirits were quickly restored by this success. Bertie was a robust child and was optimistically declared to be just like his father, reflecting the Queen's desire that he should resemble Albert in every particular. 'I hope and pray he may be like his dearest papa', she wrote, with more faith than prescience.[8] On 25 January 1842 Albert Edward was baptized in St George's Chapel at Windsor by William Howley, the Archbishop of Canterbury. At first he joined the nursery already in existence for the Princess Royal, only 18 months his senior, and the same nurse, Mrs Southey, was given charge of them both. Mrs Southey's competence, however, seems to have been limited to the very young, and she was shortly replaced by Sarah, Lady Lyttleton, a daughter of Earl Spencer, who was to prove a wise governess and surrogate mother over the next few years.[9] The Queen busily added to her responsibilities with the birth of Alice in 1843, Alfred in 1844 and Helena in 1846, proof (if any were needed) that Victoria and Albert were still deeply attached to each other.

Lady Lyttleton, however, soon encountered problems that taxed even her great resources of patience. Initially a docile, good-natured child, Albert took to her at once, but young Victoria was difficult, perhaps because she had been attached to Mrs Southey. She was what would now be called a hyperactive child, sharp, lively, intelligent and much given to extravagant tantrums. It took Sarah Lyttleton a long time and a lot of skill to win her confidence, but when she succeeded their relationship became warm and close. With Albert, the situation moved in the opposite direction. As he became a little older, his docility became a kind of sullen resentfulness and he began to appear backward. At the age of four he was noted to be 'uncommonly averse to learning'—presumably his ABC at that age—and by the time that Helena was born he was causing great distress to Sarah Lyttleton's French assistant, Mlle Hollande.[10] There were probably a number of reasons for this. He was jealous of the attention being paid to his younger siblings, and disliked Mlle Hollande. Albert began to be perceived as 'difficult', and unfortunately his parents did not attempt to disguise their disappointment. Victoria, now bright and amenable, was consistently praised and encouraged, while Bertie was just as regularly reprimanded or ignored. He developed a vicious temper and the Queen, who longed to rejoice in all her children, became increasingly anxious.

In 1847, when Bertie was just six, Albert drew up a set of instructions for educating all his children. The older two were now to be given a distinct regime, which was to commence in February 1848, and lessons in English, Arithmetic, Geography, German and French were decreed. Their religious instruction was to be supervised by another of Lady Lyttleton's assistants, Miss Hildyard, and it was stipulated that on this somewhat sensitive issue the Queen was always to be consulted.[11] Prince Albert expected to receive regular reports, and reserved all rights of punishment to himself. He was by nature somewhat austere, and this clause had the unfortunate effect of always associating their father with the whip—which he somewhat lavishly administered. Under this discipline Bertie became noticeably worse, falling behind in all his lessons except German, with which he seems to have had a natural affinity. His outbursts of temper became fiercer and more prolonged, leaving him exhausted and unable to concentrate. He developed an impediment in his speech, which turned into a dreadful stammer for which his siblings mocked him.[12]

Nowadays parents similarly placed might have sent for an educational psychologist, but such people were unknown in the 1840s. The nearest thing then available was a phrenologist, and Sir George Combe was duly consulted. His advice strikes the modern eye as sensitive and enlightened. He questioned the whole value of the 'punishment culture' to which the boy was being subjected, and suggested that a little encouragement might work wonders. He should not be forced to learn, as persistence in coercion would only further aggravate his obstinacy.[13] However, Prince Albert was not prepared to accept this implied criticism of his methods. He was steeped in the educational theories of the German enlightenment, and believed that it had been defects in upbringing that had led to the debauchery so detrimental to the British monarchy in earlier generations. The report was ignored. Anxious not to repeat the mistakes of their predecessors, both Victoria and Albert continued to pursue their hopeless quest of seeking to turn Bertie into a model Prince of Wales.

When he was about eight the boy was moved out of the female-dominated environment that he apparently found so irksome. A male tutor was appointed, one Henry Birch, a young master at Eton. Birch was handsome, well mannered and no doubt well connected, but he was not a good choice. Although he was an excellent sportsman he was a poor teacher, and his charge made little progress.[14] They also seem at first to have disliked each other intensely. Birch described Bertie as 'extremely disobedient, impertinent … and unwilling to submit to discipline'. He was a most difficult pupil, varying in mood from day to day, refusing to answer questions even when he knew the answers perfectly well, and flying into ungovernable rages. He was also a congenital fantasist, making up stories about himself, even when he knew that the truth was readily available. What Bertie thought of Birch is not on record, but it was probably equally unflattering. In his tutor's opinion, isolation was at the root of his problems. 'Boys' characters', he observed, 'are formed as much by their peers as by their tutors'.[15] Unfortunately anything approaching a normal schoolroom seems to have been thought out of the question. The only concession made was that Bertie's lessons should be shared with Alfred, who although two years younger was far more advanced in his learning. Rather surprisingly, this seems to have worked. The older boy calmed down and began to apply himself more diligently. This may have been because he did not want to be outshone by his junior, but it seems to have been rather because he just liked Alfred, and the sibling jealousies of their infancy had been forgotten. Bertie's relations with his tutor also improved, and when the latter resigned in 1852 in order to enter Holy Orders (Albert not thinking such a vocation suitable for a royal tutor), the boy was genuinely sorry to see him go. 'It has been', one observer wrote, 'a trouble and a sorrow to the Prince of Wales [who is] such an affectionate dear little fellow'.[16]

Birch was replaced by one Frederick Gibbs, an opinionated barrister who had been for a short while a Fellow of Trinity College, Cambridge, and the relationship building had to begin all over again. It did not work, because Bertie detested him, and started to take out his ill humour on his brother. Their friendship was replaced with quarrels that sometimes became violent. By this time it was clear that Bertie's lack of academic progress was not the result of a defective temperament, nor of poor relationships, nor of stupidity, but simply of a lack of aptitude for the kind of studies to which he was being subjected. He was simply not 'bookish'. The pressure from his father, however, was remorseless. The Prince was kept at work seven hours a day, six days a week, with any free time being filled with riding and gymnastics. In 1849 he accompanied his parents to Ireland, but his tutors went too, and there was no let up in the daily grind. In Albert's view, 'not a week, not a day, not an hour of the time of this precious youth could safely or properly be wasted', noted the courtier Lord Esher.[17] Albert did not believe in holidays, and even when the court had moved to Balmoral for the shooting season, the tutors were supposed to apply their labours just as diligently.[18]

Nothing would make Bertie studious, but he did have other qualities that by this time were emerging from the general fog of disapprobation. He had, for example, a very good memory and remarkable powers of observation. Above all (and this his parents should have noticed with approval), he had a very strongly developed moral sense. In spite of the arbitrariness with which his irate father had treated him, he had a keen and just sense of the difference between right and wrong. Perhaps it had been the teething troubles of that sensibility which had made him appear so short-tempered as a child. [19]

In 1855, at the age of 14, he accompanied his parents on a State visit to Paris, and if this looks like indulgence it must be remembered that the trip was heavily (not to say oppressively) supervised. Nevertheless Bertie fell in love with the city, and—his French being very reasonable by this time—began to develop some of those cultural links that would later mean so much to him. He enjoyed himself, was notably well behaved, and became very fond of the Empress Eugénie. The Emperor carefully treated him as an adult guest, not as a child, and the kilt that he habitually wore fascinated the Parisians. On his return Gibbs was at last dismissed and Bertie was sent to White Lodge with a Governor and a Director of Studies to learn how to be an enlightened gentleman. Needless to say, he found the experience boring and oppressive.[20] Two years later, however, the monotony was broken with a more extended Continental tour, taking in Germany, Switzerland and France, and no doubt exercising his excellent German. The pretext of the tour was study, and again it was strictly controlled, this time by Charles Grey, his father's Secretary. The change of air seems to have done the Prince more good—although he was required to keep a journal, and committed the appalling indiscretion of getting slightly drunk and kissing a pretty girl. He was 16, and Grey described the episode as 'a squalid little debauch'.[21]

By the time that Bertie was 17 everyone had given up trying to make him a replica of the Prince Consort. At this stage, in the late 1850s, there seems to have been some uncertainty about what sort of career he should nominally pursue. In 1858 he was gazetted as a Lieutenant-Colonel in the Grenadier Guards (without taking any of the usual examinations) and elected to the Order of the Garter in November, both of which would indicate a military training. However, these gestures may have been intended to do no more than give him established status for the visit to Berlin that he made before the end of the year—the Prussian court being famous for its military posturings. There he met his brother-in-law Frederick of Prussia, newly married to his sister Victoria, and began to establish something of a reputation as an ambassador.[22]

Almost immediately after returning from Berlin in January 1859, Bertie was despatched to Italy. Again the intention was to improve his mind, and tutors in Italian and Archaeology were engaged. In view of what had happened in Paris, General Robert Bruce, now the Prince's Governor, was given strict instructions never to let him out of his sight. Bertie enjoyed the trip, but could raise no enthusiasm for antiquities— he was much more appreciative of the beautiful Italian girls. He had an audience with the Pope (a noteworthy achievement for a non-Catholic), and the fact that it was not a success and ended up by causing offence was not his fault—rather a matter of esoteric Vatican protocol.[23] On the whole he won golden opinions in Italy, and received the Order of the Annunciation from King Victor Emmanuel, although without meeting him.

On his return Bertie was sent to Edinburgh for a further period of study—and apparently while his father considered what to do next. Then, in October 1859, he unexpectedly matriculated at Christ Church, Oxford. The reason for this move is obscure: the Prince was totally unsuited to academic study, and ill-equipped for it. He was also isolated. In Frewin Hall, a detached part of the college, he had little chance to mingle with his fellow students, an exposure that might have made the whole experience worthwhile. He was nominally tutored by Herbert Fisher, for whom he had scant respect, and the only aspect of university life that seems to have appealed to him was the opportunity to indulge in blood sports.[24] He was also noted to be rather too fond of good food and wine, but, surprisingly, did quite well in the examinations that he was required to take at the end of his first year.

During what would have been for an ordinary student his first long vacation, Bertie was given the unique opportunity of representing his mother on a visit to Canada. He was by now 19 and, although small of stature (he was 5'7"), had a good deal of polish as well as excellent manners—particularly when he was not bored. The ostensible reason for the visit was to open the Imperial Exhibition at Montreal, but plans were also put in motion for Bertie to visit the United States.

The proposed itinerary, outlined in a letter by Lord Lyons which is now held in the National Archives, was wide-ranging. It included 'as much time as is desirable politically in the great Atlantic cities', as well as a visit to the President in Washington. Lyons was conscious of the unique, and politically sensitive, nature of the tour, observing that 'As nothing at all resembling His Royal Highness's visit has ever before taken place in the United States, it is no doubt an experiment and one not to be made without considerable anxiety as to the result.'[25] Among the official concerns he describes were fears that an over-exuberant welcome might prove distasteful to one steeped in royal protocol, although Lyons was careful to note 'I have done all I have been able to do to put the Americans upon their mettle to show that they know how to behave to a Prince, and I hope I have done some good in this way.'

Bertie acquitted himself well in the Canadian part of the trip and was enthusiastically received. There was a brush with some aggressive Orangemen in Toronto—Protestant activists who objected to his courtesy to the Roman Catholic bishops—but otherwise the tour was an outstanding success.[26]

On 20 September he crossed into the United States, thinly disguised as Lord Renfrew, on what was ostensibly a private visit. However, nothing was private to the American press, and there was great interest in his visit. He met President James Buchanan and was received as an honoured guest in the Capitol. On his way home he visited New York and West Point. The reception which he received at the former was the best anywhere in the States—and a setting in which his relaxed good humour was displayed to its best advantage. Lyons observed with relief that 'the tour of the Prince of Wales has succeeded extremely well. It requires a very irksome degree of watchfulness and attention to keep the Americans from taking offence. Hitherto, however, they have behaved extremely well and are, I believe, very much pleased. His Royal Highness renders the task as easy and as agreeable as possible.'[27] Even when the floor of a ballroom collapsed under the weight of the dancers, he was able to preserve his admirable composure!

Altogether Bertie's tour was something of a triumph, thanks to his judgement and tact, and at long last he earned the accolade of parental approval. He returned to Oxford briefly, but in 1861 his father sent him to be assessed in a military camp in Ireland. The result was most discouraging. Whatever nominal rank he might be given, he was, in the opinion of his commanding officer, quite unsuited to practical soldiering, having neither the requisite energy nor will.[28] So instead he went back to that other hopeless quest, a university education, this time at Cambridge. Here he matriculated at Trinity College and went to live (with his entourage) at Madingley Hall, a nearby mansion that he rented for the purpose. In spite of the handicaps resulting from this status and isolation, he succeeded in making some friends at both universities, and some of these (notably Nathan Rothschild) remained in his circle for many years.

Bertie was now almost of age, and the question of his marriage was exercising both the Queen and the Prince Consort—but not the Prince of Wales himself. In spite of being described as 'woefully ignorant' in all such matters, he had in fact lost his virginity during a one-night stand in Ireland with an actress called Nellie Clifden. This had originated in a prank sprung on him by his brother officers, but there is no suggestion that Bertie resented it in any way, and he continued to see Nellie after his return to England.[29] For the time being this remained his secret, and his parents energetically swept through the pool of North German princely houses looking for suitable brides. The role was likely to be a demanding one, because the successful candidate needed to be pretty and healthy, intelligent but not intellectual, and wifely but not too submissive. In this search the Prince played no part whatsoever, but in the early autumn of 1861, just after he got back from Ireland, a possible bride had been spotted.

Princess Alexandra of Schleswig-Holstein, a daughter of Christian IX of Denmark, had been suggested by Bertie's sister, Victoria, although such a union was not at all in Prussia's political interests.[30] The Princess was beautiful, not at all intellectual and 17 years old. In September 1861, just before he went up to Cambridge, Bertie was persuaded to take another brief 'study tour', in the course of which it was arranged that he would meet Alexandra. They encountered at Speyer on 24 September, and the Prince was favourably impressed, but he seemed unaccountably hesitant about the idea of marriage. This, it soon transpired, was largely on account of his relationship with Nellie, and that rather squalid business was revealed during the autumn. Both the Queen and the Prince Consort were furious, there were bitter family recriminations, and Bertie was suitably penitent.[31]

Meanwhile Queen Victoria had lost her mother, who had died in November, altogether a miserable month for the royal family. Worst of all, Albert became ill. In spite of that he insisted upon going down to Madingley Hall for a heart-to-heart with his son, and when he returned took to his bed with what turned out to be typhoid fever. As his condition worsened Victoria, beside herself with anxiety, and irrationally offended with her son's conduct, declined to summon him. He, however, heard the bad news from his sister Alice, and arrived at Buckingham Palace just in time to say goodbye to his father on 14 December. The Queen was distraught, and quite unreasonably insisted upon blaming Bertie for her beloved Albert's death. For the time being she could not stand the sight of him, and all talk of his marriage was shelved together with the whole question of his future role and responsibilities.[32] The Prince Consort's wishes, as construed by the Queen, were to become sacrosanct, particularly those relating to the Prince of Wales.

Instead, in January 1862 he was packed off to the Middle East, again accompanied by General Bruce. He was supposed to be travelling incognito, but since he crossed the Mediterranean in the royal yacht, his disguise was less than paper thin, and he was recognized everywhere. To Bruce's chagrin he was far more interested in shooting crocodiles, quails and vultures than he was in the antiquities, but in terms of his behaviour the tour was an undoubted success. From Egypt he went to the Holy Land, and from there to Turkey, where he was lodged in the British Embassy and was received by the Sultan. This could have been an extremely tricky encounter for political reasons, but the Prince's tact and charm were equal to the occasion, and it passed off very well. Sir Henry Bulwer, the British Ambassador, was most impressed, as were the members of the Prince's entourage.[33] He returned in June to find his mother in a more positive frame of mind, and the question of his marriage now again high on the agenda. The story of his escapade with Nellie had reached Germany by this time, but Alexandra's parents, with more good sense than Victoria ever showed, expressed themselves happy to accept the Prince 'as he was' as their son-in-law. Fortunately Victoria liked what she had seen of the Danish Princess, and an agreement was swiftly reached.

Bertie went to Ostend to propose to his intended, and was immediately accepted. 'I really do not know whether I am on my head or my heels', he wrote with a mixture of relief and apprehension.[34] The engagement was not immediately announced, partly because of political complications arising from conflicting Danish and Prussian interests in Schleswig-Holstein, and partly because Alexandra had not yet been formally vetted by her formidable mother-in-law. So Bertie was packed off on another trip, this time to South Germany, Malta and the Riviera, in the course of which he celebrated his 21st birthday in the unlikely setting of the Bay of Naples. He arrived back at Calais in time to escort his fiancée home from her 'approval interviews', which had fortunately been most successful. The Queen with unexpected hyperbole described Alexandra as 'one of those sweet creatures who seem to come from the skies to help and bless poor mortals'. Bertie also discovered that his engagement had been made public on 16 September.[35] The

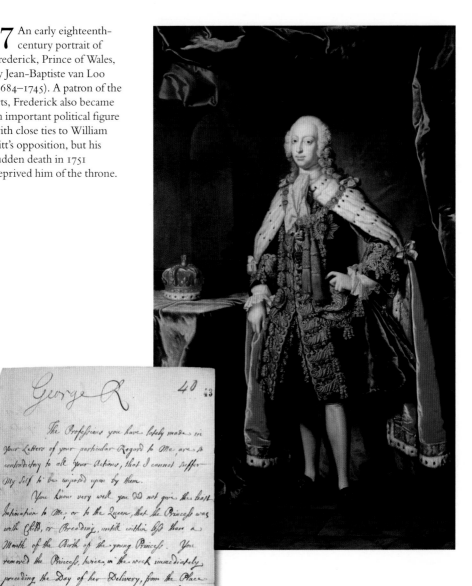

17 An early eighteenth-century portrait of Frederick, Prince of Wales, by Jean-Baptiste van Loo (1684–1745). A patron of the arts, Frederick also became an important political figure with close ties to William Pitt's opposition, but his sudden death in 1751 deprived him of the throne.

18 The acrimonious relationship between George II and Frederick is clearly illustrated by this letter of 10 September 1737 in which the King orders his son to leave St James's Palace. It follows Frederick's decision to take his wife, in the early stages of labour, away from Hampton Court where the King was resident—an action seen by his father as a deliberate insult. (TNA SP 36/42)

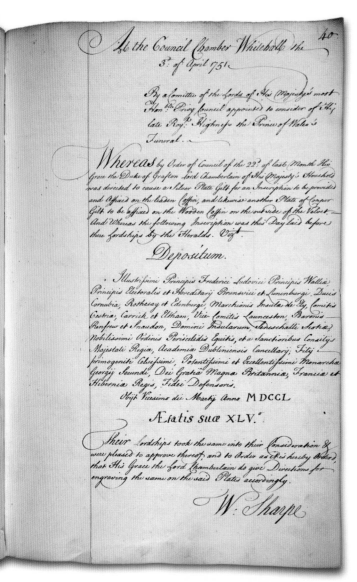

19 (*Left*) The official record of Frederick's funeral, which took place on 17 April 1751 at Westminster Abbey. His death, probably caused by an undiagnosed abscess on the lung, dramatically changed England's political scene. (TNA LC2/36)

20 (*Below*) George, Prince of Wales, later George III, received this miniature portrait, by Jean-Etienne Liotard, on his 15th birthday, 1753.

21 (*Bottom*) This note appears to show that some form of 'marriage service' took place between Hannah Lightfoot, a young Quaker, and George, Prince of Wales, in 1759. However, their union was never formally acknowledged, and Hannah lived in obscurity in later years. (TNA J77/44/R31)

22 George, Prince of Wales, later George IV, painted by John Hoppner in 1792. His poor relationship with his father, George III, was characterized by arguments over the Prince's flamboyant—and extravagant—lifestyle.

23 (*Below left*) After the Prince's disastrous marriage to Caroline of Brunswick in 1795, satirical cartoons flourished. This one shows George's ambitious cultural aspirations, symbolized by the Brighton Pavilion, eclipsed by the malign influence of his wife. (TNA TS 11/115)

24 (*Below right*) Rumours surrounding Caroline's behaviour obliged the King to establish a formal Commission of Enquiry in the summer of 1806 to investigate 'certain written Declarations touching the conduct of her Royal Highness the Princess of Wales'. (TNA HO 126/3)

A TOTAL ECLIPSE,
or, The Moon passing the Sun's disc!!

25 Four generations of royalty appear in this photograph, dating from 5 August 1899: Queen Victoria, the Prince of Wales (right), George, Duke of York and Prince Edward of York, aged five. Relations between them varied considerably.

26 A formal photograph of Albert Edward, Prince of Wales, later Edward VII, published as a collection of studio portraits in 1888. The Prince had little opportunity to engage with affairs of state, and instead became a prominent figure in society.

27 (*Below*) The description of an assassination attempt made on the Prince of Wales in Brussels, 1900. Telegrams of congratulation at Bertie's escape flooded in from royal houses across Europe, many of whom were related to the Prince. (TNA FO 10/744)

Sir F. Plunkett to the Marquess of Salisbury.—(*Received April 4, 11·30 P.M.*)

(No. 3.)
(Telegraphic.) *En clair.*   *Brussels, April 4, 1900.*
    I DEEPLY regret to announce that a dastardly attempt was made this afternoon to shoot the Prince of Wales at the Gare du Nord here, but with the blessing of God His Royal Highness has not been touched.
    Following are the details which I have just received from the Minister for Foreign Affairs :—
    The Prince on arriving soon after five had walked freely about the station without anybody paying attention to him, but the Chef de Gare, who knew him by sight, had kept as near as he could to him without attracting attention. Just as the Prince had taken his seat, and the train was about to start, a lad of about sixteen rushed at him and fired a first shot from a revolver, which fortunately hit nobody.
    The Chef de Gare seized the lad and they rolled together on the platform, during which a second shot was fired. The people near rushed to help, and the lad was at once arrested. The Prince of Wales mercifully escaped unhurt, and displayed the most perfect coolness throughout the whole affair.
    His Royal Highness has continued his journey with a delay of only a few minutes, and the police authorities are now engaged in examining the prisoner, who has declared that he intended to kill the Prince.
    Minister for Foreign Affairs has telegraphed to Prince of Wales at Cologne to congratulate him on his escape, and express deep regret that such an attack should have taken place on Belgian soil.
    (Sent to the Queen)

28 George, Prince of Wales, later George V, (right) and Tsar Nicholas II, with their sons Prince Edward (left) and the Tsarevich Alexei, at Cowes, 1911. The Kaiser, another relative, brought a highly competitive spirit to the event, which Edward VII, in particular, did not appreciate.

29 George, Prince of Wales at a Marlborough House garden party, 1 July 1907. Unlike his father, he disliked formal entertaining and resisted the efforts of Sir Arthur Bigge, his Private Secretary, to find him a house more suited to this purpose.

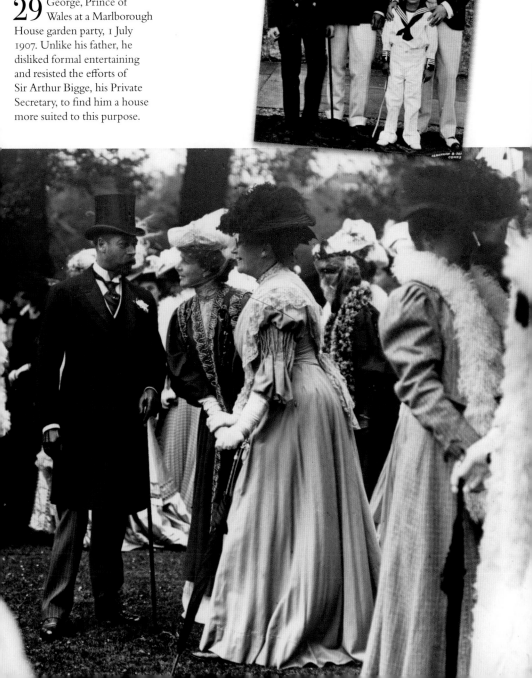

30 (*Left*) Edward's investiture as Prince of Wales took place at Caernarvon Castle on 13 July 1911. After the deliberately historical ceremony, the 16-year-old Prince was presented to the people, flanked by Queen Alexandra and George V.

31 (*Below left*) The design of a commemorative medal celebrating Edward's investiture in 1911. The medal, struck in silver and gold by the Royal Mint, features an image of Caernarvon Castle and a Welsh inscription on its reverse. (TNA HO 290/98)

32 (*Right*) Edward, Prince of Wales and his father, George V, examine gas weapons at a gas school in Helfaut, northern France, 1917. The Prince inspected troops in Flanders and later joined the Headquarters Staff in France, but his attempts to get closer to the action were repeatedly frustrated.

33 The Prince of Wales presents medals at a football match featuring teams of unemployed men in the early 1930s. His concern for the unemployed made him a popular figure with ordinary people in a country struggling with economic depression.

34 Edward undertook several visits to deprived areas of Britain during his time as Prince of Wales. Conditions at many of the mining towns were bleak, as this photograph of the Prince at Winlaton, County Durham, taken in 1929, shows.

35 The Queen presents the new Prince of Wales to cheering crowds at Caernarvon Castle, following Charles's investiture on 1 July 1969. In a ceremony devised by the Earl of Snowdon, the Prince delivered a speech in fluent Welsh and wore a sword, ring and cloak clasps dating from Prince Edward's investiture in 1911.

36 Members of The Prince of Wales Company, 1st Battalion Welsh Guards, are entertained by Prince Charles at Clarence House, London, in May 2008. The Prince presented campaign medals to soldiers of the regiment following their return from operations in Afghanistan.

Princess finally arrived for her nuptials on 7 March 1863, and endured the most exhausting public exposure on her way to Windsor with the utmost composure and good humour. Bertie and Alexandra were finally married in St George's Chapel on 10 March. It would be difficult to say who was the more relieved—the Queen, the Prince, or the country at large. Now it was up to Alexandra to do her duty.

The newly-wedded couple took up residence at Marlborough House in Pall Mall, which had been allocated to the Prince by parliament as long before as 1849, and had been expensively modernized. The Prince's resources were by now considerable. The Duchy of Cornwall had been worth no more than £16,000 a year when he had inherited it in 1841, but by 1860 it was bringing in more like £60,000. As he had not been allowed to touch this income until he came of age in 1862, a substantial balance had accumulated—some £600,000 according to one calculation.[36] In the interval between his coming of age and his marriage, Bertie had spent some £220,000 of that on acquiring the estate at Sandringham in Norfolk. This was worth about £6,000 a year in rents and other income, but was purchased mainly as a congenial retreat. Altogether by the time of his marriage, the Prince was worth about £65,000 a year. To this parliament added a Civil List quota of £40,000, plus £10,000 'pin money' for the Princess—who had no resources of her own.[37] Consequently the combined income of the Prince and Princess of Wales in 1863 was about £115,000 a year, which although large, by no means made him the richest peer in England. Before moving in to Marlborough House the couple spent a honeymoon at Sandringham. Everyone agreed that they seemed blissfully happy with each other, a perception confirmed by Alexandra's prompt pregnancy. Their first son, named Albert Victor for his grandfather, was born on 10 January 1864.

'Eddy' (as he was always known) was born prematurely, probably because of Alexandra's acute anxiety over the war that had broken out between Prussia and Denmark over her homeland. The Princess was passionately pro-Danish, but England was neutral and although Bertie was as supportive of his wife as he could be, he was solemnly warned off political interference. The Foreign Secretary, Lord John Russell, even advised him to have no independent contact with the Cabinet on the issue, and his rather desperate offer to mediate was rejected. Marlborough House may for the time being have been a love nest, but all was not well with the Prince's circumstances, quite apart from the stresses of the Prusso–Danish war.

This was almost entirely due to Victoria. Obsessed with her late husband, she was never able to forgive Bertie for failing to live up to his father's quite unreasonable expectations. She insisted on trying to choose his friends for him, and was withering in her scorn for his attachment to the (somewhat flighty) Duchess of Manchester, although Alexandra was quite relaxed about it.[38] The Queen deplored her son's enthusiasm for the club life of London, which she described as 'lax and bad', and his tendency to return home in the small hours of the morning. 'Bertie is not improved since I saw him last', she was lamenting as early as 1864, having apparently expected marriage to bring about some magic transformation in her son's character. As a result of this maternal disapproval, the Prince found himself frozen out of public affairs. In 1864 General Knollys, Comptroller-General of the Prince's Household, was rebuked for allowing Bertie to meet the Italian patriot Garibaldi privately. The legacy of the Hanoverian Princes of Wales, and their recurring interventions in party politics, cast a long shadow. 'The Queen is not disposed to let him interfere in public', it was reported in 1865, and this situation was to endure for almost a decade. The Prince held no public office, not even of an honorary nature, nor was he given access to any State papers. Instead bowdlerized summaries were prepared for him, which told him only what his mother thought were fit to divulge.[39]

Fortunately some politicians were more sympathetic, and he did in fact know quite a lot about what was going on, but in no case was his advice sought, even as a courtesy. In spite of the evidence of his tours abroad, in the course of which he had shown admirable discretion, the Queen apparently feared that in his cups, and in the company of some of his disreputable friends, he might disclose some aspects of the *arcana imperii*. The result was predictably disastrous. Deprived of any public role, the Prince of Wales became increasingly self-indulgent, on the assumption presumably that whatever he did would meet with disapproval. This situation was highlighted, and made worse, by the Queen's extravagant and protracted mourning for the Prince Consort. She withdrew from the public gaze for years, and the monarchy, which thrived on public appearances, began to slip back into that discredit from which the young Victoria had redeemed it 25 years earlier. Her refusal to allow the Prince of Wales to supply her place was in these circumstances a serious mistake. 'If more work had been found for the prince, the monarchy would never have come to such a pass', as one concerned observer wrote in 1870.[40] In the same year Charles Dilke, a well known republican, questioned the whole value of such a reclusive monarchy in the House of Commons, describing it as wasteful and unnecessary. In the circumstances, many believed he had a point. The Prince himself grew frustrated at the limitations of his role, particularly when his talent for diplomacy might be put to use.

> If only something could be done to stop this terrible war [the Franco–Prussian]. Could not England, backed by the other neutral powers, now step in and try to induce the belligerents to come to terms, as it might yet save the lives of some thousands of fellows … I cannot bear sitting here and doing nothing while all this bloodshed is going on. How I wish you could send me with letters to the Emperor [of France] and the King of Prussia, with friendly advice, even if it ultimately failed. I would gladly go any distance, as I cannot help feeling restless when so many one knows and likes are exposed to such danger....[41]

By this time, of course, Bertie's titular Principality of Wales offered no opportunities at all. The last fragment of distinctive government had been lost during the reforms of the early 1830s, when the Courts of Great Session had finally been abolished and the Welsh circuits absorbed into the Westminster system. There had been no governing role for the Prince in Wales since the 1530s, and even the revenues had ceased to be paid to him since the days of the first George. There is no evidence that Bertie ever showed interest in the country.

Nobody thought any the worse of him for that, but in other ways his own behaviour contributed to his misfortune. He was undoubtedly far too fond of raffish company, both male and female; he got into debt, became stout, and appeared as a witness in a rather sordid divorce case, all of which gave fuel to the maternal disapproval.[42] Nor were all the problems personal. Princess Alexandra was embarrassingly anti-German after the conflict over Schleswig-Holstein, and when in 1864, in the aftermath of the war, the couple visited Denmark (thereafter going on to Sweden and returning via Belgium), all sorts of hackles were raised in other parts of the extended royal family — and most of all in Prussia. In June 1865 she presented her husband with a further token of her affection in the shape of George — eventually to become King George V — and in that respect at least there seems to have been nothing wrong with their relationship. In 1866, however, when she was pregnant again, he went to Russia to attend the wedding of her sister Dagmar, and to cultivate stronger links with the Tsar on behalf of his mother's government.[43] His lack of official standing was imperfectly understood in Europe, and that could be useful on occasions. The Prince spent his 25th birthday enjoying the relaxations of St Petersburg, but all was not well at home.

During his absence Alexandra began to suffer, not emotionally but physically. She had a difficult pregnancy, and became seriously ill with an undiagnosed condition that eventually left her deaf and a little lame.[44] The pain was intense, but Bertie, to his lasting discredit, refused to take her illness seriously. When he returned from Russia he picked up the threads of his clubbing, dining and shooting parties where he had been forced to lay them down. He did not ignore his suffering wife, but he was nothing like as solicitous as contemporaries thought he should have been, or as his reputation demanded. In a sense he was right, because when Alexandra was brought to bed in February 1867 her labour was normal and the child, Louise, born healthy. Nevertheless the impression that he had neglected his wife just when she needed him most became firmly embedded, particularly in the circle surrounding the Queen.

What was to be done with the Prince of Wales? In 1868 he visited Ireland and there was talk of making him Viceroy there. As the Fenian movement was strong at that juncture, attempting to spring prisoners in Manchester and causing explosions both in London and in the colonies, such a move could have solved more than one problem.[45] However, his mother decided that he was unsuited for the job and the suggestion came to nothing. In July 1868 Alexandra presented him with another daughter, Princess Victoria, so at least the succession was secure — if (as the pessimists were whispering darkly) there was anything left to succeed to by the time that the children grew up. Gladstone himself was acutely aware of the monarchy's position, and sought to advise the Prince accordingly.

The conviction of my mind, based on no short experience, is that so long as the nation has confidence in the personal character of its sovereign, the throne of this Empire may be regarded as secure; but that the revival of circumstances only half a century old [the Prince Regent] must tend rapidly to impair its strength and might bring about its overthrow ... and such nearness to the throne as that of your Royal Highness for this purpose is almost identical with its possession....[46]

In January 1869 Bertie visited Egypt again, displaying the same suave tact and lack of interest in history that had characterized his earlier visit. Whether Victoria would acknowledge the fact or not, as her representative abroad, however unofficial, the Prince was a distinct success. In November 1869 his nursery was augmented again by the arrival of Maud, and in April 1871 by the birth of John. This time, however, the couple's luck ran out. All their previous children had survived childhood, but John died almost at once.[47] Perhaps Alexandra's infirmities were more serious than she would admit, or perhaps she was simply exhausted. Although she was only 28, with nearly 60 years of life ahead of her, there were no more children. There does not seem to have been any estrangement between husband and wife - his shabby behaviour of five years earlier seems to have been quickly forgiven and forgotten. They remained devoted to each other, but their relationship now moved onto a different plane.

The Prince was also experiencing further criticism on the political front. Republicans such as Charles Bradlaugh, author of a *Letter from a free-mason to General HRH Albert Edward Prince of Wales*, attacked his hedonistic lifestyle with a ferocity that may have contributed to Bertie's long periods abroad in 1868 and 1869. Republican sympathies increased across the country, led by charismatic figures such as Charles Dilke and Joseph Chamberlain, both of whom later became friends of the Prince. Gladstone remained concerned by the strength of the movement, recognizing that the unhappy combination of a reclusive Queen and a flamboyant Prince of Wales was costing the monarchy much popular support. Unfortunate comparisons were drawn with the Prince Regent, and perceived extravagance became a focus of demands for change.

Paradoxically, it was to be Bertie's own near fatal illness that resolved some of the problems that he and his mother were facing. In November 1871 he caught typhoid—the same disease that had killed his father 10 years earlier. For several weeks he was delirious, and his life was despaired of. Victoria could not bear the thought of losing Bertie in the same manner as his father.[48] Perhaps he was not such a bad son after all! Suddenly his life became very precious to her. The mood in the country likewise shifted from hostility to alarm. Press reports held in the National Archives reflect the scale of the nation's anxiety, noted by *The Times* in its Court Circular for 13 December 1871.

> The whole nation holds its breath and watches the struggle. We are one for the hour—one in sympathy and interest, while this death-grapple between youth and decay is going on. There is, as it seems, all across the land, only one hushed, respectful, watchful, praying crowd.[49]

Prayers for the Prince were said across the globe, and reported in the British press. Near Bombay a 'great meeting of Parsees … at the Chief Fire Temple of Hormusjee Wadia' offered prayers for Bertie's recovery, as did the Fulton-Street Prayer Meeting 'and other praying assemblies in America' where the Prince had made such an impression 11 years before. They must have been effective, as later in December—contrary to medical predictions—the Prince began to mend, and by the New Year was weak, but himself again. His mother was more relieved than she would readily admit, and a subtle change came over their relationship. Most important of all, a thanksgiving service was held in St Paul's Cathedral on 27 February, and the Queen attended. She had not been seen in public for over 10 years, and the pent-up emotion of her reception was remarkable. It was as though the entire population of London had been waiting for this opportunity to demonstrate its loyalty. Republican sentiment, which had been powerful as recently as the previous autumn, suddenly began to wane. In a sense this sea change was more beneficial to the Queen than it was to the Prince. She absorbed the lesson that it was part of her role as a ruler to be visible, and although she was never as happy in public as she had been in the days of her marriage, she now realized that total seclusion was not an option if she wished the monarchy to continue.

Bertie did not immediately spring to life politically, but the days of his rigid exclusion were over. He further defused republican sentiment by attending the opening of the Workers' International Exhibition, a ceremony performed by the declared republican Auberon Herbert in July 1870, and by establishing friendships with some of the radical leaders that were to develop over time. Henry Broadhurst, the first working man to become a Cabinet minister, was invited to Sandringham in later years, and Joseph Arch, leader of the agricultural workers' trades union, later received the Prince's support in his attempts to seek election to parliament for the Norfolk constituency that included the estate. After 1873 he also from time to time represented the Queen on State occasions, most notably on an extended tour of India in 1875–6.[50] The subcontinent was beginning to be a concern for the British authorities, and the newly formed Congress movement boycotted his visit altogether. However, the Prince's easy manners, and most particularly his courteous relations with the Indian rulers and others whom he met, made a good and lasting impression. He travelled all over that huge country, stayed for several months, took part in endless ceremonies and shook thousands of hands. A lesser man might well have wilted or become fretful, but Bertie took it all in his stride with unfailing good humour, and when he returned presented the Colonial Office with a damning report on the arrogant and unsympathetic way in which English officials were too often treating the Indians.[51] His words were heeded and a number of important changes — not least of personnel — resulted. It was believed by acute observers at the time that his visit had done 'much to increase the loyalties of both Indian princes and ordinary people to the British Crown'. However, if this was correct, the beneficial effects did not last very long.

As the euphoria induced by his recovery from illness began to wear off, some of Victoria's suspiciousness returned. In spite of the success of his visit to India, and the knowledge that the expedition had given him of the country, he was not consulted over the Royal Titles Act of 1876, which created for Victoria the title of Empress of India. This was a perfectly gratuitous snub to the Prince, who was extremely resentful.[52] Shortly afterwards he quarrelled violently with Lord Randolph Churchill, who challenged him to a duel. Fortunately such antique displays of gallantry were not only illegal but also outmoded in the England of the 1870s, and although the quarrel rumbled on until 1883 no violence resulted. Bertie was a man of moderate and liberal inclinations in his politics, and much preferred Mr Gladstone to Mr Disraeli — a taste that directly contradicted that of the Queen, who famously complained that the former addressed her as though she was a public meeting. The Prince also supported Liberal policy on Home Rule for Ireland, another issue upon which he found himself at odds with mama.[53] His sons also established connections with Gladstone, encouraged by the Prince of Wales.

15th August 1882. Wrote to Mr. Thorold Rogers—Mr. Lefevre—the Queen—and minutes of the H[ouse] of C[ommons] ... saw Mr. H[amilton]—Lord R.G. ... The Prince of Wales and the two princes [Eddy and George] who came at two. Lord Grenville—Lord Northbrook—Mr. Childres—Lord Huntington—Mrs. Bolton. Read Leckie's England—Sullivan's Ireland.[54]

He did, however, find a niche for himself at what might be described as a 'second rank' public level. In spite of his manifest lack of concern with Egyptian antiquity, he was deeply interested in the arts of Italy, and quickly became a supporter of literary and musical enterprises. He became President of the Society of Arts as early as 1863, and in the following year a Governor of Wellington College, a school established primarily for the sons of serving officers, where his rather vague military connections were an additional qualification.[55] Later the Prince became a Trustee of the British Museum, and was an enthusiastic Freemason. He was acknowledged as a leader and supporter of good causes generally, and was a committed and skilful fundraiser for those enterprises with which he became associated.[56] His military aspirations, however, look rather sad in retrospect. He was delighted to become the Regimental Colonel of the 10th Hussars, and Colonel of the Honourable Artillery Company (in succession to his father) in 1863, but these were largely honorary positions, and his uniforms were ornamental. Active service was strictly forbidden—as it was to all Princes of Wales after the fifteenth century, and there was more than a little truth in the Kaiser's later sarcastic observation that his battle experience was confined to the Battle of the Flowers, at Cannes.

Unlike the 'Leicester House set' of the 1750s, the 'Marlborough House set' after 1870 was not a political group, let alone one in opposition. It was more notable for its devotion to Newmarket and Cowes than to Westminster. The Prince ran several mistresses, or quasi-mistresses, notably Lillie Langtry, the so-called 'Jersey Lily', although it is not clear how far any of these affairs went. Alexandra seems to have remained indifferent to them, and none of them produced any acknowledged bastards. There were, of course, rumours, but Bertie rode out these low-key scandals with little trouble and the press showed surprisingly little interest. Although not quite as bad as during the Queen's reclusive years, the basic problem remained the same—he was underemployed.

Victoria seems to have been quite neurotic about surrendering any aspect of her authority, a situation that became increasingly unreal as she became old and her son was a man in his 50s.

Fortunately he found an outlet in what might be called 'family diplomacy', and his expertise in talking to his strategically placed relatives around Europe not only gave him an excellent grasp of international politics, but one that was much appreciated by successive governments. The King of Denmark was his father-in-law, the Empress of Russia his sister-in-law, the King of Greece his brother-in-law and the Kaiser his nephew, all of whom could be discreetly visited on a personal rather than an official basis. Family connections also gave the Prince an opportunity to assess Britain's image in other countries in a manner that professional diplomats could never achieve. Politicians were keen to make use of the Prince's unique status: he made three trips to Russia alone in 1866, 1874 and 1894, as well as entertaining visiting heads of state, such as the Sultan Abdul Aziz and the Tsar (in 1867 and 1895 respectively), and representing the royal family at numerous court functions. In 1878 Bertie met with the French radical Léon Gambetta to soothe ruffled feathers over Britain's acquisition of Cyprus, with notable success. Salisbury congratulated the Prince, who 'acquitted himself with great skill', and Gambetta also paid tribute to him, believing that he possessed the 'makings of a great statesman'. Four years before, *The Times* had noted the implications of his diplomatic role for the Prince's expenditure, commenting that 'the Prince of Wales has long represented the royal house of England in visits to the Chief Courts of Europe, and has been burdened with the expenditure required to discharge these duties.'

Yet for the majority of his subjects the Prince was most visible as a leader of fashionable society. Marlborough House was a famous social centre, and Bertie associated with many of the most glamorous women of the day, from actresses such as Sarah Bernhardt and Lillie Langtry to society ladies—Lady Brooke, the Hon Mrs George Keppel and Mrs Agnes Keyser. His circle of friends included wealthy Jews such as Nathan Rothschild, Sir Ernest Cassel, Baron Hirsch and the Sassoons, and the Prince's own investments benefited from their skilled financial advice. Cosmopolitan and flexible in outlook, Bertie found new wealth more stimulating than old breeding, and was predictably castigated for this by the court. The Prince relished sports such as tennis, shooting, golf and racing yachts, and frequently attended race meetings — as many as 28 in 1890 (three times the number of days that he spent in the House of Lords). He began to build up the royal stable, which was to produce a victor in the Grand National and three Derby winners — the first, Persimmon, delighting the crowds with his success in 1896.

The Prince's high profile was also due to many public engagements, from opening buildings to delivering addresses at banquets, and by the 1880s he was undertaking more than 40 such functions a year. One of particular note was the opening of Tower Bridge in London on 29 June 1886, where Bertie represented the Queen. An article in the *London Gazette*, now held in the National Archives, records the happy event.

Gentlemen, It gives the Princess of Wales and myself sincere pleasure to be permitted on behalf of the Queen, my dear mother, to drive the first pile of the New Tower Bridge, and in Her name We thank you for your loyal Address, and assure you of Her interest in this great undertaking. All must allow that this work when completed, will be one of great public utility and general convenience, as tending materially to relieve the congested traffic across this noble river. We shall always retain in Our remembrance this important ceremony.[57]

As his own children grew up, he found that his imperious mother regarded even his role as a parent with suspicion, and neither he nor Alexandra had much control over the education of their sons.[58] Born prematurely, with his mother under acute stress, 'Eddy' was always in poor health and undersized for his age. The Prince was every bit as difficult a child as his father had been, and seems to have shared all the paternal vices without any of the compensating virtues. He was un-academic and resentful of all discipline, his memory was not particularly good, nor was he notably observant. George, just over a year younger, was much more normal, and since they were tutored together the fault cannot be laid to the tuition the boys received. Predictably, when they were both sent, aged 13 and 12, to be taught as naval cadets at Dart-mouth, the regime suited George, but not Eddy — who became a trial to everyone, including (one suspects) himself.[59] Following Dartmouth, Eddy was sent, with his younger brother, on a world cruise, which lasted no less than two years (p.210). George benefited hugely from the experience, but if it made any impression on Eddy then no one noticed. His deficiency in all aspects of 'manliness' (so valued at the time) was painful to behold.[60]

Upon his return in 1882, he was sent to follow his father at Trinity College, Cambridge in 1883, and after this gesture towards the academic life he was gazetted in the 10th Hussars. Although he was well enough liked by his brother officers, as a career the army was as out of the question as everything else seemed to be. Eddy was heedless, aimless and self-indulgent. He was created Duke of Clarence in 1890, but that was more in recognition of his position as his father's heir than for any qualities that he had shown. He was charming in a languid way, and attractive to women, but that was the best that could be said for him. Indeed, the one thing that he seems to have done with any zeal was to fall in love, and that he did several times in the late 1880s. Neither marriage nor scandal resulted, however, and he appeared to be as ineffective in this mode as in all others.[61] By 1890 his grandmother, remarkably well informed of the affairs of her very extended family, was despairing of him, and even his father's good-humoured indulgence was wearing thin. Altogether Eddy was looking a most unpromising heir to the throne. However, it did not come to that. He caught cold out shooting on 7 January 1892, and within a few days the cold had turned to pneumonia. He died at Sandringham just a few days after his 28th birthday, leaving his extremely competent brother George, who had established himself as a successful naval officer, to become the heir in his place.

The Prince and Princess of Wales were deeply distressed by Eddy's pathetic end, and inclined to think the better of him in consequence, but in reality his death was a huge relief to the monarchy. It was a time of volatile politics, when calmness and stability were required from both the Prince of Wales and his heir. Bertie had engaged with some prevailing social issues, serving on the Royal Commission into the Housing of the Working Classes, at Gladstone's invitation, in 1884— an initiative which brought him into contact with slums at St Pancras and Clerkenwell, and left him genuinely appalled. In 1891 constitutional propriety denied the Prince a similar position on the Royal Commission of Labour, expected to divide along party political lines, but he did subsequently serve on the Royal Commission on the Aged Poor, where his friendship with Henry Broadhurst and Joseph Arch was to develop. The Prince was also involved with two bills seeking to legalize a widower's marriage to his late wife's sister—a major concern at a time when maternal mortality was not an uncommon event. The Archbishop of Canterbury, who opposed the principle, believed that the bill's eventual success in 1896 was due in significant part to the influence exerted by the Prince of Wales.

The late nineteenth century was also a testing time for Britain abroad, with the outbreak of the Boer War arousing disapproval on all sides. International isolation had a dangerous side, and on 4 April 1900 the Prince himself came close to assassination at the Gare du Nord, Brussels. A young Belgian anarchist, Jean Baptiste Sipido, leapt on to the royal carriage's footboard as the train was pulling out of the station and fired through the open window into the compartment. A bullet lodged in the back of the seat behind the Prince, but he was unhurt. Reports in the National Archives show that the would-be assassin was quickly apprehended; they also note Bertie's courage in 'displaying the most perfect coolness throughout the whole affair'. Telegrams of congratulation at the Prince's escape flooded in from across Europe, but, as British officials were at pains to remark 'The Belgian newspapers took no notice of the attempt upon the Prince of Wales beyond just publishing the telegraphic reports'.[62]

Time was now also running out for Victoria. At the age of 78 she celebrated 60 years of rule in 1897, and none except the elderly among her subjects could remember a time when she had not been on the throne. Age had slowed her, and she never entirely threw off the reclusive habits of her years of mourning, but her obstinacy was as marked as ever, and her political experience was without equal.[63] Over the years she had grown from being the Queen (and a fertile mother) into being a unique symbol of Britain and its Empire, and the grandmother of half the royal families of Europe. She was to die on 22 January 1901 at Osborne House in the Isle of Wight—always her favourite residence, and largely designed by the Prince Consort. Surrounded by all her immediate descendants, her end was peaceful. A new era had at last arrived.

Ten months short of his 60th birthday, the Prince of Wales became King. Out of deference to custom and public opinion he used his second name, taking the title of Edward VII. At long last he had shaken off the shadow of his overbearing father, although what his mother would have said defies imagination. The most immediate decision that he had to make was whether to let his son George go ahead with his planned visit to Australia, so soon after the old Queen's death. Considerable pressure was brought to bear.

> Mr. Balfour fully recognizes the force of all the objections which may justly be urged against the visit — at the present moment. The recent death of the Queen, the general mourning which it has occasioned, the natural emotion which your Majesty and your Majesty's subjects may well feel at seeing your Majesty's only son leave the country at such a time and on so distant an expedition, are considerations which cannot be, and ought not to be, ignored. If in Mr. Balfour's judgement, they have not conclusive weight, it is because he cannot help feeling that there are on the other side reasons to be urged which touch the deepest interests of the monarchy. The King is no longer King of Great Britain and Ireland and a few dependencies ... he is now the great constitutional bond, uniting together in a single Empire communities of freemen separated by half the circumference of the globe. All the patriotic sentiment which makes such an Empire possible centres in him, and everything which emphasises his personality to our kinsmen across the sea must be a gain to the monarchy and Empire....[64]

Needless to say, the Duke of York — and May his Duchess — undertook the tour (p.214).

As might have been expected, Edward transformed the court almost immediately. Once his mother's obsequies had been observed, he introduced his own friends. The whole atmosphere, which had become gloomy and claustrophobic in the Queen's last years, was lightened and refreshed.[65] In the same year parliament revised the Civil List, giving him an income of £470,000. A policy of shrewd and sensible investment over the years meant that Edward acceded with no debts whatsoever, and was the first monarch to be solvent for centuries.[66] Clearly his gambling, particularly on horses, had been well within his means. Nevertheless there was an early scare, and it looked for a while as though his reign might be over before it had properly begun. In the autumn of 1901 the King developed appendicitis, then a dangerous condition, and the coronation had to be postponed. Medical science, however, was advancing, and on 23 January 1902 he underwent a pioneering and successful operation. There was a huge collective sigh of relief. Convalescence was slow, in accordance with the opinion of the time, but by the summer Edward had completely recovered. He was crowned with due ceremony at Westminster on 9 August 1902, and a wait of over 60 years had finally come to an end!

King Edward reigned for less than 10 years, but they were years of ominous significance for the future. The continuing decay of the Ottoman Empire threatened conflict in the Balkans, while the personal power and eccentric ideas of Kaiser Wilhelm II began to destabilize the balance of power in the west.[67] The Kaiser was Victoria's oldest grandchild, and had been present at the Queen's death, but relations with his uncle in England were never easy—the latter making no secret of his belief that his German kinsman was slightly cracked. This being so, it made sense to seek allies where they could be found, and both the Anglo–Japanese naval treaty of 1902 and the Anglo–French alliance of 1904 must be seen in that context. Unlike the Kaiser, Edward had little personal power, and foreign policy, like all other affairs of state, was in the hands of his governments. However, his personal acquaintance with France was long and affectionate. He loved the Mediterranean, spent months on the Riviera, and had done a lot to turn Biarritz into the fashionable resort that it had become by 1900.

In May 1903 the King paid a state visit to Paris, which President Loubet returned in July. These exchanges, as well as improving the atmosphere, provided an excellent screen for the two foreign ministers, Delcassé and Lansdowne, to hold face-to-face discussions.[68] The result was the so-called Entente Cordiale, which shaped Anglo–French relations down to and including the First World War. Edward's devotion to things French—he spoke the language almost perfectly—continued to influence his choice of vacation, and he was famously in France when Herbert Asquith won the general election of 1908. There was nothing wrong with that as he had no part to play in an election, but he was disinclined to return when a new government was to be sworn in, and a new leader summoned to kiss hands as Prime Minister. He endeavoured to summon the entire Cabinet to Biarritz, and when that failed would only condescend to come as far as Paris to meet the new Prime Minister. Asquith thus became the only such office holder in history to be sworn in outside of the country.[69] The King's behaviour was regarded as not a little exasperating, particularly by those directly inconvenienced.

By 1910 a constitutional crisis was looming. It began in 1909 when the House of Lords rejected the budget offered by the Chancellor of the Exchequer, David Lloyd George, on behalf of Asquith's Liberal government. This budget was a preparation for both war and social reform, to both of which the Conservatives were opposed. The Liberals denounced the Lords' veto as unconstitutional, and indeed it ran counter to the custom of centuries. Asquith asked the King to create enough new peers to push the budget through the House of Lords. The King, sensing the political implications of the crisis, was deeply concerned, but agreed to Asquith's plan on the condition that the Prime Minister got the people's backing in a general election.

Lord Knollys asked me to see him this afternoon and he began by saying that the king had come to the conclusion that he would not be justified in creating new peers (say 300) until after a second General Election, and that he, Lord K., thought you should know of this now, though for the present he would suggest that what he was telling me should be for your ear only. The king regards the policy of the government as tantamount to the destruction of the House of Lords and he thinks that before a large creation of peers is embarked upon or threatened, the country should be acquainted with the particular object for accomplishing such destruction, as well as with the general line of action as to which the country will be consulted at the forthcoming elections....[70]

This Asquith won with a reduced majority, but before the consequences of this victory could become apparent—indeed within days of the result being called—King Edward died, and the constitutional dilemma was postponed. Edward had reigned very much as he had lived in his later days as Prince of Wales, relaxed, good humoured, disinclined to do more than was necessary, but capable of showing both wisdom and discretion when these qualities were called for. He had also shifted the monarchy back into a masculine mode after the long reign of his mother. The climate and social structure of the court could best be described as 'transitional'; it would be left to his son and grandson to reinvent the monarchy for a more modern world, after that transforming holocaust known as the First World War. Bertie's reign—something he had waited all his life to achieve—was to become in hindsight a twilight of the Gods.

CHAPTER VIII

Princes of Change –
George and David

George was the most respectable and least controversial of all the Princes of Wales, coming between his raffish father and his playboy son. He would probably have been warmly approved by his grandfather, Prince Albert, who died four years before he was born, and even by his great-great-grandfather, George III. Yet it was only by chance that he became Prince and King at all, because he was his father's second son, and it was simply by being there when his brother Eddy died that he performed his greatest service to the monarchy. George was always high in his father's confidence and affection, and theirs was perhaps the most positive relationship ever enjoyed between a King and his heir. George V's son, David, by contrast, endured a fraught association with his father, partly because the nature of the role was changing fast, a circumstance that David understood much better than the King. He was a conspicuous success as Prince of Wales—far more prominent than George had ever been—but his brief reign as King was beset by conflict. This time it was not death that imposed the solution, but constitutional politics. After Edward's abdication the Crown passed into another safe pair of hands—again those of a younger brother, who became George VI. In spite of all the problems, George V would eventually have had good cause to be satisfied with the outcome of the crisis that followed his death.

George was born at Marlborough House on 3 June 1865, the second son of the then Prince and Princess of Wales, and was baptized at Windsor Castle on 7 July. Every boy born into Victoria's expanding family was expected to bear the name Albert, but in his case it was his fourth Christian name (George Frederick Ernest Albert) and he never used it. From a very early age his elder brother, Eddy (christened Albert Victor), caused endless problems, both to his nurses and to his parents, and it was with great relief that they observed that George appeared to be more or less normal. This did not mean that he was particularly favoured, but he was the dominant partner as soon as he was able to express himself at all.[1]

Having been the victim of his own father's compulsive desire for perfection, Edward was determined not to 'overcook' his sons' education, a policy that had to be infiltrated underneath his mother's vigilant radar. In his anxiety, he probably erred too far in the other direction, because both of them underwent only limited instruction before the Rev. John Dalton was appointed as tutor in 1871. Dalton was a mild-mannered, easygoing man with whom George established an immediate bond. So good was their relationship that years later, when he came to get married, the Prince recalled his former tutor to be his domestic chaplain. However, Dalton was a man of limited accomplishments, who confined himself to English, Mathematics, History and Geography. His assistants also taught Latin and some Bible Studies, but, unlike generations of their predecessors, George and Eddy were not taught any modern languages. George's lack of French and German was subsequently to be an embarrassment to him.[2] What they did learn was a lot of sporting accomplishments—such as shooting, swimming, cricket and lawn tennis. It was an altogether different regime from that to which their father had been subjected. At the same time, unpromising though he was, Eddy was the heir—second in line to the throne—and George was destined for a career in the navy.

In 1877, aged 13 and 12, both boys were sent to HMS *Britannia* at Dartmouth, a regime that suited George's practical and rather phlegmatic nature, but was an agony to his temperamentally more fragile brother. Victoria had not been in favour of sending Eddy at all, thinking that a rough naval training would not be suitable for a boy whom she chose to regard as 'refined and amiable'. However, Dalton, who accompanied the boys as resident tutor, was quite clear that the experience would be beneficial to him—but only if George went too. As he had written in the previous year, 'Prince Albert Victor requires the company of Prince George to induce him to work at all'. There they remained for two years, while George learned the rudiments of cosmography and navigation, and Eddy learned nothing in particular. It was to prove a tough environment, with no special privileges—quite the reverse.

It never did me any good to be a prince ... the other boys made a point of taking it out on us on the grounds that they would never be able to do it later on. There was a lot of fighting among the cadets ... they used to make me go up and challenge the bigger boys—I was awfully small then—and I'd getting a hiding time and again. Then we had a sort of tuck shop on land ... only we weren't allowed to bring any eatables into the ship ... well the big boys used to fag me to bring them back a whole lot of stuff—and I always got found out and got into trouble... And the worst of it was ... they never paid me back—I suppose they thought there was plenty more where that came from, but in point of fact we were only given a shilling a week pocket money, so it meant a lot to me...[3]

Their father's reaction to this problem, and a reflection of his own restricted childhood, was to keep them moving in the hope that Eddy might be stimulated by fresh places and new experiences. George did not need such a stimulus, but seeing a bit of the world would do him no harm either, so in 1879 they were shipped aboard the *Bacchante* and sent off to the West Indies. The following year their destinations were Ireland and Spain, and later in the same year they were despatched on a round-the-world tour—an extended version of the European tours that the Prince of Wales had enjoyed when he was slightly older.[4] This took two years, and involved not a little danger. The perils of putting all his hereditary eggs in the one basket, and then sending it to sea, was pointed out at the time, but the Prince of Wales appears to have taken a sanguine view, and the Queen finally gave her consent.

The shipboard regime was tough, because this was not supposed to be a holiday, and the boys were in fact placed in some danger when the *Bacchante,* a fully rigged corvette of 4,000 tons with auxiliary engines, broke down in the South Atlantic. It was an extended itinerary, taking in South America, the Falkland Islands, the Cape of Good Hope, Australia, New Zealand and Hong Kong, before returning via the newly opened Suez Canal. It was also to prove an adventurous trip, including a futile dash to help the British soldiers in the Boer War battle at Majuba Hill in January 1881, and the sighting of a 'spectral ship'—a kind of *Flying Dutchman*—between Melbourne and Sydney. However, they returned safely and George, at least, was reckoned to have benefited greatly from the experience. John Dalton had again accompanied them, and kept a journal of the expedition that he subsequently published.[5] They returned in August 1882 and, as soon as he passed his 18th birthday in June 1883, George was commissioned as a Sub-Lieutenant and posted to HMS *Canada*. The Prince was also confirmed into the Church of England shortly after his return to England, and became committed to that middle-of-the-road Anglicanism that was to be his faith for the rest of his life.

George's naval career was no token matter. In 1884–5 he attended the Royal Naval College at Greenwich and Dartmouth, taking all the regular examinations. Most of these he passed, some with first class honours, but was chagrined to have narrowly failed Pilotage in spite of a special course on HMS *Excellent* (the shore-based establishment). However, this turned out to be a matter of relatively little importance, and on the strength of his other successes he was duly promoted Lieutenant. The Prince of Wales was particularly gratified when the First Lord of the Admiralty commented 'the capacity which Prince George has shown is unusual'. In 1889 he received his first command—the functional and unglamorous torpedo boat *79*—and in 1890 was promoted to the gunboat HMS *Thrush*. Neither of these were token commands, and he really was a competent naval officer.

Meanwhile Prince George's royal status was not ignored either. He visited Canada in a semi-official capacity in 1884, and on his return his grandmother made him a Knight of the Garter.[6] He was not to know it, but when he took command of the *Thrush* it was to be his last functional command, and a family tragedy was about to alter his life entirely. In November 1891 George contracted typhoid—that bane of the royal family—and was seriously ill, his weight dropping to nine stone. He was bedridden for six weeks and was still convalescent when the frail and unfortunate Eddy succumbed to pneumonia on 14 January 1892, just after his 28th birthday. George was suddenly catapulted into the direct line of succession to the throne.

One of the first and most immediate effects of this was that he inherited his brother's fiancée. Negotiations had been in hand for some time for a marriage between Eddy and Princess May of Teck. This had not been of Eddy's designing, but he had lacked the will power to resist.[7] He had been prompted to propose at Luton Hoo on 3 December 1891, and was rather surprised (and not a little disconcerted) to be accepted at once. May was a bright, attractive 17-year-old who seemed well suited to the difficult role; the Prince of Wales had pointed out in a letter to his mother the previous August that she would be a great help in 'managing' Eddy! Conscientious and eminently practical, she was not unduly distressed by Eddy's unexpected demise, and took her transfer to George with equanimity. They met at Cannes in March, accompanied by their respective families (it was always difficult to keep the Prince of Wales away from Cannes anyway) and the deal was done. This was not quite as heartless as it sounds, because the young couple were genuinely attracted to each other, and it would not have taken May long to realize that George was a much better prospect than Eddy.

George was also shrewd enough to know when he was well suited. He had already had at least one romance, with Julie Stonor, a grand-daughter of Sir Robert Peel, but Julie was both a commoner and a Catholic, so marriage was out of the question. They had both accepted this situation, and were to remain friends for many years. May had far too much common sense to object. Other brides had also been canvassed from within Victoria's extended family, but none was as suitable as the Princess of Teck. In 1892 George was created Duke of York and Earl of Inverness, and the following month took his seat in the House of Lords.[8] Although in the interval he had been promoted, first to Commander and then to Captain, his career as a serving naval officer had come to an end. At the same time he was given quarters of his own, both within St James's Palace and at Bachelor's Cottage, near Sandringham. A small staff was also created for him, presided over by a former shipmate, George Cust, who was to serve him as equerry and friend for over 40 years.

Meanwhile, the proprieties had to be observed. Although the newspapers were full of the intended engagement between George and May (or Mary as she was later known), it had not actually happened. It was not until 2 May, after dinner at White Lodge, that the question was properly posed—and answered. 'We walked together afterwards in the garden, and he proposed to me, and I accepted him', she recorded matter-of-factly in her journal.[9] Victoria, that most meticulous of grandmothers, was delighted. They were married on 6 July 1893 in the Chapel Royal at St James's Palace, with all the pomp of which a royal wedding is capable, but also with genuine affection on both sides. 'I love you with all my heart', she scribbled in a pencilled note to him just hours before the ceremony.

Unlike his father, George was very insular in his tastes, and in temperament has been described as a thoroughgoing Norfolk squire. This had probably as much to do with his lack of languages as his tastes, because he disliked having his limitations exposed. So the couple honeymooned in the prosaic surroundings of the White Lodge at Sandringham, where they subsequently took up residence. Meanwhile political duties began to take over from his former naval preoccupations. Like his father, he was Liberal in his sympathies, and although he remained personally on good terms with his grandmother, he was far from the extreme conservatism of the court. This was particularly the case over Irish affairs, where he backed Mr Gladstone's attempts to find a way out of that morass, and had to be sheltered by his father from the extreme Unionism that characterized the Queen and her personal advisers.[10] He had dined with Gladstone in February 1893, and when the veteran statesman died in 1898, George and his father acted as pall-bearers at the funeral. When Victoria found out (after the event), she was livid. Although George attended the House of Lords regularly, it was rather in the spirit of a student or apprentice than as a participant. He did not speak, and his voting was extremely discreet.

The Duke of York, in fact, seemed to hold all the domestic virtues that his father (and most of his ancestors) had lacked. His children appeared at regular intervals, starting with David in June 1894. Then followed Albert (1895), Mary (1897), Henry (1900), George (1902) and John (1905). May was by then 38 and, either by choice or necessity, her childbearing days were over. George was strictly monogamous and, unlike nearly all his male ancestors, his wife did not have to reproach him with any infidelities. His lifestyle, even his amusements, were more bourgeois than aristocratic. He was an excellent shot, reputedly 'the best game shot in the Empire'. He collected postage stamps, and by the end of his life had perhaps the finest collection in the world, amounting to some 250,000 in 325 large volumes, which are now preserved for the nation. He was a lifelong addict of philately, and when the Duke of Edinburgh, who was also a collector, died in 1900 Edward bought the whole collection and gave it to his son. He was also interested in constitutional history, and indulged this taste after 1894 under the scholarly eye of J.R. Tanner, a distinguished professor of that subject.[11]

There is more than one way to neglect a wife, however, and although May never had to face any rivals for her husband's affections, she did suffer from these constant distractions. She was highly intelligent, and began to feel excluded—not through any conscious intention on George's part, but rather because his favourite pastimes were not very shareable—least of all with his wife. By contrast with his raffish father, who frequently went to bed with the lark, even in later life, and entertained the ladies in all sorts of ways, George was a model of respectability. This was probably just as well, because later, as King, he was to face both at home and abroad the kind of tests that would ruthlessly have exposed any lack of moral fibre. In spite of her frustrations, May was quite shrewd enough to appreciate when she was well off; she supported him assiduously in his public duties, even (reputedly) writing some of his speeches for him. They visited Ireland together in 1897, meeting with a remarkably enthusiastic reception, and Lord Salisbury commented, 'The devotion to your person which you have inspired is not only a result gratifying to yourself ... but it will have a most valuable effect upon public feeling in Ireland'. Unfortunately appearances flattered to deceive. They also went to Berlin for Crown Prince William's coming of age in April 1900, an experience that George described as 'very disagreeable'. What his wife thought we do not know.

Victoria died on 22 January 1901, and when his 59-year-old father at last ascended the throne as King Edward VII, George became Duke of Cornwall and heir to the throne. The Duchy gave him a good income in addition to his Civil List allocation, and he had no extravagant tastes, so his competently managed finances ceased to be of interest to anyone. The most immediate concern was whether or not to go ahead with the Empire tour that was scheduled and had been a long time in the planning. In the event, and out of a sense of obligation rather than because either Edward or his son wanted it, it did go ahead, and George set off for Australia in March, accompanied by his wife, but not by their children—a wrench for the closely knit family.[12] There he opened the first parliament of the Commonwealth of Australia at Melbourne in May, before going on to New Zealand (which he was the first member of the royal family to visit), South Africa and Canada. In Canada he crossed the country on the newly opened railway link, and returned to the East Coast by the same method. This gave him ample opportunity to meet a wide variety of people, which he did with unfailing kindness and courtesy. In the course of the whole trip George is alleged to have travelled 45,000 miles, to have listened to 544 addresses, and to have shaken 24,855 hands![13] On his return he was congratulated by the King and, at the age of 36, formally created Prince of Wales and Earl of Chester.

In making you today Prince of Wales and Earl of Chester [his father wrote on 1 November], I am not only conferring on you ancient titles which I have borne upwards of 59 years, but I wish to mark my appreciation of the admirable manner in which you have carried out the arduous duties in the Colonies which I have entrusted you with. I have little doubt that they will bear good fruit in the future and knit the Colonies more than ever to the Mother Country. God bless you, my dear boy, and I know that I can always count on your support and assistance in the heavy duties and responsible position I now occupy....[14]

It was at this stage that the Prince of Wales made one of the few landmark speeches of his career, at the London Guildhall. In spite of the hedonistic atmosphere that emanated from the court, keen observers, particularly of international affairs, thought that the country, and the Empire, were in danger. The King himself was well aware of the threat posed by Germany, hence the Anglo–Japanese treaty of 1902 and the Entente Cordiale, but was perhaps less appreciative of the relative decline in Britain's industrial and economic position, or of the danger of strained relations with the United States.[15]
Nor was he inclined to take the Kaiser seriously. William II was the son of Victoria's eldest and favourite daughter, who had married Frederick William of Prussia, and was thus King Edward VII's nephew. He had always been the old Queen's favourite grandson, but he had developed an extremely autocratic streak, and his uncle regarded him as slightly unbalanced. George did not make the same mistake, and made no bones about these various threats in his speech, pointing out the need for the British government to take remedial action. 'To the distinguished representatives of the commercial interests of the empire whom I have the pleasure of meeting here today, I venture to allude to the impression which seemed generally to prevail among their brethren across the seas, that the Old Country must wake up if she intends to maintain her old position of pre-eminence'.[16] This 'wake up' speech, as it was called, was very favourably received by the press. It helped to ease the government towards that reforming agenda that was to create

a constitutional crisis between 1909 and 1911. This was not at all the kind of speech that the King would have been capable of making, but fortunately he appreciated its importance.

The relationship between Edward and his heir blossomed.[17] At no time had relations between the King and the Prince of Wales been more harmonious. It was certainly a far cry from Bertie's own strained relations with his dictatorial parents, or the fierce political infighting of the eighteenth century, and it was a harmony for which the Prince's pragmatic and peace-loving disposition can claim a lot of the credit. George was reticent by nature, but that was in no sense constrained, and he was far better informed about public affairs than his father had been at a similar stage in his career. He saw all the Cabinet papers, and was in as good a position to frame an informed judgement as the King or any of his ministers. He also benefited greatly from the appointment of Sir Arthur Bigge as his Private Secretary. Bigge, later Lord Stamfordham, held this position from 1901 to 1931 and was effectively George's political tutor.[18] As the latter observed, 'He taught me how to be a King', and the two men became close friends. The only thing that Bigge failed to do at this stage was to persuade George to move into a larger house, and take his entertainment responsibilities more seriously. The Prince was not a recluse, but he had clear preferences for the company he kept, and did not want to broaden his social—or political—horizons. Moreover he hated Osborne, Victoria's favourite residence on the Isle of Wight (which was available), and eventually had to be squeezed out of St James's Palace and into Marlborough House, which his father had vacated on his accession.

From 19 October 1905 to 8 May 1906, George and May were in India—a tricky time to be visiting the subcontinent because the Viceroy, Lord Curzon, had just resigned. Curzon was a reformer, but his abrasive personality had caused problems, not least with the rising power of the Indian Congress movement. George, like Curzon, believed that the Indians would benefit most from closer ties with Britain, and from more honest and impartial administration. The Congress, on the other hand, wanted a more representative style of government, an objective that they partly achieved in the India Councils Act of 1909, to which the Prince was opposed.[19] In the course of his visit he covered over 9,000 miles by train and several hundred more by carriage, visiting (among other places) Jaipur, Delhi, Agra, Lucknow and

Calcutta. He went north to Hyderabad and the North West Frontier before returning by way of Karachi. The Prince shot tigers, met maharajahs, talked to British officials, and allowed himself to be seen as much as possible. He showed much shrewdness and understanding of the political situation, and spent a lot of time closeted with the Viceroy's Private Secretary, Sir James Dunlop Smith.[20] In particular he was perturbed (as his father had been) by the contempt that many of the British still showed towards the Indians, even those in positions of responsibility. 'It was not the same,' he observed, 'as that of superiors to inferiors at home'—a remark that subsequently became celebrated. May also played her part, having with characteristic conscientiousness read up on the cultures and religions of the country, so that she showed herself better informed than many Raj wives of long standing—and also a good deal more sympathetic.

The royal couple had moved on to Burma when the news reached them of the landslide victory of the Liberals in the 1906 election. Arthur Balfour's Conservative and Unionist government had resigned in December 1905, and parliament had been dissolved. In the resultant election the Liberals had secured an overall majority. Logically, given his sympathies, the Prince should have been pleased, but the new Labour party had also secured 53 seats, and this evidence of popular socialism worried him. His reaction was premature, if not mistaken, but the new government had to face social and industrial issues with a very twentieth-century flavour to them—pensions, trade-unionism and women's suffrage. The Irish problem, which William Gladstone had eventually failed to solve, was also still on the agenda, and the Irish Councils Bill of 1907, designed to reorganize local government, went nowhere near far enough to satisfy the Nationalist lobby.[21] George, meanwhile, had a somewhat different agenda. He chose, wisely, not to meddle with issues of social reform, but concentrated rather on Imperial defence and the reform of the navy—both matters upon which he was well informed.

Meanwhile he also continued with the kind of roving diplomacy that his father had practiced. In an attempt to use his family connections to defuse the rising tension with Germany, he visited Berlin in 1902 and again in 1908, but he found the Kaiser increasingly contemptuous of constitutional monarchs, and not to be deflected from his 'Imperial destiny'. These visits may not have achieved much in political terms, but they did serve to emphasize the nature of the threat, and to strengthen the defence lobby. In 1908 George also revisited Canada, where his speeches contained some thinly veiled criticism of his father's government, and particularly of Lloyd George, then Chancellor of the Exchequer. It was the latter's 'people's budget' of 1909 that brought about the constitutional crisis. In an attempt to raise the money necessary for an old age pension scheme, and for the expansion of the navy, the Chancellor proposed a tax on unearned income. Convinced that confiscatory socialism was upon them, the Conservative Lords vetoed the bill. This violated constitutional convention, and the Prime Minister, Asquith, called for a new mandate.[22] He achieved this (just about), but was now more dependent than ever upon Labour support. In opening the new parliament in April 1910 the King made it clear that the constitutional powers of the Lords were under review. Within a few days Asquith introduced a Parliament Bill, and declared that if that were rejected he would again appeal to the country, and seek the King's guarantee that he would create enough Liberal peers to ensure its passage. Before this crisis could come to a head, however, King Edward died, on 6 May 1910 at Buckingham Palace — probably from severe bronchitis followed by a heart attack. George, who had been with him at the end, was distraught, and noted in his diary 'I have lost my best friend and the best of fathers ... I never had a [cross] word with him in my life.'

Not many Princes of Wales could have written that with honesty over the years. However, it could also be argued that Edward had exited with impeccable timing, leaving his heir to deal not only with the unresolved constitutional issue, but also with a mounting threat from Germany, profound discontent in Ireland, and increasing trade-union militancy.[23] King Edward's funeral was the last great gathering of European royalty before the holocaust of 1914–18 swept most of them away, but George V's coronation, which took place on 22 June 1911, was, appropriately enough, a celebration of the Empire. Troops from India, Africa and the Far East lined the route, and the King noted in his journal 'There were hundreds of thousands of people, who gave us a magnificent reception'.[24] The King was popular, and when the journalist E.F. Mylius attempted to spread the story that he had three children by a bigamous marriage contracted during a visit to Malta, he was accused of criminal libel, and convicted. Neither the story (which was intrinsically implausible) nor the trial did the monarch's image any harm at all.

By the time that this happened, the constitutional crisis had been largely resolved. A further general election in December 1910, after the failure of an all-party conference, had resulted in deadlock. However, most of the Tory peers had no desire to see themselves swamped with a new Liberal intake, and passed the Parliament Act in August 1911 by the simple process of abstaining. The prerogative powers had not eventually been called on and the new King's role was little more than that of an interested spectator. However, the effectual demise of the House of Lords as a constitutional force was a symbolic development for a new century.

About a month before the passage of the crucial Bill, there had also been another symbolic beginning. The King's eldest son, David, was invested as Prince of Wales at Caernarfon Castle in July 1911.[25] There had hardly been the slightest connection between Wales and its Princes since the days of Arthur at Ludlow in 1502, but Lloyd George was the member for the Caernarfon boroughs, and with the King's agreement decided that this time it would be different. The hapless 17-year-old was dressed up in an 'historic' costume devised for the occasion, and taught to say in Welsh 'Thanks from the bottom of my heart to the old land of my fathers', and 'all Wales is a sea of song'. The whole ceremony was thoroughly contrived, and an excellent example of Lloyd George's style of showmanship, but it was extremely well received, and that was what mattered. David was thoroughly disgruntled at having to jump through these particular hoops, but his mother succeeded in averting a head-on family row, and eventually he went through the whole ceremony word perfect.

The passage of the Parliament Act enabled the Government of Ireland Act to pass also, and the King's willingness (under extreme pressure) to create Liberal lords in sufficient numbers thus constituted the most effective intervention of the prerogative in Irish affairs since the eighteenth century—even though it had not eventually been called upon.[26] It was also an intervention against the entrenched Unionist interest, which included his own Secretary and strained their otherwise excellent working relationship. All this was behind the scenes, and his subjects knew little about it. The King had more public appearances in mind, not least upon the larger stage of India. Although he was not an extrovert in any sense, George demonstrated that he had learned the lessons of his father's and grandmother's reigns. Victoria as a young woman and mother had been a happy, popular figure, but her with-drawal into morose seclusion after Albert's death had done her image immeasurable harm. Edward, by contrast, for all his raffishness, had been a cheerful, popular figure. George was keenly aware that, just as he did not have his father's weaknesses, he did not have his *bonhomie* either, and that other ways to display the monarchy had to be found.

As early as the autumn of 1910 he wrote to Lord Morley, the Sec-retary of State for India, that 'ever since I visited India five years ago I have been impressed by the great advantage which would result from a visit by the sovereign to that great Empire'.[27] He proceeded to propose a coronation Durbar at Delhi, where he could meet Princes, officials and 'a great number of people'. The Durbar was the King's idea, and in November 1911 he set out for India, accompanied by the Queen. In one sense the great celebration was a huge success, but there were troublesome details. He could not be symbolically re-crowned, because that had been a Christian ceremony and his Indian subjects were mostly Hindus or Muslims. Nor could he take the English crown with him for legal reasons, so a special crown was made for the King. He wore it throughout the homage ceremony, which took place on 12 December, despite great personal discomfort.[28] Also, the reforms that he announced on that occasion went nowhere near meeting the demands of what was now the Congress Party, a movement beginning to look for the ending of British rule altogether. The royal couple returned to England on 12 February 1912, having made a great impression but solved none of the problems of the subcontinent.

They returned to find a country in the grip of industrial recession and labour strikes. Between 1900 and 1911 the purchasing power of the pound had dropped by 25 per cent, and wages had scarcely increased at all. It was all very tiresome, the Queen decided, but worse was in store. Although George visited Berlin for the wedding of the Kaiser's daugh-ter in 1913, nothing could disguise the deteriorating relations between the two countries, and in August 1914 war broke out. At first the conflict was popular; it was going to be 'over by Christmas', and the country was gripped by khaki fever.[29] Industrial action was suspended, and the munitions manufacturers prospered. However, the euphoria was short lived. The war dragged on and the casualties became ever more appalling. There was little that the King could do, beyond wear uni-form in public and remain at his post in Buckingham Palace. What he could, he did indefatigably, paying 450 visits to the troops, many times within reach of the front line in Flanders. Over 300 times he went to hospitals, shipyards and munitions factories, and his lifestyle became ostentatiously frugal. This was no hardship to him, or to May, and he felt that he could look his hard-pressed subjects in the face. In these encounters, which became increasingly frequent, his no-nonsense manner and lack of bombast or pretentiousness went down extremely well.[30]

Although David, as the heir to the throne, was by custom exempt from active service, his brother Albert served in the navy, and was present as a Sub-Lieutenant on HMS *Collingwood* at the battle of Jutland—a situation that caused both his parents acute anxiety. The war, moreover, created particular problems for a monarchy so closely associated with Germany by heredity and custom. The sheer power of the xenophobia that gripped the nation appears to have taken the King by surprise. While he had no doubts about the need for war, or the justice of it, the sheer visceral hatred that it aroused was not in his nature. When the republican H.G. Wells alluded to him in 1917 as 'alien and uninspiring', he is alleged to have responded 'I may be uninspiring, but I'll be damned if I'm an alien'. But changes had to be made. The King was reluctantly persuaded to strike off the German knights from the Order of the Garter, and on 17 July 1917 he officially changed his own name —and that of his family—from Saxe-Coburg-Gotha to Windsor. He abandoned his German titles in the process.[31] George's own insularity was thus confirmed by necessity rather than choice, but in fact he cut loose from a sinking ship. The Kaiser was driven into exile at the end of the war, and the German aristocracy collapsed as a political force.

It was a brutal war in every way, and although constitutional and social issues, not least in Ireland, were temporarily put on hold, there were few other advantages from the conflict. The most difficult (and controversial) decision that George V was called upon to make followed the overthrow of his cousin Tsar Nicholas II by the Bolsheviks in October 1917. Nicholas clearly expected that he and his family would be given refuge in England, as had happened with the Emperor Louis Napoleon of France. The request was refused, and the Tsar and his entire family were executed by the revolutionaries.[32] When the news of the murders reached him, George was deeply (and understandably) distressed. On a more positive note, the Companions of Honour were created for the purpose of honouring civilians of distinction in 1917, and the Order of the British Empire in 1918. The war had left both the King and the country emotionally and physically exhausted, and although the victory celebrations were protracted and turbulent, all the problems suppressed by the conflict re-emerged after 1918. A virtual civil war in Ireland, in which George sought earnestly but ineffectually to intervene, resulted in the formation of the Irish Free State on 6 December 1921.[33] In 1926, nearly a decade of social unrest was to culminate in the General Strike.

There were two positive achievements during these years, however, which were to be of lasting significance: the granting of the vote to women, who achieved equality in the franchise in 1929, and the constitutional accommodation of the Labour Party. This last was achieved when the General Election of December 1923 returned 258 Conservatives, 191 Labour members and 159 Liberals. Stanley Baldwin, the Conservative Prime Minister, did not immediately resign, but there was panic in some Conservative and Liberal quarters at the prospect of a Labour government.[34] When the government was defeated in January 1924, and the Prime Minister resigned, the King called upon Ramsay MacDonald, the Labour leader, to form a new government. Although George permitted himself a wry speculation as to what his grandmother would have thought of such an outcome, it was the only sensible course. MacDonald's government lasted only 10 months, but they were in fact a sober and serious minded group of men, and the King accepted them as such, thereby securing both the future of the party and the constitutional stability of the country. In May 1929, when a further General Election returned Labour as the largest single party, George had no hesitation in sending for Ramsay MacDonald.

By this time, however, his health was failing. In February 1925 he developed severe bronchitis, and the supposedly restorative cruise in the Mediterranean that followed was a failure.[35] In the autumn of 1928 the King was ill again, this time much more seriously, and had to undergo two operations from which he barely recovered. All this served to focus attention upon the heir to the throne, and unfortunately relations between the King and his eldest son were far from relaxed and amiable. Where his own position as Prince of Wales had been easy, there were unfortunate echoes in the 1920s of his father's unhappy experience with his grandmother. Edward Albert Christian George Andrew Patrick David (always known as David until his accession) was born at White

Lodge in Richmond Park on 23 June 1894, and 'both grandmothers pronounce[d] him to be the most beautiful strong and healthy child'. Such an accolade from Victoria was a moment to be treasured. In spite of (or perhaps because of) the fact that she produced 5 more children over the next 10 years, May farmed out the nursery duties to an extensive staff.[36] This, of course, encouraged the siblings to be close to each other, and David soon became inseparable from his younger brother Albert, born in 1895.

Unfortunately their father had no gift with children, appearing gruff and censorious in a manner sadly reminiscent of his grandfather, as perceived by the young Edward. The Duke of York had fixed ideas of discipline and decorum, and although the story that he avowedly set out to terrify his children is probably apocryphal, it contains more than a grain of truth The children were cared for by governesses, and allowed only very limited access to other children of similar age. Most of their own kindred were in Germany, and their father was a man of limited vision, even if relations between the two countries had not been deteriorating.

In 1902, at the ages of seven and six, the two older boys were place in the care of a tutor, one Henry Hansell. Hansell was a schoolmaster by profession, and was well liked by his charges, but he was a man of distinct limitations. Hansell has been described as 'representing everything that was most philistine and blinkered about the English upper middle classes', and if this is a little harsh, he did appear to have a most deleterious effect upon his charges.[37] He was possessed of a self assurance that squeezed the life out of a naturally adventurous child like David, who was later to describe his time under Hansell's supervision as 'five curiously ineffectual years'. It is perhaps not surprising that the children made very little academic progress under his supervision, and equally unsurprising that their parents did not appreciate the situation. Fortunately separate tutors were employed to teach the boys French and German, and in those subjects their progress was normal. Both were intelligent boys, but they grew up with no appreciation of books, or what could be learned from them. 'We have taken no end of trouble with their education', May wrote in 1907, with a degree of self-deception that tells its own story.[38] David had a naturally enquiring mind, but never learned any of the means by which his curiosity could be satisfied. Hansell was great at organizing football matches, and that certainly had managed to reduce the isolation of his charges, but apart from that he appears to have been less than successful.

David, however, was not another Eddy, that damaged uncle who had died before he was born. From an early age he was noted for his charm and good looks, features which for many years led to over-indulgent assessments of his character. The veteran courtier Lord Esher noted in his journal in about 1908 that 'Prince Edward [is] as com-posed and clever as ever.... He has the mouth and expression of old Queen Charlotte, but the look of Weltschmertz in his eyes I cannot trace to any ancestor of the house of Hanover'.[39] Eventually suspicions of Hansell's incompetence began to sink in, when George discovered that his son was unable to carry out even simple arithmetical calcula-tions and realized that he would need the services of a specialist maths tutor. Even May (highly educated herself, but not overly observant) began to notice that something was amiss, particularly as their parents began to contemplate the next stage of David and Albert's progress.

George had enjoyed his naval training, and perhaps could not imag-ine any more suitable upbringing for his own sons. At any rate in 1907 David was subjected to the ordeal of the entrance examination for the Royal Naval College at Osborne. He passed the oral with flying colours, but narrowly failed the written papers, his spelling and arithmetic being particularly weak, thanks to Henry Hansell's inattention to such details, and the late date at which these omissions had been detected. Nevertheless, he was admitted, and subjected to the usual rites of pas-sage that afflict new boys at boarding school—a particularly painful experience for one with virtually no experience of dealing with boys of his own age. However, he coped remarkably well, and succeeded in concealing any qualms that he might have felt from his sanguine par-ents.[40] He did well enough, his natural intelligence balancing the defects in his earlier training, and finished about the middle of his class of 60; well enough, certainly, to justify his admission.

In 1909, on the completion of his course at Osborne, he proceeded to Dartmouth, in the footsteps of his father; he was to be tracked in turn by his brother Albert. There was, however, a difference for the boys. In 1910, with the death of his grandfather, David became heir to the throne, and while there was a realistic chance that Albert could pursue a naval career, this was now impossible for David. It was prob-ably just as well that his course came to an end just a term later. He was gazetted as a Midshipman in the following year, but this was a mere formality as he would never see active service.

Other rites of passage followed quickly. David was created Duke of Cornwall as soon as his father succeeded to the throne, and in 1911 he was confirmed in the Church of England and made a Knight of the Garter in preparation for his role in his father's coronation.[41] Of course as a minor he did not dispose of the revenues of his Duchy, but it was estimated that by the time he achieved that status there would be a capital accumulation of some £400,000 in the account. These dignities in a sense caught David off balance, because one of the features of his naval training had been its egalitarianism. On his father's insistence, no special consideration was shown to the Prince, and the regime was physically very demanding. It is not surprising that he conceived a slight contempt for those who had been through more academic public schools, in spite of the fact that they had been much better trained for their roles in adult life than he was.

On 13 July 1911, as we have seen, David was invested as Prince of Wales at Caernarfon. Lloyd George, the Constable of the castle, devised the ceremony, including the dutifully rehearsed phrases of Welsh. In spite of the contrived nature of the ceremony itself, the College of Arms went to considerable pains to ensure that his heraldic achievement was authentic, even conducting some historical research into the creation of Henry of Monmouth in 1399, which seems to have been taken as a model. The powerful ritual of the ceremony was to be re-enacted after 600 years.

> We have made and created Henry, our very dear eldest son,
> Prince of Wales, Duke of Cornwall, and Earl of Chester, and
> have given and granted, and by our charter confirmed, to him the said
> Principality, Dukedom and Earldom, and invested him with the same
> Principality, Dukedom, and Earldom … by a coronet on his head and
> a gold ring on his finger and a gold staff according to the custom.[42]

In theory David was a naval officer, but in practice he became something of a full-time hedonist, smoking heavily and indulging in what his father considered to be quite excessive amounts of physical exercise, having apparently become convinced that he was running to fat.[43] In the summer of 1912 he was sent on a carefully chaperoned visit to France. Although the trip was informal, an interview with the President was arranged, and David's general awareness of the European situation probably benefited rather more than his knowledge of French. He was accompanied by Hansell, in whom the King retained an inexplicable confidence, and struck his hosts as being rather undersized and young for his age. On his return, in October 1912, he was sent to Oxford, and matriculated at Magdalen College. The reason for this gesture is obscure. He was no better prepared for a university education than his grandfather had been, and in spite of the attentions of Herbert Warren, the President of Magdalen, who acted as his tutor, benefited little from the regime.[44] He was still accompanied by the inevitable Hansell, and by an equerry, but was not secluded from his fellow students to the extent that Bertie had been. The Prince found the social aspects of college life attractive, and made one or two lasting friends, but in the traditional manner of the young nobleman, he did not complete any course, or take a degree.

In the summer vacation of 1913 he escaped both from Oxford and from his parents, and visited Germany. This time Hansell did not accompany him, and his replacement, William Cadogan, was more a companion than a tutor. The Prince, by this time 19, enjoyed himself a good deal, particularly the night life, but found no sports to his taste and was bored by the earnest attempts to improve his mind. He found Germany more to his taste than France, and his charm made a very good impression—even on the Kaiser—but time was running out for that relationship. By the summer of 1914 war was clearly imminent, and David quit Oxford with relief for a commission in the Grenadier Guards.

During the war, his father had a good deal of difficulty in finding him work which satisfied his natural desire for action without exposing him to unnecessary danger. His commission in the Guards was little more than an excuse to put him in the fashionable khaki.[45] Like his father, he undertook 'royal' duties, inspecting the troops in Flanders, often quite close to the front line, and visiting field hospitals. He became president of the National Fund, a civilian organization set up to support the armed forces, and in 1915 joined the Headquarters Staff in France as an aide-de-camp to the Commander in Chief. Wherever David went he was popular, his charm proving a great asset when it came to liaison work with the French high command. His reports were of little value, but his contribution to mutual goodwill was considerable. Despite the Prince's wishes, however, his attempts to get closer to the action were repeatedly frustrated. He even tried (without success) to persuade the King that he was expendable as he had three brothers, leaving Lord Kitchener to point out that this was hardly the point— the real danger was that the Prince of Wales might be taken prisoner.

In 1916 David took a welcome break from his duties in France to visit the Middle East, spending most of his time in Egypt and the Canal Zone. As a public relations exercise the tour was a huge success, and he learned to handle crowds with some aplomb.[46] His relations with his father also improved. Once back in France, he quickly became bored and frustrated once more, realizing that he was being given trivial tasks to keep him occupied. Yet this was partly his own fault, because unsympathetic observers noted that in spite of his charm, the Prince was in many ways chronically immature. Most particularly he appeared to lack the application to do the paperwork which a staff position really required. He was, in short, reluctant to read. He made a few friends, but as 1917 advanced became increasingly depressed by the human carnage that the war had become. Like many of his contemporaries, the Prince could see no end to the conflict.

> Oh this **** war [he wrote to his father]… I feel as if we are in for at least another ten years of it… Ours is by far the most solid [monarchy] though of course it must be kept so and I more than realise that this can only be done by keeping in the closest possible touch with the people, and I can promise you that this point is always at the back of [my] mind and that I am and always will make every effort to carry it out….I also feel that we have good reason to be confident in the good sense and calmness of our race, anyhow just now, though one knows there are many and great dangers…[47]

At one point he even appears to have contemplated suicide. On another occasion he got close enough to the action for a shell to land within thirty yards of him, and the fright seems to have temporarily banished his depression.[48]

There was, nevertheless, a positive side to all this relative inaction. The Prince became very interested in the new technology of warfare, particularly in tanks and aeroplanes. He even assured his mother (after a brief experience) that flying was far safer than motoring! He spent time with the Canadian forces in northern France, and with the newly arrived Americans, an experience which broadened his mind considerably. The Americans were allies who knew their strength, and had no particular respect for old-fashioned royalty. Above all, he acquired a profound admiration for the ordinary British soldier—particularly the long-suffering conscripts, who stuck to their disagreeable and extremely dangerous job with such commendable tenacity. He was a good morale booster, and years later one ex-soldier wrote that the sight of him at Arras in 1917 'gave me the courage to carry on'. In so far as he later became 'the people's Prince', that affection had its roots in the last two years of the war.[49]

In 1918, and at the age of 24, David had finally grown up. This was also true in a more obvious sense. In 1916 two of his equerries, going well beyond the call of duty, had introduced him to an experienced prostitute in Amiens, who 'brushed aside his extraordinary shyness' according to one bowdlerized version of what occurred.[50] It could be argued that, at the age of 22, this had happened none too soon, but unfortunately he then set out to make up for lost time. A series of affairs ensued, so that by the time that the war ended he was well on the way to becoming an experienced *roué*.

The war had focused everyone's mind, and when it was over at last, two things happened. On the one hand a hedonistic atmosphere prevailed, while everyone tried to forget the horrendous casualties, and the destruction of so many lives. And on the other hand domestic social and political conflicts, suppressed by patriotic fervour, began to resurface strongly. The Prince returned to his royal duties, touring Newfoundland, Canada and the US in 1919, in an effort to reinforce the alliances which had been forged during the war. The governments of Britain and the United States were not always in agreement, but both had now come to the conclusion that in the uncertainties of the twentieth-century world, they could not afford to fall out. The Prince's visit served to strengthen that impression without actually committing the government to anything.

In 1920 a similar visit was paid to Australia and New Zealand, not least to express the gratitude of the British people for the way in which the dominions had stood beside them in the recent war. In 1921–2 a different experience awaited the Prince in India. The country was by this time in a very disturbed state, with several senior officials at the Colonial Office advising against the tour. The result was predictable. The Congress Party boycotted the entire event, and they now spoke for the majority of educated opinion in India. David also had to maintain his position with an extreme formality which did not suit his developing style at all.[51] At times he became acutely depressed, feeling that the whole thing was a disaster, but in fact that was not the case. Not only were the crowds in some places much more favourably disposed than the Congress leaders wanted, but the Prince also developed a sharp and observant eye which disclosed to him much of what was right, as well as most of what was wrong, with the regime in India. He observed to the Viceroy, Lord Reading, that the ostensible purpose of his visit had been to meet and get close to as many Indians as possible, and 'Well, I have not had many opportunities of doing this, either in British India or in the native States....' [52] However, his doubts were not shared by David's own police officer who summed up the positive aspects of the tour when he said that it had 'gone infinitely better than he had thought possible, and ... the good that it had done was incalculable.'[53] From India the Prince went on to Japan, where his shrewd appreciation of the country's growing power was mixed with a bilious disapproval of the Imperial family, and where his relaxed and informal approach impressed the excessively formal Japanese—on the whole favourably. When he returned in July 1922, he was described—not unjustly—as 'a great ambassador for the Empire'.

At home he began to busy himself with issues of public concern, where his status and independence of political ties gave him an advantage. He paid his first visit to South Wales in 1919, drawn by the stories of poverty and deprivation, and spent four days visiting the slums of Cardiff and going down the neighbouring mines. It was to be the first of many such visits around Britain. His concern for mining communities was genuine, and in 1920 when there was a miners' strike in South Wales, he was keen to be kept informed of its development. A telegram sent by one of his staff to the Colonial Office, and now in the National Archives, describes the Prince as 'very anxious for fullest possible information' on the strike, noting that 'We are practically without news.' It requested both a summary of the current position and briefings on future developments, reflecting the Prince's deep and ongoing concern.[54]

The Prince of Wales attempted to be a responsible landlord, and set up farming projects on co-operative principles. He monitored urban developments on Duchy land at Kennington in London, and invested heavily in new machinery for the Cornish tin mines, also an aspect of his management of the Duchy of Cornwall. In an important sense, this level of social concern was new. His mother, Queen Mary, was a great encourager of philanthropy, for centuries a prerogative of royal ladies, but she had also passed the impetus on to her sons. David's younger brother Albert established the Duke of York's camps in 1921, borrowing ideas from Baden-Powell's scouts. The Prince became the first (and so far the only) Chief Scout of Wales.

Nevertheless the positive side of the Prince of Wales's life in the 1920s was very much bound up with the Empire. In 1922 he even established a base in North America, when he bought the Bedingfield ranch, near Pekisko in Alberta—a base which he visited twice between 1922 and 1925.[55] In 1924 he spent three weeks in New York, which although not part of the Empire, served much the same purpose, and in 1925 he completed his tours of the Dominions with a visit to South Africa. He was touring in East Africa late in 1928 when news of his father's illness brought him home. The king, who had suffered from a pleural abscess, recovered, but was obviously in a fragile condition, and that set a term to the Prince's international trips.

There was also a negative side. With his good looks and superficial charm, David was far too close to being an idol on the new Hollywood model for the comfort of his family and friends. He adored the night life of London, and followed it with the same passionate enthusiasm that his grandfather had displayed, becoming a leader of the 'fast set'. He also indulged in a series of affairs, most notably (and scandalously) with Freda Dudley Ward, the wife of the Chamberlain of the Household, who was to divorce her husband in 1931, and with whom he professed himself 'passionately in love'—until the advent of Wallis Simpson.[56] The fashion icon Diana Vreeland described him as 'the Golden Prince', and declared that all the women of her generation were in love with him.[57] All this placed a great strain upon his relations with his parents, particularly as he showed no interest in their various matrimonial schemes. As he himself was later to write, he became 'an unconscious rebel against his position', and to his father the very embodiment of that 'modern age' which he so much deplored.[58] The negative side of his war experience was that he had picked up populist attitudes; they endeared him to the London crowds, but not to the courtiers, officials and politicians with whom he had mostly to deal. The Prince of Wales was cutting across tradition, and was in danger of becoming a kind of anti-establishment hero. This perception of him was not altogether accurate, because in fact he continued to take his official duties very seriously, but it did mean that there was a kind of tension between hedonism and duty which was potentially destructive. There was probably also a degree of jealousy in his relationship with his father, as there had been between previous Princes and Kings, because the latter realized that his son had tapped a vein which he could never reach. This meant that the King failed to give him the credit for the duties which he performed—and that increased the alienation between them.

David had, as we have seen, a genuine sympathy with the workers and the unemployed, and he subscribed to the South Wales miners' fund when they were caught up in the general strike of 1926.[59] He visited the slums of Glasgow, and the *New Statesman* applauded his 'welcome desire to look beneath the surface'. In one sense he was feeling his way towards a new style of monarchy, but the establishment was not yet ready for such radical innovation, and he made himself a fiercely controversial figure. He warmly approved of President Roosevelt's 'New Deal' policy in the United States, and told the American ambassador in 1934 that Britain could do with a similar social initiative.[60] His attitudes, both at the level of amusement and of engagement with the poor, were seen as 'advanced' and not at all respectable. He was even interested in migration schemes to give children in institutional care a chance of a better life in the Commonwealth. He invested heavily in the Fairbridge Farm School movement in Western Australia, and in other similar Schools elsewhere in Australia and in Canada—another concern which caught the public imagination through its combination of philanthropy with a wider Imperial vision. The Prince's high-profile commitment included launching an appeal in *The Times* in June 1934 for £100,000 to establish more schools on the Fairbridge model, observing that 'this is not a charity, it is an Imperial investment, and it is as such that I commend the Society's appeal ... with all my heart for your generous consideration.'[61]

In 1930 David met Wallis Simpson. Already once divorced, she was the wife of Ernest Simpson, an American shipping magnate. Two years younger than the Prince, she was blessed with neither beauty nor intellect, but possessed a formidable personality. Immediately she took over his private life, to the impotent rage of the King and the despair of Queen Mary. Their affair blossomed during a cruise on the *Rosaura* in the summer of 1934, an episode which caught the attention of the world's press, but was censored in Britain. As 1936 opened, several things were obvious. The first was that the King's health was in terminal decline, and it was questionable how long he would last. The second was that Ernest Simpson was about to divorce his wife; and the third was that the Prince of Wales was hell-bent on marrying her.[62]

The entire political establishment was appalled by the prospect which was opening up before them. Early in January Sir Lionel Halsey, the Prince's Chief of Staff, in consultation with Clive Wigram, the King's Private Secretary, drew up what was effectively an ultimatum for Stanley Baldwin and Ramsay MacDonald, the leaders of the two main political parties, to lay before the Prince of Wales. His private life, it was pointed out, had usurped his public one, and this could not be tolerated.[63] The future of the monarchy and of the Empire depended upon his returning to his traditional duties, and upholding traditional values. The King's health was being undermined by anxiety, and the Prince's excesses were destroying public trust. All the good work which had been done in the 1920s was being destroyed, and in short he was not likely to be a fitting monarch. When George V died, therefore, at midnight on 20 January 1936, a constitutional crisis was already in the offing. The new King, who took the title Edward VIII, indulged himself for some days in what seemed to some observers to be extravagant grief.

H is emotion was frantic and unreasonable... In its outward manifestation it far exceeded that of his mother and his three brothers, although they had loved King George V at least as much as he had... While he demanded attention for his own feelings, he seemed completely unaware of those of others...[64]

Edward's desolation was probably a counterpoise to the extent to which he had been willing to try the old man's patience.[65] At first all the proprieties of a new accession were observed, but Mrs Simpson remained in the wings, and there were from the start well-informed observers who had a fair idea how it would end. It was convenient that the King had that ranch in Canada.

At first all such thoughts were put on hold, and Edward swept into office upon a wave of innovation and modernization. He economized, sacking old retainers, and even flew in a aeroplane—not for the first time, but no one remembered that. He returned to South Wales in

November, a visit that aroused great anticipation in the region and anxiety amongst those involved in its planning and preparation. An official of the Welsh Board of Trade stressed the urgency of seizing this opportunity 'for the King to see not so much what has been done ... *but what remains to be done for industrial recovery*'. He favoured an informal visit that would maximize the opportunity to show the 'close personal touch between sovereign and subject' at which Edward had long excelled.[66]

In the event, the tour was more formal and structured, working to a tight schedule—Llanfrechfa, Pontypool, Blaenavon, Garn-yr-Erw, Abertillery and Rhymney were among the towns visited on 19 November, with stops of 20 or 30 minutes at training centres, housing schemes and (at Rhymney) a social centre for the unemployed.[67] Edward was greeted in Wales, severely hit by the economic depression, with enthusiasm and banners proclaiming 'Croeso i'r Brenhin' (welcome to the King). He visited the mining towns and villages of Monmouthshire, recalled his institution as Prince 25 years before, and made a powerful speech at Mountain Ash on 21 November, pledging that his interest in the Principality would never diminish.

However, in spite of all this rapport, Mrs Simpson had no intention of going away, nor would the King have allowed it. There was talk of creating her Duchess of Edinburgh, there was talk of a morganatic marriage. There was even talk of the king taking his fate to the country in an unprecedented constitutional move that all parties viewed with alarm.[68] Dominion governments were consulted and all, although to varying degrees, pronounced themselves hostile to his intended marriage. It was a question of irresistible force and immovable matter, only in this case the political matter proved more obdurate than the royal force.

On 7 December 1936, without having ever undergone a coronation, King Edward VIII abdicated in favour of his brother Albert, the Duke of York. This diffident 40-year-old, who took the title of George VI, now faced the immense task of reinventing the monarchy. After Edward's hurricane-like few months, a return to George V's staid conventionalism was unthinkable, but his brother's 'modern morals' were equally unacceptable. Happily married himself, George settled down instead to domesticate the monarchy, in a fashion which was to be curiously assisted by the traumas of the Second World War.

Created Duke of Windsor, and immediately shunted into exile, Edward (as it is now proper to call him) departed within days. Within six months he had married Wallis Simpson (with a wedding ring made from an ounce of Welsh gold) against the freezing background of family disapproval, which embraced his mother, his brother and his sister-in-law.[69] Only late in 1940 did the Duke receive an official posting—as Governor General of the Bahamas—and there, safely out of the way, the Windsors were to sit out the war.[70] They were not forgotten, and admiration for the Duke remained strong in some quarters, but politically and constitutionally they had become an irrelevance. After the war they returned to France, and Edward tried in vain to obtain some proper employment or appropriate recognition from successive British governments. He was to outlive his brother by 20 years, and his mother by 19, but was never reconciled to his family. He found this cruel, and many sympathized with him, but in marrying Wallis Simpson he had burned his boats. Edward visited Britain from time to time, and was visited in Paris just days before his death by his niece, Queen Elizabeth II. He died on 27 May 1972, and his body was flown back to England for burial.

Edward was 77 years old, and had spent the last 36 of them in exile. As Prince of Wales he could hardly have been a bigger contrast to his father. Where George had been staid, restrained and almost unobtrusive, David had been glamorous and flamboyant. He had worn his heart on his sleeve, both socially and personally, and although that had won him a large measure of popular approval, it had not earned the approbation of the people who mattered—even within the Labour Party. He was in some ways a throwback to his eighteenth-century ancestors, but none of them had paid such a bitter price. Ironically, the British monarchy was undoubtedly in need of modernization—but he had chosen the wrong way to go about it.

CHAPTER IX

Charles, a Modern Prince of Wales

Prince Charles was born on 14 November 1948, into a country shattered by war and a monarchy only recently refashioned. The trauma of Edward VIII's abdication only 12 years before had led to a conscious shift in how the royal family presented itself, and in how it was perceived. Two world wars and political upheaval had also taken their toll, leaving this latest Prince of Wales with a society very different from that of his predecessors. Prince Edward, for all his modernity, had been born in Victorian times; his great-nephew Charles would grow up among the diverse—often undefined—expectations of a volatile post-war world.

King George VI, precipitated to the throne in 1936, did not seek to emulate his flamboyant brother. He already had an heir presumptive in his 10-year-old daughter Elizabeth, and together with his wife Elizabeth Bowes Lyon (the first Queen consort to have been born within the realm since Catherine Parr had married Henry VIII in 1543), they recreated the role of Britain's 'first family' as a model of domestic harmony and peace. Portraits and photographs assiduously enhanced the image, in which their growing daughters played a leading role.[1] In this respect, it is probably just as well that George and Elizabeth had no son, because their daughters could be quietly educated at home and the cycle of confrontation between father and son—most recently between David and George V—was naturally broken. External events were soon to have an impact, however, as the menace of Nazi Germany that dominated the first years of George's reign cast an increasingly dark shadow across Europe. When Elizabeth was 13 and her sister Margaret was nine, the country became engulfed in the Second World War, and the role of the royal family suddenly achieved a new importance.

It soon became obvious that this was to be a different kind of war from that which had raged just 20 years earlier. Now the deployment of Luftwaffe bombers brought the civilian population into the front line; by 1940 London was being 'blitzed', and that created a wholly new situation.[2] While George V and the then Prince of Wales had donned uniforms and gone off to rally the troops during the First World War, George VI became the symbolic leader of the Home Front, as it was called. A frugal lifestyle and the shared experience of the blitz created a new and different kind of bond. The royal couple toured the bombed parts of the city assiduously, and when Buckingham Palace received a direct hit, the Queen exclaimed significantly that 'now she could look the people of the East End in the face'.[3] When Princess Elizabeth joined the ATS in 1944 and started learning how to assemble motor car engines, the re-invention of the monarchy was almost complete. This was not a staff job, or a symbolic diplomatic posting. She was the heir to the throne, and she was getting her hands seriously dirty.

By the time that victory was achieved in 1945, Britain was a changed place. Morally triumphant but physically exhausted, the country was in no mood for the political false starts and broken promises of the 1920s. The first post-war election in July 1945 installed a socialist government committed to a programme of radical change, but this did not touch the popularity of the royal family.[4] On the contrary: Elizabeth's marriage to Philip Mountbatten, a 26-year-old naval officer, son of Prince Andrew of Greece and Denmark and Princess Alice (a great-granddaughter of Queen Victoria) was just the glamorous tonic needed by austerity Britain.[5] Tens of thousands of people turned out in November 1947 to line the processional route to Westminster Abbey, and millions more listened to the commentary on the radio. After the honeymoon, Philip went back to Malta, where he was serving in the Navy, returning for the birth of their first son a year later. In December the baby was christened Charles Philip Arthur George by the Archbishop of Canterbury, Dr Geoffrey Fisher, in the Music Room at Buckingham Palace, and the future of the monarchy was secure. 'The representative monarchy', *The Times* declared optimistically in the wake of Charles's birth, 'has made every one of its subjects feel friend and neighbour to the royal family; and so it is that the simple joy which the coming of this child has brought to them is shared by all.' Society had changed indeed since 1901.

In 1949 the Princess and the Duke of Edinburgh (as Philip had become on their marriage) moved out of Buckingham Palace into the newly refurbished Clarence House, where a nursery was established under the control of Helen Lightbody and Mabel Anderson.[6] Princess Anne was added to the family in 1950, but inevitably the two young children were to have no ordinary childhood. Philip was still a serving officer and spent much of his time abroad, while Elizabeth found that her father's increasing ill health placed more and more of the formal work of the monarchy upon her shoulders. She did her best to find 'family time', but it became increasingly constrained, a situation that Queen Victoria would have understood. Anne, very much her father's daughter, quickly began to adopt his direct approach to life while Charles, by contrast, was reticent and rather shy. He became close to both his maternal grandparents, a bond cemented with a stay at Sandringham over Christmas 1950, while his parents were in Malta; and although Charles was shortly to lose his grandfather, his warm relationship with Queen Elizabeth was to last for more than half a century.

In May 1951 the King inaugurated the Festival of Britain, designed partly to celebrate the centenary of the Great Exhibition and partly to stimulate the country out of its post war economic lethargy. The subcontinent of India had been partitioned into the independent countries of India and Pakistan in 1947, not without great turmoil and loss of life, and various African colonies were also seeking greater autonomy.[7] Against this background, Philip and Elizabeth set out at the end of January 1952 on a five-month tour of Africa, Ceylon, Australia and New Zealand, intended to bolster Imperial and Commonwealth ties. George was suffering from cancer of the lung, and although he came to the airport to see the couple leave, he looked extremely frail. At Sandringham, on the morning of 6 February, he was found dead by the valet who went to wake him.[8] Elizabeth and Philip had only reached Kenya, on the first leg of their tour, when the long distance telephone informed them of George's death. Cancelling the remainder of their engagements, they flew home at once, and Queen Elizabeth II was proclaimed in London on 8 February. Charles, now Duke of Cornwall and Rothesay, had become, at the age of three, the direct heir to the throne.

King George's death was greeted with a wave of emotion ('he had seen us through the war', it was frequently said) and few monarchs can have come to the throne with a greater fund of goodwill than Elizabeth II. Perhaps most important of all was the sense of a new beginning.

There was much talk of 'a new Elizabethan age', and—as in 1841 when Bertie was born to Victoria—the young Queen with a young family was the principal beneficiary. The four-year-old Duke of Cornwall was still too little to be anything other than a spectator when his mother was crowned in the summer of 1953, although he and his sister were photographed in a family group at Buckingham Palace after the ceremony, proudly wearing their coronation medals. Charles's day-to-day care in his early years was in the hands of an experienced primary teacher named Catherine Peebles; her sympathetic approach drew him out, so that his basic education progressed quite satisfactorily.

Then in 1956 the Queen decided to send Charles to school—a remarkable precedent, as no previous heir to the throne had been. (Both George and David had become naval cadets, but the boys had been in adolescence and neither had been the direct heir at the time.) In November of that year, just before his eighth birthday, Charles was taken to a private preparatory school in West London called Hill House. It was all very discreet and well managed, and the aim was to give the Prince a more normal childhood and education. The results were satisfactory and Charles spent a year at Hill House before moving on to Cheam School in Berkshire.[9] Known as the 'Little House of Lords', this was hardly a normal boarding school; it had been founded in the seventeenth century specifically for the sons of noblemen and gentlemen.[10] In 1957 it housed about 80 boys between the ages of 8 and 14, and formed a sensible compromise between the seclusion of a home education and the rough and tumble of an ordinary school. Again it enabled the Prince to make new friends, learn how to box and 'scrum' and generally look after himself, while at the same time living in a protected and controlled environment.

During the summer of 1958, at the age of nine, Charles was created Prince of Wales and Earl of Chester—an elevation on which his school friends hastened to congratulate him—and a fortnight later, when the royal yacht called at Anglesey, he was given a wildly enthusiastic reception. For the first time in nearly half a century, Wales had its own Prince again.[11] The last one had aroused great hopes but had eventually been a disappointment—could Charles do better? Meanwhile the Prince went back to school, where he learned to play team games with some enthusiasm and discovered a talent for acting, any shyness seeming to disappear in front of the footlights. In 1962 he became Head Boy. Cheam seems to have been Philip's choice, because it had been there that his own introduction to England had taken place, and the next step most certainly was. Gordonstoun, to which Charles next proceeded, was a kind of 'alternative Eton', near Elgin in Morayshire. Devised and originally directed by Kurt Hahn, it was dedicated to physical sports and self-reliance, instilling in its pupils the conviction that actions speak louder than words.[12] Charles enjoyed the outdoor pursuits, gaining silver in the Duke of Edinburgh's Award Scheme in 1965, and through Gordonstoun's engagement with deprived communities was able to develop a sense of social action. He also developed his acting talent, starring as Macbeth in a school production that same year, and acquired a taste for music, including an ability to perform. Such public display was a new departure for the heir to the throne: his mother and her sister had both taken part in family pantomimes before the war, but they had been strictly for domestic consumption, so Charles's activities were rather different. Then, after careful consultation, it was decided that some familiarity with the Empire would be beneficial, and in 1965, at the age of 16, Charles travelled to Geelong in Victoria, Australia.

The Prince spent two terms at Timbertops, an offshoot of Geelong Grammar School, and the experience was wholly positive. He loved the country and its people, and while he was there went on an organized trip to New Guinea, where he was recognized and greeted as 'a mighty chief'—very much to his surprise. He also learned to play polo (which was to become an enduring enthusiasm), to muster cattle on horseback and to go deep-sea fishing, all of which added to that love of outdoor pursuits acquired at Balmoral and Gordonstoun. In the intervals the Prince taught himself A-level French and History, and when he returned to Scotland in 1966 he was much changed. Charles had in a sense crammed his adolescence into those two terms in Australia, and came back far more mature and self-confident. He was elected Guardian, or Head Boy, at Gordonstoun, a position that carried certain privileges such as a room of his own—which threw him into company with a new art teacher, one Robert Waddell.[13] He encouraged Charles's literary and artistic appreciation and took to playing classical music with the maturing Prince, of whom a friend wrote to Lord Louis Mountbatten, his uncle, 'This is a young man who reminds me very much of you; he's immensely interested in humanity, and in the details of human suffering.'[14]

In July 1967 Charles again broke new ground by becoming the first member of the royal family to sit routine public examinations. His father and his grandfather had both taken naval examinations, but that was in a rather different context. The Prince took A-levels in French and History, and the special examination (for university entrance) in the latter subject, gaining a C and a B, with a mark of distinction on the special paper. This was a respectable result in the years before grade inflation, and in the circumstances a considerable achievement.[15] It was, at all events, a sufficient justification for him to continue his education, and in October 1967, shortly before his 19th birthday, he matriculated at Trinity College, Cambridge. He had chosen to read for the joint honours degree in Archaeology and Anthropology—a course upon which he had insisted in preference to the contrived 'special menu' that had been prepared for him.

By this time the Prince was living in two separate worlds. On the one hand he was an undergraduate, if not quite a normal one, attending lectures, making friends and honing his gifts as a comic actor. He took part with some acclaim in several Footlights productions, being on one celebrated occasion incarcerated in a dustbin—what his noble ancestors would have thought of such a performance beggars belief! On the other hand he was a public figure—a member of the Council of State, Knight of the Garter and on certain State occasions representative of the Queen. Late in 1967 he travelled back to Australia to attend the funeral of Prime Minister Harold Holt, and was greeted with enthusiasm, both for what he represented and for what he was.[16] Then, having completed his Part I at Cambridge successfully in the summer of 1968, he opted to read History as his Part II subject. It had already been decided that he should be formally invested as Prince of Wales, and that in the new political climate—Welsh Nationalism was gaining ground in the Principality—this was a chance to recover some initiative. The perfunctory injection of a couple of phrases of rote-learned Welsh, which had done for Lloyd George in 1911, would not suffice, and in January 1969 his studies at Cambridge were intermitted in favour of a term at the University College of Wales Aberystwyth. He went to study Welsh language and history, intending to acquire a working knowledge of the language.[17] This decision marked the first serious involvement of a Prince with Wales since the sixteenth century, and probably the first time ever that an English Prince was expected to be able to express himself in Welsh. The Prince was greeted at Pantycelyn Hall with warm applause, symptomatic of his favourable reception in Wales, and he relished the chance to engage more closely with the Principality. Nor did he shy away from the issues behind Welsh Nationalism, appreciating the underlying concern for the country's language and culture. He made his first public speech in Welsh at the Urdd Gobaith Cymru (Welsh League of Youth) Eisteddfod at Aberystwyth, two months before the investiture itself, and it was well received.

Charles's investiture took place on 1 July 1969, amid security concerns that nationalist extremists, although a small and unrepresentative minority, might attempt to disrupt proceedings. It was on a less lavish scale than Prince Edward's ceremony in 1911, involving about one-fifth of the number of troops and limiting the number of seats for official guests. Those planning the event had to balance the magnificence of a State ceremony with the need for economy, and documents in the National Archives note the meticulous preparations and careful budgeting surrounding the event. Charges were made for seats, apart from those issued to official guests, and all save Ambassadors and High Commissioners were expected to pay for transport to Caernarfon, meals and accommodation. Stools, chairs and programmes designed for the occasion were offered for sale as souvenirs, and both the BBC and Independent Television had to pay for any special services required.[18] Royal permission was given to feature certain arms, emblems and portraits on commemorative souvenirs, the selection reflecting the complex history of the Prince of Wales's role and including:

> The Royal Arms differenced for the Prince of Wales and component parts thereof; The Prince of Wales' badge of the Ostrich feathers (with coronet and motto 'Ich dien'); The Prince of Wales' Cypher; The augmented Royal Badge for Wales; the Arms of the Princes of Gwynedd (as appearing in the inescucheon in the Arms of the Prince of Wales); and the Arms of the Earl of Chester.[19]

The Prince's cloak and gold investiture coronet, set with emeralds and diamonds, were newly designed for the event, but other items, such as the sword, rod, ring and cloak clasps, dated from Prince Edward's investiture in 1911.[20] The ceremony itself, devised by the Earl of Snowdon, Charles's uncle by marriage and Constable of Caernarfon Castle, was both moving and beautifully staged. Traditions and resonances of the past blended in the powerful addresses—delivered in Welsh and English—with the enduring commitment to the present and future.

> And him Our most dear Son
> Charles Philip Arthur George
> As has been accustomed We do ennoble
> And invest with the said Principality and Earldom
> by girding him with a Sword
> by putting a coronet on his head
> and a Gold Ring on his finger
> and also by delivering a Gold Rod into his hand
> that he may preside there
> and may direct and defend those parts.
> To hold to him and his heirs
> Kings of the United Kingdom of Great Britain and Northern Ireland
> and of our other realms and territories
> Heads of the Commonwealth for ever.[21]

The Prince spoke in fluent Welsh, and the crowds cheered him to the echo. Caernarfon had not seen such a day since 1911, and that had been a stilted, artificial event by comparison.[22]

There then followed a week-long progress through Wales, covering Llandudno, Bala, Newtown and Aberystwyth; Fishguard, Carmarthen, Morriston and Swansea; Neath, Aberdare, Merthyr Tydfil, Ebbw Vale and Newport; and a whole day of events in Cardiff.[23] Crowds grew in size and enthusiasm, and contrary to earlier speculation, the whole event was a great success. A warm letter of congratulations from Charles's uncle, Lord Louis Mountbatten, reflected the scale of the achievement: 'Confidential reports on naval officers are summarised by numbers ... pretty poor, 2 or 3, very good 7 or 8. Once in a way a naval officer achieves 9, your father did it ... your performance since you went with Fleet coverage to Wales ... rates you at 9 in my opinion.'[24]

After the tour, the Prince theoretically returned to Cambridge in October 1969 to complete his final year, but in practice there were many calls on his time. In February 1970 he took his seat in the House of Lords, and three weeks later flew off for an official tour of Australia, New Zealand, Hong Kong and Japan. This was highly successful and the Prince made his usual good impression, but he was hardly back in the United Kingdom when he had to return to Cambridge to sit his finals.[25]

When the results were declared, he was placed in the lower half of the second class—but given the distractions to which he had been subjected, that was little short of a triumph, and the plaudits which he received were well deserved. No member of the royal family, let alone the heir to the throne, had been required to take examinations for a degree before, but if the future of the monarchy was to be more democratic, then here was a man well qualified to take it forward. HRH The Prince of Wales, BA (and with a half blue for polo), was the first of his kind. However, possessing a degree was one thing, and knowing what to do with it was something else entirely. There was no question of the Prince entering a normal graduate profession. Quite apart from anything else the public duties that he was increasingly called upon to discharge—particularly overseas—would have made routine responsibilities impossible. So the Duke of Edinburgh advised that he should enter the Britannia Royal Naval College at Dartmouth. By this time Charles had a very healthy respect for Philip's judgement in practical matters, so to Dartmouth he went in the autumn of 1971, and in preparation underwent four months flying instruction at RAF Cranwell.[26]

He was not a beginner, having flown with the Air Corps as a student, but his progress was remarkably rapid. He made his first solo flight only three weeks after arriving, on 31 March, and within five months had earned his wings. He loved flying, undertook parachute training, and became in the eyes of the media an all-round Action Man. After this exhilarating interlude, Dartmouth was a dull grind, but by the beginning of November he had passed all his exams (a feat at which he was becoming adept), and flew out with the rank of Sub-Lieutenant to join the destroyer HMS *Norfolk* at Gibraltar.

Charles was to spend the next five years on active service. He was promoted to Acting Lieutenant in 1973 and became a qualified helicopter pilot in 1974, followed by a spell on HMS *Hermes*, a commando carrier. The Prince then returned to Greenwich to take the Lieutenant's course, and was given command of HMS *Bronington*, a coastal minehunter, early in 1976.[27] He remained in command for the rest of the year, but it had never been intended that he should devote his life to the Royal Navy, any more than his great-grandfather, the future George V, had been able to do (see p.211).

The Prince left the service in 1976, and the inevitable question was asked—what was his future to be? Should he be given 'a job' at all?

Any overtly political role was out of the question, and a quasi-political job could easily run out of control. David Checketts, the Prince's private secretary, could not see that there was a problem—or rather, the real problem was not the ostensible one. 'I find it most revealing,' he wrote, 'that the question "What is Prince Charles going to do now that he is out of the navy?" is still being raised, when even a brief investigation of the problem would reveal that the true question is "How is Prince Charles going to be able to do all that there is for him to do?"'[28]

Checketts then went on to list the Prince's current involvements, which included managing the Duchy of Cornwall, the Prince's Trust, the Prince of Wales Environment Committee for Wales, the United World Colleges, the Joint Jubilee Trusts, the Chancellorship of the University of Wales, the Colonel-in-Chiefship of the Welsh Guards and four other regiments, and the patronage of the Royal Anthropological Institute and the British Sub-Aqua Club. The Duchy was a business, and could be as 'hands on' as he chose to make it, but the emerging Prince's Trust was clearly an ideological commitment. In 1979 *The Times* noted over 150 engagements for the Prince, including opening the European Centre for Medium Range Weather Forecasts on 16 June, and diving on the *Mary Rose* on 3 August. On 10 September it also noticed the publication of *The Old Man of Lochnagar*, a children's book that this versatile young man had originally written for his brothers Andrew and Edward, now the Duke of York and Earl of Wessex and, respectively, 12 and 16 years younger than Charles. Drawing on the countryside around Balmoral, *The Old Man* has been made into an animated film, play and ballet, with the Prince's Trust receiving many of the proceeds.

The Prince's Trust had been mooted as long ago as 1972, when the long hangover from the cultural revolution of the 1960s was beginning to take hold, and there was much public concern about 'disenchanted youth'. Charles, who shared that concern, offered his help, and so the concept of the Prince's Trust was born. It did not happen immediately, partly because the Prince was then a full-time serving officer, but with the assistance of George Pratt, a professional probation officer, his enthusiastic ideas were put into a practicable shape. As soon as Charles left the Navy, the trust was officially launched, established with the Prince's £7,400 severance pay. Since then it has remained extremely important to him, becoming a 'flagship enterprise' of social responsibility and epitomizing Charles's determination to use his unique position to make a difference to individual lives. There were, inevitably, doubters and opponents from the beginning, but during the economic recession of the 1980s, with unemployment high and social tensions explosive, the trust repeatedly justified both its existence and its strategy. It has helped over 550,000 young people through practical support, from financial assistance to training and mentoring, and seeks to encourage confidence and motivation among those in difficulties. Helping 100 more young people a day, the trust has become a major enterprise.[29] It is also a symbol of the Prince's involvement with, and attitude towards, the society that has evolved over the last 30 years. As far as possible he has worked to defuse ethnic tensions, often in consultation with the police and with community leaders, using his own flexibility of mind to reinterpret his role as he has gone along.[30] The trust's programmes have a proven track record, with almost three-quarters of those assisted in 2007 entering work, education or training and starting to rebuild their lives.

The Prince's Trust is a very personal initiative, and one that the Queen would be constitutionally unable to take. Charles's status as Prince of Wales has given him more latitude, and his military training would have been relished by previous generations in his role — although perhaps fortunately he was no longer a serving officer when the Falklands War erupted in 1982. It was left to his brother Andrew (then aged 21) to fly helicopters in the conflict zone and to capture the headlines. Yet Charles has been subjected since childhood to media scrutiny of unique intensity, with a technology of intrusion never before available. One wonders how Bertie or the Prince Regent would have fared under such a spotlight, instead of the irreverent cartoons and critical pamphlets with which they had to contend.

Nowhere has this scrutiny been more remorseless or more opinionated than on the subject of the Prince's private life.[31] His marriage to Lady Diana Spencer, descended from an old aristocratic family who had welcomed James I's queen, Anne of Denmark, and her son Henry to their seat at Althorp, Northamptonshire, in 1603, took place on 29 July 1981. Full of glamour and pageantry, the event was shown to audiences worldwide, and was celebrated with some magnificent formal photographs by Lord Lichfield. A year later, on 21 June 1982, their son William was born at St Mary's Hospital, Paddington, becoming second in line to the throne. Not only was it unprecedented for a royal child to be born in a public hospital, it was also unprecedented for the father to be present at the birth, but both things happened on this occasion.[32] The press hailed Charles as a 'thoroughly modern dad' and everybody, including the principal parties, was extremely happy. By the end of the following year Diana was pregnant again, and on 15 September 1984 Prince Harry made his appearance at the same hospital and under similar circumstances.

The Prince and Princess of Wales were separated in late 1992 and formally divorced in 1996. Both parents enjoyed good relationships with their sons, now schoolboys at Eton—a credit to all concerned— and when Diana was killed in a car accident in Paris at the age of 38, Prince Philip, Prince Charles, Prince William and Prince Harry, as well as Diana's brother, now Earl Spencer, walked together behind the hearse. Many years later, as a widower of long standing, Charles married his companion Camilla Parker Bowles at the Guildhall in Windsor on 9 April 2005. As David Starkey has noted, this was 'the humblest location' for a royal wedding since the secret marriage of Edward IV to Elizabeth Woodville in 1464.[33] It was also the first time a Prince of Wales in good standing had been married in a civil ceremony. His wife is now styled Her Royal Highness Camilla, Duchess of Cornwall, and will in due course be known as the Princess Consort when Charles comes to the throne. Changing circumstances, and new situations, have made the protocol of royalty flexible.[34]

Through various biographies, films and television interviews, the present Prince of Wales is far better known than any of his predecessors. He appears a modest, self-critical man, with a multitude of interests, several of which have evolved in public consciousness from the avant-garde to the mainstream. Charles's love of physical activity remains strong; he went on playing polo until November 2005, mostly in aid of charitable appeals, and continues to be a keen skier, usually taking skiing holidays with the equally enthusiastic Princes William and Harry. He learned to dive in the navy, and in 1975 became the first member of the royal family to see the *Mary Rose* since Henry VIII watched her sink in 1545. In a more sedentary mode, he is a keen painter in watercolours, and lithographs of his work are sold in aid of the Prince's Charities Foundation. For many years he has designed and developed the organic gardens at Highgrove, his country residence near Tetbury in Gloucestershire. The Prince has overseen the creation of new features such as the woodland garden's stumpery, and gardening is one of his most relaxing occupations.

The Prince is an intensely busy man.[35] Although excluded by constitutional custom from any role in active politics, he is in fact very well informed about public business, and acts as a surrogate Head of State when called upon to do so. He specializes in slightly tricky overseas assignments, when being 'not quite the monarch' is the most appropriate status, and the Prince's very personal touch is acknowledged as an important diplomatic tool. As long ago as 1970 the newly invested Prince of Wales attended the Fijian Independence celebrations, conferring, as it were, the blessing of the former colonial power. They were held over two days—on 9 and 10 October—to honour the last lowering of the Union flag at sunset and the raising of the Fijian one the following morning. The report of the British High Commissioner in Fiji, now held in the National Archives, commends the 'immense personal contribution' of the Prince to the event's success, noting the tiring schedule that took Charles straight from a long flight from Britain to parts of the islands previously unvisited by any of the Royal Family. The Commissioner's praise for Charles's skilful navigation of the assignment is unreserved:

> He always seemed to have an extra effort in reserve to make an unexpected excursion to greet some character in a crowd who caught his eye ... His interest in local activities never flagged. He spoke on formal occasions with an authority beyond his years and at informal gatherings with charm, humour and a lightness of touch which delighted his audience. He won universal admiration and affection and the sincerity of his farewell words of thanks and praise for the Fijian peoples was deeply appreciated.[36]

The Prince himself responded with pleasure to a welcome 'overwhelming' in its warmth and happiness, and this early visit ended, like many others in the future, in mutual goodwill and satisfaction.

Much more recently, in 2007, he and the Duchess of Cornwall travelled to Uganda where they visited several charity-backed aid projects. There the Prince attended an overseas Commonwealth Heads of Government Meeting, joining the Queen for the first time at an overseas meeting and discussing issues with many of the Commonwealth leaders. He and the Duchess also visited Turkey, and on both occasions they could act on behalf of the UK government in a way that a minister of that government could not have done.[37] In spring 2008 the Prince and the Duchess toured the Caribbean, discussing climate change, youth opportunities and anti-drug initiatives with the appropriate agencies, and Prince Charles attended meetings in Brussels with the European Commission President, to explain the work of his charities. In a speech to the European parliament there, he also proposed an alliance of public, private and non-governmental organizations to address climate change issues. The Prince carried out over 600 official engagements in 2007–8 — an average well exceeding one a day — of which 77 were overseas, while the Duchess, who actively supports the Prince in Britain and abroad, undertook 201, of which 50 were overseas.[38] Charles's other recent activities included hosting the first May Day Business Summit on Climate Change in 2007, visiting Shetland with the Queen of Norway (also in May 2007) and celebrating the contribution of Black Majority Churches to national life in November 2007.

The most conspicuous theme connecting these engagements has been an intense concern with environmental responsibility. This is in essence a personal philosophy for Charles — and one he held long before it was fashionable. In delivering the Roscoe Lecture at St George's Hall, Liverpool, in April 2007, the Prince described the modern world's loss of 'an understanding of our interconnectedness with Nature and a world beyond the material.'[39] Whilst acknowledging the many benefits of technology and progress, he noted how the 'worrying imbalance' such a loss created impacted upon many aspects of everyday life, from urban developments focused upon 'single-use zones' to certain approaches of medicine and agri-industries.

Unsurprisingly, such areas lie at the heart of several of the Prince's initiatives, from The Prince's Foundation for Integrated Health, now working with Barts, a leading London medical school, to his passion for quality local food produced through sustainable farming techniques. Home Farm at Highgrove is famous as a Soil Association demonstration farm, and the Prince has recently set up a Food and Farming Summer School to introduce farmers, policy makers and those involved in every aspect of the food industry to sustainable agriculture. In an interview for the National Trust, of which he is President, Charles applauds 'an entire culture' of local food production that maintains the natural balance of its specific environment. He pays personal tribute to family farms (many run by National Trust tenant farmers) and their contribution to 'the whole remaining delicate fabric of the countryside', and approves the success of two farmers' marketing initiatives that he has recently established in the North Highlands of Scotland and the Peak District.[40] These help farmers to increase their incomes by better marketing of their products.

The Prince has also set his own house in order in environmental terms, despite the inevitable 'carbon footprint' made by his frequent and extensive travel. He has set carbon emission targets for his household, and converted all his cars to run on biodiesel made from cooking oil; unlike their national equivalents, his emissions targets have been met (and indeed exceeded), so that his new target for 2007–12 is no less than 25 per cent.[41] No one could claim that the heir to the throne is not setting a good example. In a sense this is unknown territory, not only for a Prince of Wales but also for any business or political leader, and it is an area in which Charles has been quick to engage. Going beyond his own household, he has set up the May Day Network, consisting of a nearly 1,000 companies accepting a commitment to tackle climate change. Information on new technologies and best practice strategies is shared amongst the network members, and other business contacts and employees are encouraged to follow their lead. A second May Day Summit in 2008 provided a running check on progress, and to date more than 5,000 pledges of support have been made, with almost all agreeing to measure their own carbon footprints. In 2006 the Prince also established an Accounting for Sustainability project, with the aim of helping companies and organizations to develop sustainable policies in day-to-day business activities. This has now been completed, and the results are being assessed.

On a global scale, The Prince's Rainforests Project, launched in October 2007, has brought 15 of the world's largest and most influential companies together with experts on economics and the environment to address the devastating climatic impact of deforestation. The project aims to persuade governments to take effective measures to curb deforestation (which as Charles has observed 'is likely to be one of the quickest and most cost-effective means of reducing carbon dioxide emissions'), in addition to encouraging the recycling of water vapour into rain.[42] Uniquely placed above both the political and business sphere, the Prince uses his role as an internationally powerful convener to develop practical forums for change. Two of his charities, The Prince of Wales's Business & the Environment Programme and Business in the Community, have worked closely with the insurance industry (often badly hit by the cost of natural disasters) to promote Climate-wise Principles, and similar projects are under development with the world's eight largest companies managing public pension funds.

The Prince is probably still best known for his unique brand of 'charitable entrepreneurship': of the 19 separate charities embraced by The Prince's Charities Foundation, Charles personally founded 17. Dr Starkey has recently noted how his achievements reflect a 'necessary combination of social and economic power—and imagination' and the success of the Prince's charities has proved startling.[43] In 2007–8 they raised £122 million, with the Prince helping, directly or indirectly, in all these efforts.[44] Among the best known are The Prince's Trust itself, The Prince's Youth Business Trust and The Prince's Scottish Youth Business Trust, founded in 1989. Their focus upon young people is complemented by the organizations PRIME (The Prince's Initiative for Mature Enterprise) and PRIME–Cymru, which offer support and advice on self-employment and enterprise to workers aged 50 or over. The Prince's most recent charity, the British Asian Trust, seeks to create an investment fund for employment, training, enterprise and sustainable social initiatives. With activities spanning five countries—India, Pakistan, Bangladesh, Sri Lanka and Britain— the new trust reflects Charles's awareness of the variety and importance of Britain's Asian communities.

The Prince's consistent approach to this work is to identify an unserved need and establish a charity to fill the gap, then to embark on strategic and fundraising activities to sustain it into the future.[45] Many of the charities emerge via an active research and development programme and address issues ranging from social cohesion and poverty to international regeneration and the arts. Charles's commitment to encouraging socially responsible business is longstanding, and a new 'Seeing is Believing' project seeks to introduce high profile and local business leaders directly to deprived areas. Recent visits to Burnley in Lancashire, under the auspices of the Prince's charity Business in the Community, have already brought pledges of financial support for improved facilities within the town.

The Prince has also become the celebrated champion of a variety of social and cultural causes. His School of Traditional Arts celebrates the arts of the world's great religions and attracts a strong international student base, while The Prince's Foundation for Children & the Arts seeks to introduce schoolchildren to a range of cultural and artistic experience. Charles is President of the Royal Shakespeare Company and his longstanding appreciation of Britain's literary heritage has led to some penetrating observations about the nation's educational provision: 'In Italy, France and Belgium every child under five receives nursery education from the state. Here, less than half our children have the right... It is almost incredible that in Shakespeare's land one child in seven leaves primary school functionally illiterate'.[46] Another of Charles's charities, The Prince's Teaching Institute, provides training to teachers in English, History, Science and Geography, emphasizing the acquiring of knowledge and understanding as well as skills.

Charles has also famously promoted traditional architecture in a variety of ways—not always through incisive criticism, although that has tended to capture the headlines. The model community of Poundbury, an urban extension to Dorchester in Dorset, has earned considerable praise in this regard. The Prince's Foundation for the Built Environment, based in East London, promotes and practices traditional and ecological methods of building and planning. Among its projects is the Coed Darcy Urban Village, a proposed development of a 1,300-acre site in Wales. Working with companies and regional authorities, the plans are to integrate living and working areas and community facilities, providing 4000 new homes in the region.[47] The Prince's Regeneration Trust seeks to preserve historic structures and nurture regeneration schemes in conjunction with local organizations, while his Turquoise Mountain initiative is undertaking restoration work with locally trained craftspeople in Kabul, the war-torn capital of Afghanistan.

Preservation of the historic Dumfries House in East Ayrshire was a dramatic recent success, with the Prince leading a consortium that raised £45 million for its purchase and restoration. The successful acquisition, driven by the Prince's provision of £20 million, was achieved only days before the house and contents were scheduled for sale at auction, when the fine furniture collection would have been irrevocably separated from the elegant mansion, designed by the Adam brothers in the 1750s. The feat has been described as 'one of the most remarkable heritage rescue acts in British history'[48] and the house itself is now open to the public, providing jobs and additional income in this deprived area of Scotland. Furthermore, the Prince has embarked upon a regeneration scheme for the area through the development of a sustainable, mixed-use community nearby.

Such a project is typical of the Prince of Wales, who is not just a philanthropist with a taste for fashionable causes. He is also a businessman with a desire to use his expertise in the service of the same causes. Most obviously he runs the Duchy of Cornwall, a vast private estate consisting of 54,521 hectares of land in 23 counties, seeking not only to make it profitable but also to hand it on in a flourishing condition to his own heir.[49] The estate is made up of agricultural, commercial and residential properties, and a portfolio of financial investments, and Charles's management is acknowledged to be shrewd, businesslike and principled. Unlike some of his predecessors the Prince has maintained a keen interest in Wales, not least through his role in its main university, and through the various properties that he owns in the Principality. The Duchy has recently bought the 78-hectare Llwynywermod Farm near Myddfai in Carmarthenshire, with the intention of creating a home in Wales for Charles and the Duchess of Cornwall. A local workforce is converting the farmhouse to accommodate biomass woodchip heating and other environmentally friendly features.[50]

It is now over two decades since the Duchy's biggest development, Poundbury, was established, and the community has pioneered a number of important experiments in which the Prince has been closely involved. Private and social housing has been intermixed, and offices, commercial premises and light industrial buildings have been woven into residential areas to reduce the strains of commuting. Poundbury's buildings reflect the region's character and tradition, and designs for a new centrepiece, Queen Mother Square, have been recently approved. About half of the town has now been completed, and it receives over 80 official visits per year.

The Prince's own business, Duchy Originals, was established to promote organic food, together with concern for the countryside and wildlife, in 1990. It has expanded dramatically from the biscuits made from wheat and oats organically grown at Highgrove to over 300 types of food and drink, creating an annual profit for The Prince's Charities Foundation of over £1 million (£7.5 million since inception). Despite the huge increase in scale, the business's commitment to the 'virtuous circle'—whereby high quality products make money for charity while supporting the environment and wildlife—is as strong as ever. All Duchy Originals products are made in Britain and many ingredients still come from the Home Farm: milk from the Ayrshire herd, vegetables for chutney and crisps, an old type of barley, Plumage Archer, for the ale and, of course, the wheat and oats for its legendary biscuits. Scottish honey is sourced from Balmoral and organic pork from a nearby estate in Tetbury. Following the success of Duchy Originals further 'social enterprises' have been set up on similar principles, including the Highgrove shop, which sells gifts and produce from the gardens and has recently opened a new retail outlet in Tetbury, Gloucestershire. Like the original onsite shop in the Orchard Room at Highgrove, its profits go to The Prince's Charities Foundation.[51]

Rather similar to Poundbury, but taking place in a completely different context, is the North Highland Initiative, founded in 2005. The Initiative is an attempt to regenerate the economy of Caithness, Sutherland and Ross.[52] It has involved beef and wool production, the encouragement of tourism, and a sensitive care for the built environment. The aim, once again, is sustainable development and an economic growth that improves the quality of life for the resident community, and provides an attractive environment both for new residents and investors. This enterprise has now entered its third and final stage. In its second full year of trading North Highland Products generated a turnover of £8.6 million, and plans are now in progress to establish other regional farmers' marketing schemes in the Cambrian Mountains and Dartmoor.

An area of the Prince's activities with which his predecessors would certainly have identified is his commitment to the armed forces. Charles's own years of active service have given him a good understanding appropriate to a future Commander-in-Chief, and he holds the rank of Admiral in the Royal Navy, General in the Army and Air Chief Marshal in the Royal Air Force. He also has a close relationship with several individual regiments such as the Black Watch, the Royal Gurkha Rifles, the Queen's Own Yeomanry and the Army Air Corps. Some of these associations go back many decades; the Prince has been Colonel of the Welsh Guards since 1975 and Colonel-in-Chief of the Parachute Regiment since 1977. Others are more recent, like the

Mercian Regiment (created by the merger of the Cheshire, the Stafford-shire and the Worcestershire and Sherwood Foresters), whose formation parade at Tamworth Castle was attended by the Prince in 2007. Family connections to the armed forces are of course strong: both William and Harry are serving officers in the Blues and Royals regiment of the Household Cavalry, and the Duchess of Cornwall is Royal Colonel of the 4th Battalion The Rifles, Commodore-in-Chief of Naval Medical Services and Honorary Air Commodore of RAF Halton and RAF Leeming.[53]

Presentation of campaign medals is an important aspect of the royal couple's work, with servicemen and their families often invited to their London home, Clarence House, for the occasion. Recent presentations at Clarence House have included the 9 Regiment, Army Air Corps in 2007 and the 1st Battalion Welsh Guards in 2008; soldiers from both received medals following their return from operations in Afghanistan. The Prince makes regular visits to the Royal Centre for Defence Medicine at Selly Oak and the Queen Elizabeth Hospital in Birmingham, where those injured in the conflicts in Afghanistan and Iraq are treated. He is also patron of the Falklands veterans' organization, the South Atlantic Medal Association, and was recently involved in events to commemorate the 25th anniversary.

The shared military connections have highlighted, but by no means defined, the Prince's excellent relationship with his sons. In the years after Diana's death the relaxed settings of his winter sports holidays with William and Harry served to provide the media with some of its happier (and more permitted) intrusions into the family's private life. Both are now grown men, and he has consistently fostered their talents and encouraged their ambitions—and sympathized with the frustrations of a royal position that limits the scope of service in their chosen field. The Princes' comfortable association with the Prince of Wales has been matched in the position's recent history only by George's relationship with Edward VII, and more than six centuries ago in the mutual respect of Edward III and the Black Prince.

The honour of being the nation's longest serving Prince of Wales, for so long held by his great-great-grandfather Bertie, looks sure soon to pass to Prince Charles himself. Yet his achievement is far more than mere length of service. Where he has exceeded Bertie, and indeed all his predecessors, is in the skill with which he has adapted to changing circumstances, political, social and religious. No previous Prince of Wales has had to cope with the kind of transformation wrought in our national life by a combination of technology, investigative journalism and fluid migration. It could be said that the Prince has become a specialist in lateral thinking, and has identified with great accuracy and sensitivity those issues and causes that need to be addressed, but that tend to fall outside the remit of government. In a sense the traditional trappings—the titles of honour, the military ranks and so on—are deceptive. Queen Elizabeth II has had to be a different kind of Head of State from her father or her grandfather, let alone such remote fore-bears as the first Elizabeth. The constitution has changed, with devolved government in Wales and Scotland, and a reformed House of Lords, which still awaits the final touch of the legislator. Her heir has got to be prepared for a world with different preoccupations, and different priorities from those with which he grew up. Will he, as David Starkey recently asked, even have a coronation? Or will it be replaced by some kind of civil inauguration?[54] Whatever befalls, it seems that Charles is equipped—perhaps uniquely equipped—to succeed. With his breadth and depth of interests, business acumen, consistent personal philos-ophy and skills as a convener, he has relished the role of Prince of Wales and redefined it for our age.

Notes on the text

Introduction

1. Micheal Prestwich, *Edward I*, 1988. H. Johnson, *Edward of Caernarfon, 1284–1307*, 1946.
2. The title of Prince of Wales was recognized in 1265 in a treaty negotiated on the King's behalf by Simon de Montfort and confirmed two years later in a second treaty signed by the King personally and negotiated by the Papal Legate, Cardinal Ottobon. See J. Goronwy Edwards, *The Principality of Wales, 1267–1967*, 1968, pp.2–3. See also J.R. Maddicott, *Simon de Montfort*, 1994, pp.337–8. R.R. Davies, *The Age of Conquest: Wales 1063–1415*, 1992, p.391.
3. Davies, *Age of Conquest*, pp.391–2. The Principality involved both Lordship and Overlordship, so that all Welsh barons in theory held their lands of the Prince rather than the King. It would probably have been news to most of them that they had any connection with the King at all—but they did after 1267. They were particularly required by the terms of the treaty to give up their rights to private warfare.
4. At the same time Flint was erected into a county, and placed under the jurisdiction of the Earldom of Chester. Each county had its own Sheriff and Escheator, but these officers were answerable to the Chancery and Exchequer established at Caernarfon rather than to those at Westminster. An official called the Justiciar acted on the King's (or Prince's) behalf in each part of the Principality. He appointed the officers, but they were not accountable to him. Davies, *Age of Conquest*, p.396.
5. These were controlled by Stewards and Constables appointed by the Lords, and followed distinctive customs. For example authorized travellers were protected by 'Letters of the March'—a kind of safe conduct—and boundary disputes were settled by meetings known as 'Love days'. Davies, *Age of Conquest*, p.392.
6. *English Historical Documents, 1189–1327*, ed. J.B. Roskell, 1975, pp.422–3. *Statutes of the Realm*, I, pp.55–68.
7. Within the Principality a distinction was recognized between Pleas of the Crown (which related to major crimes) and other pleas. In the case of the former the English common law was used, while for the latter practice varied. Pleas involving Englishmen (for instances burgesses of the towns) would normally be heard by English law, whereas disputes between Welshmen would be heard by Welsh customary law. The Marcher Lordships used an eclectic mixture of English and Welsh law, depending upon location and custom.
8. W.M. Ormrod, *The Reign of Edward III: Crown and Political Society in England, 1327–1377*, 1990. Nigel Saul, 'The Despensers and the Downfall of Edward II', *English Historical Review*, 99, 1984, pp.1–33.
9. Davies, *Age of Conquest*, p.398. The Black Prince also presented two of his clerks, John Gilbert and William Spreadlington, to the sees of Bangor and St Asaph, a prerogative normally reserved to the King.
10. Richard had three uncles at this point: John of Gaunt, Edmund of Langley and Thomas of Woodstock. It was probably John who was feared.
11. For a full discussion of these events, see R.R. Davies, *The Revolt of Owain Glyn Dŵr*, 1995.
12. W.R.D. Griffiths, 'Prince Henry and Wales, 1400–1408', in *Profit, Piety and the Professions in Later Medieval England*, ed. M. Hicks, 1990.
13. R.A. Griffiths, *The Reign of King Henry VI*, 1981, pp.666–72.
14. Edwards, *The Principality of Wales*, p.9. Charles Ross, *Edward IV*, 1974, pp.194–8.
15. Glanmor Williams, *Recovery, Reorientation and Reformation: Wales, 1415–1642*, 1987, p.52. The Prince's council wielded equity jurisdiction within its sphere of influence, and such common law functions as might be delegated to it by the central courts at Westminster. John Alcock, then Bishop of Rochester, became its President.

16. S.B. Chrimes, *Henry VII*, 1972, p.249.

17. R.A. Griffiths, *The Principality of Wales in the Later Middle Ages, I, South Wales 1277–1538*, 1972. T.B. Pugh, 'The Indentures for the Marches between Henry VII and Edward Stafford, Duke of Buckingham, 1477–1521', *English Historical Review*, 71, 1956, pp.436–41.

18. Chrimes, *Henry VII*, pp.284–5. John Leland, *De Rebus Brittanicus Collectanea*, ed. T. Hearne, 1715, IV, pp.352 *et seq.*

19. Williams, *Wales, 1415–1642*, p.55.

20. Henry Fitzroy (1519–36) was illegitimate by anyone's standards, his mother being Elizabeth Blount. Edward was illegitimate by Catholic standards because his parents (Henry and Jane Seymour) had married while the realm was in schism—when no lawful marriages could be celebrated.

21. J.J. Scarisbrick, *Henry VIII*, 1968, p.296 and n. *Lords Journals*, I, p.284.

22. Statute 1 Mary sess.2, cap.1. J. Loach, *Parliament and the Crown in the Reign of Mary Tudor*, 1986, pp.78–9.

23. G.R. Elton, *The Tudor Constitution*, 1982, p.202. The Duke of Buckingham's attainder highlighted the need for stronger central control; Carole Rawcliffe, *The Staffords, Earls of Stafford and Dukes of Buckingham*, 1978, p.182.

24. Part of the problem was that the customary use of Welsh law continued, and Welsh law, with its extensive use of fines and compensation, even for serious crimes such as homicide, did not provide an adequate deterrent; Williams, *Wales 1415–1642*, p.35. T.M. Charles Edwards, *The Welsh Laws*, 1989.

25. *Statutes of the Realm*, III, pp.500–503. A start was made with the statute of 26 Henry VIII, cap.6, 'An act for murders and felonies committed within any Lordship Marcher of Wales', which decreed that all Pleas of the Crown (that is felonies) were to be tried henceforth, not in the Marcher courts, but by the justices of the peace and gaol delivery in the nearest adjoining English shire. This was a revolutionary procedural change, and spelled the beginning of the end for Marcher jurisdiction. That end came more rapidly than anyone at the time can have been expecting.

26. *Statutes of the Realm*, III, pp.555–8.

27. Crown appointees included the newly constituted commissioners of the peace and gaol delivery. Each county was henceforth to send two representatives to parliament, and each county town one. The only distinctive features remaining were that the county officers accounted to their own Exchequers and Chanceries at Caernarfon and Carmarthen rather than to Westminster, and that the Assizes were the Justices of Great Session, and not answerable outside Wales. See Elton, *Tudor Constitution*, p.33. The Courts of Great Session were, however, just as much the King's courts as the King's Bench or Common Pleas.

28. Peter R. Roberts, 'Wales and England after the Tudor Union; Crown, Principality and Parliament, 1536–1641' in *Law and Government under the Tudors*, ed. J. Scarisbrick et al., 1988.

29. The appointment of Justices of the Peace by the Lord Chancellor minimized the risk of personal feuds being carried into the commissions. Roberts, *op.cit.* Penry Williams, *The Council in the Marches of Wales under Elizabeth I*, 1958. When the Reformation arrived, both the Prayer Book and the Bible were immediately translated into Welsh on the initiative of the government. Glanmor Williams, *Welsh Reformation Essays*, 1967. *Tudor Wales*, edited by Trevor Herbert and Gareth Elwyn Jones, 1988, pp.126–8.

30. *Statutes of the Realm*, III, p.926. Williams, *Council in the Marches.*

31. David Loades, *Tudor Government*, 1997, p.215. *Statutes of the Realm*, loc.cit.

32. David Loades, *Politics and the Nation, 1450–1660*, 1999, p.280. The High Commission was the first prerogative court to be assailed by the common lawyers, on the grounds that it was poaching business from the Court of Common Pleas. After 1625 it came to be regarded as an instrument of royal oppression because of its role in enforcing Laudian standards of conformity. Other attacks were then launched on the Star Chamber and the regional councils, and it was finally abolished in 1689 along with the anachronistic courts of Chancery and Exchequer. See Edwards, *The Principality of Wales*, p.12. The statutes that

occasioned the end of the Council in the Marches and the other legislative bodies were Statutes 16 Charles I, cap. 10 (Star Chamber etc.) and cap. 11 (High Commission).

33. Edwards, *The Principality of Wales*, p. 14. Such residual functions of oversight as the council was still performing were transferred to the Courts of Great Session. Throughout the eighteenth and the early part of the nineteenth century these courts were the sole relics of the once distinctive governmental system of Wales; they survived until 1830, when they too were abolished by statute, the Welsh circuits being transferred to the control of the central courts.

34. Geoffrey Holmes and Daniel Szechi, *The Age of Oligarchy, 1722–1783,* 1993, p. 8.

35. Edwards, *The Principality of Wales*, p. 16.

36. *Age of Oligarchy*, p. 247.

37. A.W. Purdue, 'Edward VIII', in *The Reader's Guide to British History,* 2003, I, p. 441.

38. Sarah Bradford, *King George VI,* 1989.

39. Anthony Holden, *Charles: A Biography,* 1998.

40. *The Prince's Charities; The Prince of Wales and the Duchess of Cornwall: Annual Review 2008*, pp. 26–7.

i. The First Princes of Wales

1. Holinshed's *Chronicle*, ed. 1807, II, p. 487.

2. The origin of this story seems to have lain in David Powell's *History of Cambria*, 1584.

3. Hilda Johnstone, *Edward of Caernarfon, 1284–1307*, 1946. Mariota (or Mary) was granted 100 shillings a year in 1312 from the King's mills at Caernarfon, and in 1317 received a burgage and 73 acres of land in the town. Alice was later in the service of Queen Isabella.

4. Ibid.

5. The King later granted him the manor of Langley, which was clearly his favourite residence.

6. H.R. Luard, ed., *Annales Monastici*, Record Society, 1864–9, III, p. 392.

7. *ODNB*.

8. M.C. Prestwich, 'Edward I and the Maid of Norway', *Scottish Historical Review*, 69,

1990, pp. 157–73.

9. Johnstone, *Edward of Caernarfon*. The resentment was largely over his demand for subsidies, and this was aggravated by the Papal Bull *Clericis laicos*, which forbade such payments from the clergy without Papal consent.

10. Johnstone, *op. cit.*

11. Michael Prestwich, *Plantagenet England, 1125–1360*, 2005, pp. 232–9.

12. P. Chaplais, *Piers Gaveston, Edward II's Adoptive Brother*, 1994, p. 10.

13. J. Goronwy Edwards, *The Principality of Wales*, 1968, p. 10.

14. Ibid., p. 12.

15. *English Historical Documents, 1189–1327*, p. 251. *The Chronicle of Pierre de Langtoft, 1297–1307*, edited by T. Wright (Rolls Series, 1866–8, II, pp. 265–83. In French.).

16. M.C. Prestwich, 'Italian Merchants in Late Thirteenth and Early Fourteenth Century England', in *The Dawn of Modern Banking*, 1979, pp. 99–100.

17. Johnstone, *Edward of Caernarfon*.

18. Ibid.

19. N. Denholm Young, *History and Heraldry, 1254–1310*, 1965, pp. 25, 49.

20. *Calendar of the Patent Rolls, 1301–1307*, p. 424.

21. Prestwich, *Plantagenet England*, pp. 179–80.

22. The gross revenues totalled £8,775. Johnstone, *Edward of Caernarfon*.

23. Chaplais, *Piers Gaveston*, pp. 27–34.

24. Prestwich, *Plantagenet England*, pp. 179–80.

25. Chaplais, *Piers Gaveston*, p. 68.

26. J.C. Davies, *The Baronial Opposition to Edward II*, 1918, p. 372.

27. N. Denholm Young, ed., *Vita Edwardi Secundi*, 1957, p. 21.

28. Prestwich, *Plantagenet England*, p. 189.

29. *Vita Edwardi Secundi*, edited by Wendy Childs, Oxford 2005, p. 69.

30. J.R. Maddicott, *Thomas of Lancaster, 1307–1322*, 1970, p. 165.

31. Ibid., pp. 213 *et seq.* The negotiations have been described as 'complex to reconstuct'.

32. Prestwich, *Plantagenet England*, pp. 197–8.

33. R.M. Haines, *King Edward II: Edward of Caernarfon, his Life, his Reign, and its Aftermath, 1284–1330*, 2003, p. 174.

34. *ODNB*.

35. Davies, *The Age of Conquest*, p.397.
36. *ODNB*.
37. C. Shenton, 'Edward III and the coup of 1330', in J.S. Bothwell, ed., *The Age of Edward III*, 2001, pp.13–34.
38. Richard Barber, *Edward, The Black Prince*, 1978, p.41.
39. *Calendar of the Patent Rolls, 1343–1345*, p.114. 20 September 1343.
40. *ODNB*.
41. *Calendar of the Patent Rolls, 1343–1348*, p.12. 8 November 1345.
42. Prestwich, *Plantagenet England*, pp.266–9.
43. William Montague, Robert Ufford and William Clinton, all of whom had been present at Nottingham in 1330 became Earls of Salisbury, Suffolk and Huntingdon respectively, while Montague was also granted extensive lands in Wales, including the Lordship of Denbigh. The chronicler Robert of Reading considered them to be worse than Piers Gaveston, *Flores Historiarum*, ed. H.R. Luard, Records Society, 1890, III, p.178.
44. Prestwich, *Plantagenet England*, p.275.
45. R.M. Haines, *Archbishop John Stratford, Political Revolutionary and Champion of the Liberties of the English Church, c.1275/80–1348*, 1986, pp.296–305.
46. *Calendar of the Patent Rolls, 1345–1348*, p.123. 2 June 1346.
47. For a full discussion of the battle, and the stories relating to it, see A. Ayton, ed., *The Battle of Crécy*, 2005.
48. *Knighton's Chronicle, 1337–1396*, ed. G.H. Martin, Oxford 1995, pp.61–3.
49. Barber, *The Black Prince*, pp.68–9. The quote is attributed to one John Ardenne.
50. *ODNB*.
51. Davies, *Age of Conquest*, p.409.
52. J.B. Smith, 'Crown and Community in the Principality of North Wales', *Welsh History Review*, 3, 1966–7, pp.145–71. Davies, *Age of Conquest*, p.411.
53. Barber, *The Black Prince*, p.81.
54. *ODNB*. For a full discussion of these troubles, see below.
55. Davies, *Age of Conquest*, p.411.
56. A.D. Carr, 'An Aristocracy in Decline', *Welsh History Review*, 5, 1970–71, pp.103–29.
57. Goronwy Edwards, *The Principality of Wales*, p.14.

58. Davies, *Age of Conquest*, p.420.
59. A.D. Carr, *Medieval Wales*, 1995. Prestwich, *Plantagenet England*, pp.141–64.
60. M. Vale, *Edward III and Chivalry*, 1983, pp.76–91.
61. N.A.M. Rodger, *The Safeguard of the Sea*, 1997, p.104.
62. *ODNB*.
63. *English Historical Documents, 1327–1485*, edited by A.R. Myers, 1969, pp.110–11. Pedro Lopez de Ayala, *Cronicos de los eyes de Castilla*, Tom.1, 1779, pp.407 *et seq.*, In Spanish.
64. C.W. Previte Orton, *The Shorter Cambridge Medieval History*, 1962, II, p.885.
65. E.B. Fryde et al., eds., *The Handbook of British Chronology*, 1986, pp.39–40.
66. Prestwich, *Plantagenet England*, pp.538–46.
67. John Julius Norwich, *Shakespeare's Kings*, 2001, p.53.
68. J.B. Smith, 'Crown and Community in the Principality of North Wales'.
69. Ways round the Welsh system's limitations had been discovered, either by establishing a trust to use in the English manner or by using a type of perpetual mortgage called *tir prid*.
70. Waters, *Edwardian Settlement*, p.82.
71. Barber, *The Black Prince*, p.41.
72. John Julius Norwich, *Shakespeare's Kings*, 2001, p.44.
73. *ODNB*, Richard II.
74. Ibid.
75. TNA E403/475, m.8.
76. R.H. Hilton and T.H. Aston, eds., *The Peasants Revolt of 1381*, 1884.
77. *Handbook of British Chronology*, p.494.
78. A. Goodman, *The Loyal Conspiracy. The Lords Appellant under Richard II*, 1971.
79. Ibid., *ODNB*.
80. Anthony Tuck, *Richard II and the English Nobility*, 1974. *ODNB*.
81. Anthony Goodman and James Gillespie, eds., *Richard II. The Art of Kingship*, 1998.
82. Anthony Goodman, *John of Gaunt. The Exercise of Princely Power in Fourteenth Century Europe*, 1992.
83. Geoffrey Barraclough, 'The Earldom and County Palatine of Chester', *Transactions of the Historical Society of Lancashire and Cheshire*, 103, 1952, pp.23–57.

84. Michael Bennett, *Richard II and the Revolution of 1399*, 1999.
85. C. Given Wilson, ed., *The Chronicle of Adam of Usk, 1377–1421*, 1997.
86. Ibid., p.63.
87. Papal rights of provision had been attacked in the Acts of Provisors and Praemunire of 1393. England adhered (with qualifications) to Pope Boniface IX (in Rome) while the French recognized Benedict XIII (in Avignon).

ii. A Dangerous Inheritance

1. *ODNB*, Henry V.
2. C. Allmand, *Henry V*, 1998.
3. Ibid.
4. R.R. Davies, *The Revolt of Owain Glyn Dŵr*, 1995, p.102.
5. J.L. Kirby, *Henry IV of England*, 1970, p.106.
6. *ODNB*, Henry V.
7. *Chronicles of London,* edited by C.L. Kingsford, 1905, p.51. BL Cotton MS Julius B.II, f.47.
8. Davies, *The Revolt of Owain Glyn Dŵr,* pp.102–29.
9. *Chronicles of London,* pp.224–5. BL Cotton MS Vitellius A.XVI, f.174.
10. J.E. Messham, 'The County of Flint and the Rebellion of Owen Glyndŵr in the Records of the earldom of Chester', *Flintshire Historical Society Transactions, 23,* 1967–8, pp.1–34.
11. There had been revolts before—Rhys ap Meredudd in 1287, Madoc ap Llewellyn in 1295, Llewellyn Bryn in 1316, Wynion Eden in 1345, and Owain Lawgoch in 1378 —but none had had the power or pretensions of Glyn Dŵr.
12. J.B. Smith, 'Crown and Community in the Principality of North Wales', *Welsh History Review, 3,* 1966–7, pp.145–71.
13. Statutes, 2 Henry IV, caps. 12, 16, 17, 18. 4 Henry IV, caps. 26, 28. In theory Englishry and Welshry had been separate since the conquest; distinct settlements that were differently administered, but in practice the distinctions had become blurred. Now they were to be reinforced and taken seriously.
14. Davies, *Revolt,* p.102.
15. J.E. Lloyd, *Owen Glendower*, 1931, pp.58–9.
16. Davies, *Revolt,* p.107 and n.
17. William Shakespeare, *King Henry IV, Part I,* Act V, Scene IV. J.M.W. Bean, 'Henry IV and the Percies', *History*, vol.40, pp.212–27.
18. Titus Livius Forojuliensis, *c.*1437, quoted in *Shakespeare's Kings*, John Julius Norwich, pp.140–41.
19. *ODNB. Calendar of the Patent Rolls, 1401–5,* p.216.
20. Ibid., p.311.
21. Lloyd, *Owen Glendower*, pp.82–6.
22. In this he was greatly assisted by the adherence of two of Wales's most senior ecclesiastics, Lewis Byford, the Bishop of Bangor, and John Trefor of St Asaph. Trefor, who had been Chamberlain of Chester since 1399, was a particularly valuable acquisition. Davies, *Revolt,* p.187.
23. E.F. Jacob, *The Fifteenth Century*, 1961, p.47.
24. Led by the Archbishop, Richard le Scrope. Jacob, *Fifteenth Century*, pp.59–61.
25. A.D. Carr, 'Gwilym ap Gruffydd and the Penrhyn Estate', *Welsh History Review*, 15, 1990–91, pp.1–21.
26. Davies, *Revolt,* pp.169–72. Benedict XIII was recognized by the French, while the English remained loyal to Innocent VII in Rome.
27. TNA SC6/1216, m.6.
28. Davies, *Revolt,* pp.123–4.
29. Glanmor Williams, *Recovery, Reorientation and Reformation: Wales 1415–1642*, 1987, p.6.
30. Ibid., pp.7–8.
31. Ibid, p.15.
32. Ibid., p.8, p.12. Guto'r Glyn, although ostensibly writing in the cause of the Yorkist William Herbert, was actually issuing a call to national redemption.
   'Dwg Forgannwy Gwynedd/ Gwna'n im o Gonwy i Nedd/ O digia Lloegr a'i chigiaid/ Cymru a drg yn dy raid...'
   (*Bring Wales from Glamorgan to Gwynedd under thy sway/ unite it all from Conwy to Neath./ If England and her Dukes are offended,/ Wales will rally to thy cause.*)
   Nor were these feeling unrequited. 'The Libel of English Policy', written about 1435, contained the lines 'Beware of Wales,

Christ Jesus must us keep, That it make not our child's child to weep....'

33. *ODNB*, Henry IV.

34. Jacob, *Fifteenth Century*, p.112.

35. *ODNB*, Henry V. C.T. Allmand, *Henry V.*

36. W.T. Waugh, 'Sir John Oldcastle', *English Historical Review*, 20, 1905, pp.434–56, 637–58.

37. T.B. Pugh, *Henry V and the Southampton Plot of 1415*, 1988.

38. *ODNB*, Henry V.

39. Agnes Strickland, *The Lives of the Queens of England*, 1902, III, p.110.

40. *Handbook of British Chronology*, 1986.

41. Renée was Duke of Anjou, Lorraine and Bar, and titular King of Naples, Sicily and Jerusalem. He was not himself a member of the royal family, but his sister was married to Charles VII. The betrothal took place before it was clear that the result would be a truce and not a peace.

42. For a full discussion of this declaration and what followed, see R.A. Griffiths, *The Reign of King Henry VI*, 1981, pp.275–95.

43. G.L. Harriss, 'Cardinal Beaufort—patriot or userer?' *Transactions of the Royal Historical Society*, 5th series, XX, 1970, pp.129–48.

44. J.J. Bagley, *Margaret of Anjou, Queen of England*, 1948.

45. J. Stevenson, ed., *Letters and Papers Illustrative of the wars of the English in France during the Reign of Henry the sixth*, 3 vols. Record Society, 1861–64, II, ii, pp.639–42.

46. By 1449 Suffolk was completely dominant. The Earl of Somerset was trying to hold together the dwindling English presence in France, and the Duke of York had gone off in disgust to take up his appointment as Lieutenant in Ireland. His appointment was officially for 10 years, with a starting 'salary' of 4,000 marks. N.H. Nicolas, ed. *Proceedings and Ordinances of the Privy Council*, Records Commission, 1834–37, VI, p.89. *Calendar of the Patent Rolls, 1446–52*, p.185.

47. Stevenson, *Letters and Papers*, II, ii, p.630.

48. N.H. Nicolas and E. Tyrell, eds, *A Chronicle of London, 1189–1483*, 1827, pp.137–8.

49. A.R. Myers, ed., *English Historical Documents*, vol. iv, 1327–1485, 1969, p.272.

50. R.A. Griffiths, *Henry VI*, pp.719–25.

51. *Calendar of the Patent Rolls, 1452–1461*, p.172. 32 Henry VI, m.9.

52. *ODNB*, *sub* 'Edward of Westminster'.

53. J.R. Lander, *Conflict and Stability in Fifteenth Century England*, 1969. D. Loades, *Politics and the Nation, 1450–1660*, 1999, pp.36–57.

54. C.A.J. Armstrong, 'Politics and the battle of St Albans, 1455', *Bulletin of the Institute of Historical Research*, 33, 1960, pp.1–72.

55. *ODNB*.

56. N. Davies, ed., *Paston Letters and Papers of the Fifteenth Century*, 2 vols, 1971–76, II, p.221.

57. Griffiths, *Henry VI*, p.857.

58. Hall, *Chronicle*.

59. *Rotuli Parliamentorum*, V, pp.375–83.

60. Contrary to the story perpetuated by Shakespeare, Margaret was nowhere near Wakefield at the time of the battle, and was not responsible for Richard's death.

61. A.H. Thomas and I.D. Thornley, eds., *The Great Chronicle of London*, 1938, pp.193–4.

62. M-R. Thielemans, *Bourgogne et Angleterre; relations politiques, 1435–1467*, 1968, p.398.

63. *ODNB*, citing Fortescue, *De Laudibus Legum Angliae*.

64. Charles Ross, *Edward IV*, 1974, pp.137–45.

65. J. Bruce, ed., *Historie of the Arrivall of King Edward IV*, Camden Society, 1838, pp.18–21.

66. *ODNB*, *sub* 'Margaret of Anjou'.

67. Ibid., *sub* 'Edward V'.

68. *Handbook of British Chronology*, p.457.

69. *Calendar of the Charter Rolls, 1427–1516*, p.239.

70. *Calendar of the Patent Rolls, 1467–77*, pp.283, 361, 365–6, 429. P. Williams, *The Council in the Marches of Wales under Elizabeth I*, 1958, p.7.

71. Ross, *Edward IV*, pp.196–8.

72. *ODNB*.

73. The civil wars had brought an unprecedented number of Lordships into the King's hands, but this provided only a partial solution. R.A. Griffiths, 'Wales and the Marches in the Fifteenth Century', in Griffiths, ed., *King and Country, England and Wales in the Fifteenth century*, 1991, pp.55–82.

74. Ross, *Edward IV*, p.408. *Cal.Pat., 1467–77*, p.429.

75. Williams, *Council in the Marches*, p.9.

76. Ross, *Edward IV,* p.197.

77. *Rotuli Parliamentorum*, VI, pp.202–4. *Cal.Pat. 1476–85*., pp.59–60, 94, 339.

78. Ross, *Edward IV*, pp.246–7. T. Rymer, *Foedera etc.*, 1704–35, XII, pp.142–5.

79. Charles Ross, *Richard III*, 1981, pp.65–7.

80. Ibid.

81. C.T. Wood, 'The Deposition of Edward V', *Traditio*, 31, 1975, pp.247–86.

82. 'Historiae Croylandensis Continuatio' in *Rerum Anglicarum Scriptores Veterum*, ed. W. Fulman, 1684, p.565.

83. Dominic Mancini, *The Usurpation of Richard III*, ed and trs, C.A.J. Armstrong, 1969, pp.94–7.

84. Ross, *Richard III*, pp.96–104. The bones recovered in 1674 were scientifically examined in 1933, and found to be those of young males, aged about 12 and 10 — which is suggestive but not quite conclusive.

85. *ODNB sub* 'Edward of Middleham'.

86. *Handbook of British Chronology*, p.481.

87. *ODNB*.

88. *Calendar of the Charter Rolls, 1427–1516*, p.260. 24 August 1483.

89. The eldest son of Richard's elder brother, George, Duke of Clarence, who had forfeited his Dukedom for treason in 1478. Edward, who was born in 1475, was recognized as Earl of Warwick from his birth, in the right of his mother. In 1483 Richard claimed that his title to the throne was invalidated by his father's attainder. He was eventually executed by Henry VII in 1499.

iii. The Tudor Princes

1. G.R. Elton, *The Tudor Constitution*, 1982, p.1.

2. W.S.K. Thomas, *Tudor Wales*, 1982, pp.1–21.

3. *ODNB, sub* 'Arthur'.

4. T.B. Pugh, *The Marcher Lordships of South Wales*, 1963, p.257.

5. *Calendar of the Patent Rolls, 1485–1494*, p.438.

6. S.B. Chrimes, *Henry VII*, 1972, p.98.

7. *Calendar of the Patent Rolls, 1485–1494*, p.407.

8. *ODNB*.

9. André subsequently wrote an encomium on his pupil's skill with the Latin authors — but that is hardly evidence. He wrote that he had 'either committed to memory or read with his own eyes', the works of Thucidedes, Ceasar, Livy and Tacitus. W. Nelson, *John Skelton, Laureate*, 1939, p.15.

10. M.K. Jones and M.G. Underwood, *The King's Mother; Lady Margaret Beaufort*, 1992.

11. Chrimes, *Henry VII*, pp.272–7. Pope Innocent VIII had been the first continental power to recognize him.

12. This failed because Henry was only prepared to contribute to a defence force, and Maximilian, who was supposed to do the actual fighting, allowed himself to be bought off. Henry did wage war in 1492, but his campaign came very late in the season, and he too allowed himself to be bought off at Etaples on 3 November. Rymer *Foedera etc*, XII, pp.497 et seq.

13. Ibid., pp.787, 793, 803.

14. Ibid, pp.741–9. TNA E 30/677.

15. S. Anglo, *Spectacle, Pageantry and Early Tudor Policy*, 1969, p.57.

16. There are three narrative accounts of these pageants. The first is College of Arms 1st MS 13, ff.27–74, published in *Antiquaries Repertory*, ii, pp.259–82; the second appears in A.H. Thomas and I.D. Thornley, *The Great Chronicle of London*, 1938, pp.297–310; and the third in C.L. Kingsford, *Chronicles of London*, 1905, pp.234–48.

17. *Chronicles of London*, p.241. BL Cotton MS Vitellius A.XVI, f.189.

18. Anglo, *Spectacle*, pp.56–97.

19. Catherine's command of English is very seldom commented upon, but it must have been sufficient for her to sustain life at court, where relatively few women would have spoken anything else. Her own servants at this stage were predominantly Spanish. Garrett Mattingly, *Catherine of Aragon*, 1963.

20. Penry Williams, *The Council in the Marches of Wales under Elizabeth*, 1958, p.10.

21. Mattingly, *Catherine of Aragon*, p.328. *Cal.Span.*, I, no.327.

22. Edmund, his third son, lived only from 21 February to 19 June 1500.

23. *Cal.Span.*, I, no.351. Rymer, *Foedera*, XIII, pp.76–86.

24. Chrimes, *Henry VII*, pp.206–7.

25. J.B. Smith, 'Crown and community in the principality of North Wales in the reign of Henry Tudor', *Welsh History Review*, 3, 1966, pp.145–71.

26. The burgesses of the English boroughs complained against such emancipation, but did not, as far as we know, offer any legal challenge.

27. For example David Phillips and David Cecil, both of who received lands in Northamptonshire. D. Loades, *The Cecils*, 2007, pp.10–27.

28. *Correspondencia de Gutierre de Fuensalida*, ed. Duque de Alba, 1907, p.449. J. Scarisbrick, *Henry VIII*, 1968, pp.5–7.

29. Ibid.

30. Henry Kamen, *Spain 1469–1714; a Society of Conflict*, 1983. Richard Bonney, *The European Dynastic States, 1494–1660*, 1991, pp.90–91.

31. G. Burnet, *History of the Reformation*, ed. N. Pocock, 1865, IV, pp.17–18. Sir Francis Bacon, *History of the Reign of Henry VII*, ed J.R. Lumby, 1885, p.146.

32. Mattingly, *Catherine of Aragon*, pp.46–64.

33. Ibid., pp.75–6.

34. Ibid., p.108.

35. There were rumours of an affair with Anne Hastings, a married sister of the Duke of Buckingham, which may have been based on no more than conventional 'courtly love' play. D. Loades, *Henry VIII*, 2007, p.42.

36. D. Loades, *Mary Tudor; A Life*, 1989, pp.14–15.

37. B. Murphy, *Bastard Prince: Henry VIII's Lost Son*, 2001, pp.27–8.

38. TNA SP1/35, pp.261–2. *Letters and Papers*, IV, no.1577.

39. BL Cotton MS Vitellius C.i, f.23.

40. W.R.B. Robinson, 'Princess Mary's Itinerary in the Marches of Wales; a provisional record', *Historical Research*, 71, 1998, pp.233–52.

41. BL Cotton MS Vitellius C.1, f.23.

42. Ibid.

43. C. Rawcliffe, *The Staffords: Earls of Stafford and Dukes of Buckingham*, 1978, pp.37–44.

44. For a discussion of the problems afflicting the Council, see Penry Williams, *The Council in the Marches of Wales under Elizabeth*, 1955.

45. The problem with settling for Mary was that her husband would claim the Crown Matrimonial, and that would almost certainly mean a foreign King, because a domestic marriage would raise the problem of kinship factions. Neither Henry nor most of his subjects wanted a foreign King. Loades, *Henry VIII*, pp.78–9.

46. What Henry wanted was not a divorce (which was virtually impossible) but an annulment, and that could only be obtained on the grounds that the marriage had been invalid in the first place—and that Mary, in consequence, had been born out of wedlock. He rejected the argument that the marriage was valid because it had been contracted in good faith. For a full discussion of the issues, see Scarisbrick, *Henry VIII*, pp.163–97.

47. D. MacCulloch, *Thomas Cranmer*, 1996. Loades, *Henry VIII*, p.87. TNA E30/ 695.

48. Mattingly, *Catherine of Aragon*, pp.258–69. Loades, *Mary Tudor*, pp.74–9.

49. For a discussion of Cromwell's strengths and weaknesses, see G.R. Elton, *Thomas Cromwell*, 1991, pp.18–35.

50. Statute 26 Henry VIII, cap. 6, *Statutes of the Realm*, III, pp.500–503.

51. By a series of Acts, the most definitive of which was 28 Henry VIII, cap. 10, 'An act extinguishing the authority of the Bishop of Rome'.

52. Statute 25 Henry VIII, cap. 22 and 28 Henry VIII, cap. 7, required by the failure of the King's first two marriages.

53. 27 Henry VIII, cap. 24. *Statutes of the Realm*, III, p.555.

54. Statute 27 Henry VIII, cap. 24. *Statutes of the Realm*, III, pp.555–8.

55. J. Goronwy Edwards, *The Principality of Wales*, p.25.

56. 27 Henry VIII, cap. 26. *Statutes of the Realm*, III, p.563.

57. Edwards, *Wales*; G.R. Elton, *The Tudor Constitution*, p.33. This provided the integration between local self-government and the central administration of justice that had long been needed, and helped to reconcile the Welsh gentry to the loss of some of their more disreputable freedoms.

58. 27 Henry VIII, cap. 5.

59. The prayer book was translated in 1549, and in 1563 it was declared by statute that public worship in Wales should be conducted in the vernacular, as it was in England. Sir John Price's awkward translation of the 1549 book was therefore replaced; the New Testament was translated into Welsh in 1567 and the whole Bible in 1588.

60. Edwards, *Principality, passim*.

61. J. Loach, *Edward VI*, 1999, pp.9–17.

62. Glanmor Williams, *Wales, 1415–1642*.

63. Williams, *Council in the Marches under Elizabeth*.

64. Ibid., p.335. Whereas there were only nine such cases in the four years from 1559 to 1563, there were 243 between 1592 and 1597. Admittedly these numbers fell off in the last five years of the reign, but the tendency to resort to the courts rather than to self-help was by then firmly established.

65. T.F. Tout, 'The king's Courts of Great Session in Wales', *Y Cymmrodorion*, XXVI, 1916.

66. Williams, *Wales 1415–1642*, p.335. The Council became, in effect, an alternative route to Great Sessions.

67. For the story of this Welsh 'idol', and its part in the demise of Friar Forrest, see John Foxe, *Acts and Monuments*, 1583, pp.1100–01.

68. Glanmor Williams, *The Reformation in Wales*, 1989. Thomas *Tudor Wales*, pp.104–8. It is sometimes said that the popular religion of Wales, particularly in the remoter parts of the north, was so conservative as to be primitive, and it is true that Catholic missionaries who visited the region from the 1580s found their task almost as daunting as that of the Protestant evangelists.

iv. The Stuart Princes

1. James had been born in June 1566. His mother had been imprisoned and forced to abdicate in July 1567. She had fled to England in 1568, and they had never met since.

2. The story that she acknowledged him on her deathbed is an uncorroborated report by Camden. Elizabeth never allowed the succession to be discussed in her presence, but she had been very careful to reassure James that his claim was not jeopardized by his mother's attainder.

3. D. Loades, *The Cecils*, 2007, p.221.

4. *ODNB*, sub 'Henry Frederick, Prince of Wales'.

5. Ibid.

6. T. Birch, *The Life of Henry, Prince of Wales*, 1760.

7. E.C. Wilson, *Prince Henry and English Literature*, 1946, pp.18–19.

8. *ODNB*.

9. *Ambassades de M. de la Broderie en Angleterre*, 1750, I, 31 October 1606.

10. Penry Williams, *The Council in the Marches of Wales under Elizabeth*, 1958.

11. The deputies were chosen from within the commissions of the peace, nominally from those with military experience, but in practice the Lord Lieutenant's patronage tended to prevail. C.G. Cruikshank, *Elizabeth's Army*, 1966, pp.19–20. G. Scott Thompson, *Lords Lieutenants in the Sixteenth Century*, 1913, pp.43–83.

12. To what extent this was due to the fact that Essex directed his activities elsewhere, and to what extent to Pembroke's vigilance is not entirely clear. Long before the mess was finally cleared up, Pembroke had died.

13. Williams, *Wales 1415–1642*, p.340.

14. Thomas, *Tudor Wales*, pp.146–7. Bristol had originally been included in its orbit, but that emancipated itself in 1562. Chester followed, as we have seen in 1569. Worcester struggled unavailingly for many years to escape its embrace, as did Gloucester.

15. By the terms of the statute of 1536 there should have been 8 JPs in each Welsh county, but already by 1575 the average was 12 or 13 per county, and counting.

16. Penry William, *The Tudor Regime*, 1979, p.104.

17. A.P. McGowan, *The Jacobean Commissions of Enquiry, 1608, 1618*, Navy Records Society, 1971, p.xv.

18. Loades, *The Cecils*, p.239.

19. *ODNB*. W.W. Seton, 'The early years of Henry Frederick, Prince of Wales and Charles, Duke of Albany, 1593–1605', *Scottish Historical Review*, 13, 1915–16, pp.366–79.

20. *Proceeding in the Parliament of 1610*, ed. Elizabeth Read Foster, Vol.1, 1966, pp.3–5.

21. Pauline Croft, 'The parliamentary installation of Henry, Prince of Wales', *Historical Research, 65*, 1992, pp.177–93.

22. Ibid.

23. Speech by the Earl of Northampton, *Proceedings*, I, pp.262–3. BL Cotton MS Titus C.VI, f.456.

24. *ODNB sub* 'Charles I'.

25. Barry Coward, *The Stuart Age, 1603–1714*, 1994, pp.158–60.

26. Charles was created Duke of Albany about a month after his birth, but he was regarded as Duke of Rothesay and Cornwall only after the death of his brother. Rothesay was the traditional title of the heir of Scotland, as Cornwall was of England.

27. Conrad Russell, ed., *The Origins of the English Civil War*, 1973. A.G.R. Smith, *The Emergence of a Nation State, 1529–1660*, 1984, pp.277–84.

28. *ODNB*. TNA SP13/89, no.7.

29. Ibid. McGowan, *Commissions*, xxvi-xxvii.

30. Roger Lockyer, *James VI and I*, 1998.

31. Richard Bonney, *The European Dynastic States, 1494–1660*, 1991, pp.189–92. N.G. Parker, *The Thirty Years War*, 1985.

32. *ODNB*.

33. T. Cogswell, 'England and the Spanish Match', in R. Cust and A. Hughes, eds, *Conflict in Early Stuart England*, 1989.

34. Coward, *The Stuart Age*, p.156.

35. Sir John Chamberlain to Sir Dudley Carleton, 22 February 1623. *Calendar of State Papers, Domestic, 1619–23*, p.495. TNA SP13/138, no.39.

36. Ibid. Cogswell, 'England and the Spanish Match'.

37. *Calendar of State Papers Domestic, 1623–25*, p.315. TNA SP13/170, no.69.

38. T. Cogswell, *The Blessed Revolution. English Politics and the Coming of War, 1621–24*, 1989.

39. Coward, *The Stuart Age*, p.160.

40. C. Carlton, *Charles I*, 1983, pp.58–9.

41. Williams, *Wales 1415–1642*, p.340.

42. J.P. Kenyon, *The Stuart Constitution*, 1966, p.192.

43. Statute 16 Charles I, cap. 10. *Statutes of the Realm*, V, pp.11–12.

44. There was a natural tendency for feuding kindreds to take advantage of whatever national polarities there were in order to disguise their real motivation. See above.

45. R. Hutton, *The Royalist War Effort, 1642–6*, 1982, parts 2 and 3.

46. See Coward, *The Stuart Age*, p.224 for a discussion of the significance of this tactic.

47. Jenkins, *The Foundations of Modern Wales*, p.21.

48. The Instrument of Government, 1653, para. XVIII. Kenyon, *Stuart Constitution*, p.344.

49. Jenkins, *Foundations*, p.32.

50. V.F. Snow, 'Parliamentary Re-apportionment Proposals in the Puritan Revolution,' *English Historical Review, 74*, 1959, pp.409–42.

51. Jenkins, *Foundations*, p.33. Typical of these was Colonel John Jones of Maesgarnedd in Glamorgan, who was the husband of the Protector's sister, and Sergeant John Glynne of Caerarvonshire who became Lord Chief Justice in 1655.

52. Ibid, p.34.

53. Ibid, p.36. *Hen Gerddi Gwleidyddol*, 1901, p.33.

54. Kenyon, *Stuart Constitution*, pp.361–5.

55. *ODNB*.

56. *Handbook of British Chronology*, p.455.

57. PRO 22/60/74.

58. Coward, *Stuart Age*, pp.329–32. J.R. Jones, *The First Whigs*, 1971.

59. J.R. Jones, *The Revolution of 1688 in England*, 1972.

60. Printed in *A Collection of Papers relating to the present juncture of affairs in England*, 1688–9; PRO 30/53/11/38.

61. Jenkins, *Foundations*, p.147.

62. *ODNB sub* 'James Francis Edward'.

63. Coward, *Stuart Age*, pp.356–9.

64. Statute 7 & 8 William III, cap. 27. *Statutes of the Realm*, VII, p.114.

65. Coward, *Stuart Age*, pp.390–91.

66. *English Historical Documents, Vol. VI, 1660–1714*, ed. Andrew Browning, 1953, p.462. Daniel Defoe, *A Tour Through Great Britain*, ed. 1724–27, II, pp.78–102.

67. Sir Charles Sedley on the alleged extravagances of the Civil List. *English Historical Documents, 1660–1714*, p.107. *Somers Tracts*, ed. 1809–15, X, pp.331–2.

v. The Princes of Leicester House

1. Ragnhild Hatton, *George I: Elector and King*, 1978. Derek Jarrett, *Britain, 1688–1815*, 1965, pp.151–2.
2. Jarrett, p.152.
3. John Baynes, *The Jacobite Rising of 1715*, 1970.
4. *ODNB*, 'George II'.
5. Ibid. Paul Langford, *The Eighteenth Century, 1688–1815*, 1976.
6. Jarrett, p.155. There was a clause in the Act of Settlement that required the King to get the permission of Parliament to leave the country, and this had to be repealed before George could go.
7. W. Michael, *England Under George I*, vol. I, 1936.
8. Jarrett, p.160. R. Walcott, *English Politics in the early Eighteenth Century*, 1956.
9. Jeremy Black, *Sir Robert Walpole and the Nature of Politics in Early Eighteenth Century Britain*, 1990.
10. John Carswell, *The South Sea Bubble*, 1993.
11. *The Diary of Mary, Countess Cowper 1714–20*, ed. S. Cowper, 1864.
12. Jarrett, p.163.
13. *Journals of the House of Commons*, 1803, Vol. IX, p.627. B.W. Hill, *Sir Robert Walpole*, 1989, p.109.
14. Black, *Walpole and the Nature of Politics*.
15. Jarrett, p.174.
16. S.W. Baskerville, *Walpole in Power, 1720–1742*, 1983.
17. John, Lord Harvey (Vice Chamberlain of the Household, 1730–40), *Some Materials towards a Memoir of the Reign of King George II*, ed. R. Sedgewick, 1931, II, pp.485–8.
18. 9 and 10 William III, cap. 23. Paul Langford, *A Polite and Commercial People*, 1989, p.15.
19. *ODNB*, 'Frederick'.
20. He was gazetted by that title on 11 January 1718, but it was never officially conferred. He was created Duke of Edinburgh on 26 July 1726. G.C. Cockayne, *Complete Peerage*, 1926, Vol. V, p.703.
21. *ODNB*.
22. J.H. Plumb, *The First Four Georges* (2nd ed., 1975.

23. *ODNB*.
24. This was one of the troubles that afflicted the royal family. 'It is doubtful', one observer wrote, 'whether royalty has ever been the object of more obloquy than it was during these years....' Langford, *A Polite and Commercial People*, p.34.
25. Jarrett, p.199–200.
26. Black, *Britain in the Age of Walpole*.
27. TNA SP36/42.
28. A.N. Newman, 'The Political Patronage of Frederick Lewis, Prince of Wales' *Historical Journal*, I, 1958, pp.68–75.
29. P.P. Powney in 1784. Ibid. Most of his direct loans appear to have been repaid.
30. Jarrett, p.207. Rohan Butler, *Choiseul: Father and Son, 1719–1754*, 1980.
31. Baskerville, *Walpole in Power*.
32. *ODNB*.
33. Linda Colley, *In Defiance of Oligarchy: The Tory Party, 1719–1754*, 1982.
34. R. Harris, 'A Leicester House Political Diary, 1742–3', *Camden Miscellany*, 31, 1992, p.393.
35. TNA SP36/69.
36. Ibid.
37. Colley, *The Tory Party*. A.N. Newman, 'Leicester House Politics, 1748–1751', *English Historical Review*, 76, 1961, pp.577–89.
38. A.N. Newman, 'Leicester House Politics, 1750–1760, from the papers of John, second Earl of Egmont', *Camden Miscellany*, 23, 1969, pp.88–238.
39. *ODNB*.
40. Ibid. It is possible that this interest derived from his mother, who kept a botanical collection.
41. TNA LC2/36.
42. Langford, *A Polite and Commercial People*, p.221. She wrote 'I throw myself together with my children at your feet. We commend ourselves, Sire, to your paternal love and royal protection'.
43. Cockayne, *Complete Peerage*, III, pp.173, 178.
44. *ODNB*, 'George III'.
45. Christopher Hibbert, *George III: A Personal History*, 1998.
46. James, Earl Waldegrave, *Memoirs from 1754 to 1758*, 1821, pp.8–10. Waldegrave was Governor to the Prince of Wales from 1752 to 1756.

47. Langford, *A Polite and Commercial People*, p.223.
48. Hibbert, *George III*.
49. *ODNB*.
50. John Bullion, 'The Prince's Mentor; A New Perspective on the Friendship between George III and Lord Bute during the 1750s', *Albion*, 21, 1989, pp.34–55.
51. TNA J77/44/R31.
52. *ODNB*.
53. Jarrett, pp.266–7.
54. Lewis Namier, *The Structure of Politics at the Accession of George III*, 1973, pp.173–234.

vi. Prince Regent

1. George (1762–1830); Frederick, Duke of York (1764–1827); William, Duke of Clarence [William IV] (1765–1837); Charlotte (1766–1810); Edward, Duke of Kent (1767–1820); Augusta (1768–1840); Elizabeth (1770–1840); Ernest, Duke of Cumberland (1771–1851); Augustus, Duke of Sussex (1773–1843); Adolphus, Duke of Cambridge (1774–1850); Mary (1776–1857); plus Sophia, Octavius, Alfred and Amelia, who died as infants.
2. Christopher Hibbert, *George IV, Prince of Wales*, 1972, p.3.
3. Bonomy Dubree, *The Letters of King George III*, 1968, p.27.
4. James Greig, ed., *Northumberland Diaries … 1716–1776*, 1926, p.63.
5. *ODNB*, 'George IV'.
6. Hibbert, *George IV*, p.5.
7. He and his brother Frederick were 'flogged like dogs' according to one memoir. *Recollections of the Early Years of the Present Century by the Hon. Amelia Murray*, 1868.
8. A. Aspinall, *The Correspondence of George, Prince of Wales*, Vol.1 (1770–1789), 1963, no.27, 4 May 1778. Aspinall comments 'In all his letters to the king the glaring contrast between promise and performance is notable'.
9. When Cumberland was 25 his brothers had had to find £10,000 to compensate the Earl of Grosvenor, whose wife had committed adultery with him. The Duke of Gloucester was banished from the court in 1766 for marrying the widow of Lord Waldegrave without the King's consent.
10. Statute 12 George III, cap. 11. *Statutes at Large*, Vol.11, p.335.
11. On George's relationship with Mary Robinson, see Hibbert, *George IV*, pp.14–19. On his behaviour in 1781, see ibid., pp.23–4.
12. Ibid., p.27.
13. L.G. Mitchell, *Charles James Fox and the Disintegration of the Whig Party, 1782–1794*, 1971.
14. J.W. Derry, *British Politics in Age of Fox, Pitt, and Liverpool*, 1990.
15. Dobree, *Letters of George III*, p.176.
16. A. Aspinall, ed., *The Correspondence of George, Prince of Wales, 1770–1812*, 1963–71, I, p.113.
17. The architect of his choice was Henry Holland, whose work on Brook's Club in 1776–8 had brought him into contact with the Whig aristocracy. Holland began work at Carlton House in the autumn of 1783.
18. Statute 12 George III, cap. 11. *Statutes at Large*, xxix, pt 2, pp.11–12.
19. Charles Langdale, *Memoirs of Mrs Fitzherbert*, 1856, p.142.
20. *The Diaries and Correspondence of James Harris, 1st Earl of Malmesbury*, 1844, II, p.130.
21. Hibbert, *George IV*, p.71.
22. Clifford Musgrove, *The Royal Pavilion: An Episode in the Romantic*, 1964, pp.1–8.
23. The Duke of Buckingham and Chandos, ed., *Memoirs of the Court and Cabinets of George III*, 1855, II, p.445.
24. Hibbert, *George IV*, pp.90–103, p.125.
25. Aspinall, *Correspondence*, II, pp.446–7.
26. Hibbert, *George IV*, p.132.
27. Even in that country 'where they were not at that period very nice about female delicacy'. Henry Edward, Lord Holland, ed., *Memoirs of the Whig Party during my Time*, 1852–4, II, pp.145–6.
28. TNA FO 93/20/2.
29. Aspinall, *Correspondence*, III, pp.172–3.
30. Ibid., III, p.232.
31. Hibbert, *George IV*, pp.163–4.
32. When the decision was announced, the Prince declared that Roman Catholicism was 'the only religion for a gentleman' (*The Times*, 4 July 1800). This did not eventually make him any more amenable to Catholic Emancipation.

33. Aspinall, *Correspondence*, IV pp.463–4. The actual falling out was over a command that the Duke of York was alleged to have issued as Commander-in-Chief.

34. Hibbert, *George IV,* pp.185–6.

35. Ibid, p.200.

36. TNA HO 126/ 3.

37. James Grieg, ed., *The Farington Diary* (1922–28), VII, p.158.

38. E.J. Evans, *Political Parties in Britain, 1783–1867*, 1985.

39. Hibbert, *George IV,* p.227.

40. Ian Fletcher, ed., *The Peninsular War; Aspects of the Struggle for the Iberian Peninsular*, 1998. Philip J. Haythornthwaite, *The Napoleonic Sourcebook*, 1990, p.33.

41. The scandal was over the death of his valet, Joseph Sellis, whom the Duke was alleged to have murdered. Hibbert, *George IV*, pp.269–70.

42. E.J. Evans, *The Forging of the Modern State, 1783–1870*, 1996, p.64.

43. Hibbert, *George IV, Regent,* [II], 1973, p.10.

44. Grieg, *The Farington Diary*, VII, 27 August 1811.

45. Hibbert, *George IV*, p.13.

46. The Duke of York to the Prince Regent, 25 July 1811. Aspinall, *Correspondence*, VIII, no.311.

47. Evans, *Forging of the Modern State*, pp.67–8.

48. Hibbert, *George IV,* II, p.21.

49. TNA TS I/ 115/ 70; TNA TS 11/ 115/ 69.

50. *The Life and Times of Henry, Lord Brougham, written by himself*, 1871. R.Stewart, *Henry Brougham; his Public Career*, 1985.

51. Hibbert, *George IV,* II, p.92.

52. J. Stevenson, *Popular Disturbances in England, 1700–1870*, 1979.

53. M. Philip, ed., *The French Revolution and British Popular Politics*, 1991.

54. *ODNB*, 'Victoria'.

55. Hibbert, *George IV*, II, p.154. *ODNB*.

56. Ibid.

57. A. Aspinall, ed., *The Letters of King George IV*, 1938, II, pp.377–8.

58. Ibid, pp.453–64.

59. W. Hinde, *George Canning*, 1973.

vii. The Prince of Pleasure

1. Christopher Hibbert, *George IV*, 1972, pp.242–6.

2. Roger Fulford, *Royal Dukes; the Father and Uncles of Queen Victoria*, 1933.

3. *ODNB*.

4. Viscount Esher, ed., *The Girlhood of Queen Victoria* (extracts from Victoria's Journals), 1912.

5. *ODNB sub* 'Albert'. S. Weintraub, *Albert; uncrowned king*, 1997.

6. Eric J. Evans, *The Forging of the Modern State, 1783–1870*, 1996, p.260.

7. *ODNB, Handbook of British Chronology*, pp.254–6.

8. Christopher Hibbert, *King Edward VII*, 1976, p.3, citing Victoria's Journals.

9. Ian Dunlop, *Edward VII*, 2004, p.28. Sarah was the widow of Lord Lyttleton.

10. Hibbert, *Edward VII,* p.5.

11. Ibid, p.6.

12. *ODNB*.

13. Hibbert, *Edward VII,* p.7.

14. Dunlop, *Edward VII,* pp.30–31.

15. As his observations demonstrate, Henry Birch was neither stupid nor insensitive, but he was quite out of his depth in attempting to deal with parents as intransigent and opinionated as Victoria and Albert.

16. Hibbert, *Edward VII,* p.11; Philip Magnus, *King Edward VII*, 1964, p.7. The reason for the opposition to Birch's plans for ordination are unclear.

17. Maurice V. Brett, ed., *The Journals and Letters of Reginald Viscount Esher*, 1934, I, p.23.

18. Albert's attitude towards relaxation can be traced indirectly through Queen Victoria's Journals.

19. Bertie was credited particularly with a meticulous respect for the truth, which stayed with him in spite of the peccadilloes of his later life.

20. Hibbert, *Edward VII,* p.21.

21. Ibid., p.23.

22. Frederick was at that time the Crown Prince (he succeeded in 1871), and died in 1888.

23. The fault seems to have lain with General Bruce, who misunderstood the protocol.

24. Dunlop, *Edward VII*, p.33. The inhibiting presence of Bruce seems to have prevented any other indulgence.
25. TNA 30/22/34.
26. At the Laval University of Quebec, the Prince offended Roman Catholic sensibilities by addressing the Bishops as 'gentlemen'. When the Duke of Newcastle apologized for the discourtesy, the Orangemen in turn were outraged. Dunlop, *Edward VII*, p.34.
27. TNA 30/22/34.
28. Hibbert, *Edward VII*, p.37.
29. Ibid, p.41.
30. Dunlop, *Edward VII*, p.36.
31. Bertie seems to have been determined on a love match, and was for the time being quite uncertain where his affections lay. His father had not the slightest comprehension of such a scruple.
32. Lytton Strachey, *Queen Victoria*, 1921. There seems little doubt that the balance of the Queen's mind was disturbed by her loss.
33. Hibbert, *Edward VII*, p.54.
34. Ibid., p.57.
35. Ibid., p.59. He arrived back in England on 3 December.
36. *ODNB*. Hibbert, *Edward VII*, p.65.
37. King Christian is alleged to have observed that this was more money than he could dispense himself!
38. Hibbert, *Edward VII*, p.72. The Queen's anxieties were studiously ignored, which did not improve her temper.
39. Ibid., p.74.
40. *ODNB*.
41. The Prince of Wales to the Queen, 1870. Dunlop, *Edward VII*, p.52.
42. *ODNB*.
43. An attempt was being made to guarantee the neutrality of Luxembourg, in which all the Great Powers were engaged. There was a treaty in 1867.
44. Hibbert, *Edward VII*, pp.87–8.
45. Evans, *The Forging of the Modern State*, p.289. R. Foster, *Modern Ireland, 1600–1972*, 1988.
46. W.E. Gladstone to the Prince of Wales, cited by Dennis Judd, *George V*, p.16.
47. He was born on 6 April and died the following day.
48. Dunlop, *Edward VII*, pp.62–3.
49. TNA LC2/ 88.
50. *ODNB*.
51. Ibid.
52. Ibid.
53. K.T. Hoppen, *Elections, Politics and Society in Ireland, 1832–1885*, 1984.
54. H.G.C. Mathew, *The Gladstone Diaries*, X, p.313.
55. David Newsome, *The History of Wellington College*, 1959, pp.170–72.
56. *ODNB*.
57. TNA HO 49/ 9662/ A43356.
58. Hibbert, *Edward VII*, p.180.
59. Ibid., p.185. Dennis Judd, *George V*, 1973, pp.28–9.
60. Judd, *George V*, p.36.
61. James Pope-Hennessy, *Queen Mary*, 1959, pp.189 et seq.
62. TNA FO 10/ 744; FO 10/ 745.
63. *ODNB, sub* Victoria
64. Letter from Prime Minister Balfour to King Edward VII, 6 February 1901. *English Historical Documents*, ed. W.D. Hancock, 1977, X, p.40.
65. Dunlop, *Edward VII*, pp.167–71.
66. Ibid.
67. A.J.P. Taylor, *The First World War*, 1963.
68. Dunlop, *Edward VII*, pp.213–18.
69. R. Jenkins, *Asquith*, 1964.
70. Memorandum by Vaughan Nash, Asquith's Private Secretary, 15 December 1909. *English Historical Documents*, X, p.41.

viii. Princes of Change – George and David

1. Sir Harold Nicholson, *George V; his Life and Reign*, 1952, pp.3–17.
2. For a brief account of the Dalton regime, see Judd, *George V*, p.22.
3. George recalls his days on *Britannia*. Dennis Judd, *George V*, p.25.
4. *ODNB, sub* George V. Queen Victoria had not approved of both boys entering *Britannia*, pointing out that 'it is not intended that they should both enter the navy', but she gave the final authorization for both princes to sail on the *Bacchante*.
5. Ibid.
6. Judd, *George V*, p.41.
7. For an account of Eddy's love affairs, see Pope-Hennessy, *Queen Mary*, pp.189–212.

At the time of his death he was apparently more enamoured of Princess Hélène of Orleans than he was of his fiancée.

8. *ODNB*.

9. Pope-Hennessy, *Queen Mary*, p.259.

10. Richard Shannon, *Gladstone: the Heroic Minister, 1865–1898*, 1999, pp.406–42.

11. Tanner was Fellow and Tutor in Modern History at St John's College, Cambridge from1882 until his death in 1931.

12. Pope-Hennessy, *Queen Mary*, pp.364 et seq. May wrote to her aunt 'we should leave the children in charge of my parents-in-law … as you know what a bad sailor I am'.

13. Kenneth Rose, *King George V*, 1983, 45.

14. Judd, *George V,* p.74.

15. Feiling, *History of England*, pp.1043–4. On the Entente Cordiale, see Dunlop, *Edward VII*, pp.210–18.

16. Nicholson, *George V*, pp.73–4.

17. *ODNB*.

18. Nicholson, *George V,* pp.64–5.

19. Judd, *George V*, p.201. George was opposed to all concessions to Indian nationalism, as he made clear when he met Gandhi at the second Round Table Conference in London in 1931, but he did not attempt to obstruct the Government of India Act of 1935.

20. Smith observed that 'at Barrackpore I found that he has distinct ability, great shrewdness, and a wonderful memory', Martin Gilbert, *Servant of India: Sir James Dunlop Smith*, 1966, p.32.

21. T.K. Hoppen, *Ireland since 1800: Conflict and Conformity*, 1999. T. Garvin, *The Evolution of Irish Nationalist Politics,* 1981.

22. It had long been an accepted constitutional custom that the Lords did not obstruct revenue acts. For a summary account of the crisis, see R.C.K. Ensor, *England 1870–1914*, 1963, pp.414–20.

23. Judd, *George V*, p.98. Ensor, p.391. See also R. Jenkins, *Asquith*, 1964.

24. From the King's own account, cited by Judd, p.92.

25. Philip Ziegler, *King Edward VIII*, 2001, pp.26–7. The suggestion for such a ceremony had been raised by the Empress Frederick, David's great aunt, before her death in 1901.

26. Garvin, *Irish Nationalist Politics*. Ivor Richard and Damien Welfare, *Unfinished Business: Reforming the House of Lords,* 1999.

27. Cited by Judd, *George V*, p.100.

28. He later wrote that the ceremony made him 'Rather tired after wearing the crown for 3½ hours, it hurt my head, as it is pretty heavy'.

29. J.M. Winter, *The Great War and the British People*, 1986. Trevor Wilson, *The Myriad Faces of War*, 1986, pp.1–40.

30. *ODNB*.

31. Ibid.

32. Judd, *George V*, p.148. A. Bone, *The Bolsheviks and the October Revolution*, 1974.

33. T.P. Coogan and George Morrison, *The Irish Civil War*, 1998. *ODNB*.

34. Judd, *George V*, p.169. C.L. Mowat, *Britain Between the Wars*, 1955.

35. See, for example, Dunlop, *Edward VIII*, pp.193–212. Frank Hardie, *The Political Influence of the British Monarchy, 1868–1952,* 1970.

36. Ziegler, *King Edward VIII*, pp.6–9.

37. Ibid., p.14.

38. Pope Hennessy, *Queen Mary*, p.393.

39. Frances Donaldson, *Edward VIII*, 1986, p.20.

40. Many of his letters to his mother survive in the Royal Archives. They were thoroughly investigated in 1990 by Philip Ziegler.

41. His mother confided to her aunt that David had looked 'too sweet' in his Garter robes—not a sentiment that he would have appreciated. Ziegler, *Edward VIII*, p.26.

42. TNA PC8/706.

43. Ziegler, *Edward VIII*, pp.35–6.

44. The Prince of Wales confided to his diary on 18 October 1913 that he thought Warren 'an awful old man'. He was also taught by other tutors for whom he had more respect.

45. Ziegler, *Edward VIII*, p.65.

46. Sir Almeric Fitzroy, *Memoirs*, II, 1926, p.780.

47. Ziegler, *Edward VIII*, pp.78–9.

48. Ibid, p.76.

49. Donaldson, *Edward VIII*.

50. Lees-Milne, *The Enigmatic Edwardian*, p.301.

51. P.M.H. Bell, 'Appeasement' in Martin Pugh, *A Companion to Modern History, 1871–1945,* 1997, pp.300–321.

52. Prince of Wales to the Viceroy, 28 December 1921, cited by Chandrika Kaul in *Reporting the Raj: the British Press and India, c.1880s–1922*, 2003, ch.9.
53. Ziegler, *Edward VIII*, p.144.
54. TNA C323/ 841.f.512.
55. Ziegler, *Edward VIII*, p.144.
56. *ODNB*.
57. Diana Vreeland, *D.V.*, 1984.
58. Ziegler, *Edward VIII*, p.140.
59. The Duke of Windsor, *A King's Story: The Memoirs of H.R.H. the Duke of Windsor*, 1951, p.133.
60. Susan Williams, *The People's King*, 2003, p.50.
61. TNA MH 102/1400/12.
62. Michael Bloch, ed., *Wallis and Edward: Letters, 1931–1937*, 1986.
63. Memo by Halsey, 10 January 1936. Cited by Ziegler, p.221.
64. Helen Hardinge, *Loyal to Three Kings*, 1967, p.61.
65. Judd, *George V*, pp.211–12.
66. TNA MH 58/309.
67. Ibid.
68. Michael Bloch, *The Reign and Abdication of Edward VIII*, 1990.
69. Duchess of Windsor, *The Heart has its Reasons; the Memiors of the Duchess of Winsdor*, 1956. Ziegler, pp.363–5. She was refused the title of Her Royal Highness, which the Duke of Windsor saw as an insult he could never forgive.
70. Ziegler, *Edward VIII*, pp.437–9.

ix. Charles, a Modern Prince of Wales

1. Sarah Bradford, *George VI*, 1989. The celebrated group portrait of the family at tea was painted after the war.
2. Calder, *op.cit.* Basil Collier, *The Defence of the United Kingdom*, 1957.
3. These words were widely reported at the time, and appeared in several contemporary papers.
4. Trevor Burridge, *Clement Attlee; A Political Biography*, 1985. K.O. Morgan, *The Labour Party in Power, 1945–51*, 1984.
5. Elizabeth Longford, *Elizabeth R.A Biography*, 1983. Morgan, *The Labour Party in Power*.

There is no scholarly biography of the Queen Mother, but a useful summary of her life to that point can be found in D.S. Duff, *Elizabeth of Glamis*, 1973. See also Donald Zec, *The Queen Mother*, 1990. For a different perspective, see the Duchess of Windsor's own account, *The Heart has its Reasons*, 1956.
6. Howard Hodgson, *Charles; The Man who Will be King,* 2007, p.13.
7. C.H. Philips and Mary Wainwright, eds., *The Partition of India; Policies and Perspectives, 1935–1947*, 1970.
8. Wheeler Bennett, *George VI.* Pope Hennesey, *Queen Mary*, p.619.
9. Jonathan Dimbleby, *The Prince of Wales, A Biography*, 1994.
10. For Charles's period at Cheam, see Hodgson, pp.25–30.
11. Philip Ziegler, *Edward VIII*, pp.106–8. Alan Butt Philip, *The Welsh Question; Nationalism in Welsh Politics, 1945–1970*, 1971.
12. Louis Wulff, *Elizabeth and Philip*, 1947, pp.22–4.
13. Hodgson, *Charles*, pp.72–3.
14. Letter from a friend to Lord Louis Mountbatten, 1967. Cited by Charles Hodgson in *Charles; The Man who Will be King*, 2007, p.79.
15. At that time the standard 'offer' to an A level candidate for university admission was a B and two Cs. Charles took only two A levels instead of the usual three, but the scholarship paper counted instead.
16. Anthony Holden, *Charles; A Biography*, 1998, p.35. Hodgson, p.78.
17. The great majority of Welsh people (whether they spoke the language or not) accepted the gesture as appropriate, although Nationalist circles in Wales were traditionally suspicious of Englishmen who learned Welsh. Peter B. Ellis, *Wales, A Nation Again. The Nationalist Struggle for Freedom*, 1968.
18. TNA HO 290/28.
19. Ibid
20. *Charles, Prince of Wales: a Birthday Souvenir Album*, Royal Collection Publications, 2008, pp.35–6
21. TNA HO 290/28
22. Ziegler, *Edward VIII*, pp.26–7.
23. TNA HO 290/28

24. Cited by Hodgson, pp.89–90.

25. When Charles was there, he played a full part in university life, with both theatrical and sporting interests. He took his exams (and received his results) in the normal fashion, but the usual residence qualifications seem to have been waived for him.

26. Peter Lane, *Prince Charles; A Study in Development*, 1988.

27. *Charles, Prince of Wales*, pp.44–5.

28. Hodgson, p.155.

29. *The Prince's Charities*, 2008, p7.

30. This aspect of the Prince's work, which is distinct from the operations of the Trust, has not been properly studied; biographers' comments are laudatory but vague. The range of the Prince's interest as a charitable entrepreneur is truly formidable. He is either patron or president of some 380 organisations; and of the nineteen which form the group of 'Prince's Charities', he personally founded fifteen. *www.royal.gov.uk/output/Page 5572.asp.*

31. Concordats were negotiated between the palace and the media from time to time to protect Princes William and Harry as they grew up, with 'photo opportunities' being provided at regular intervals. On the whole this has worked. Piers Morgan, *The Insider*, 2005. However, his relationships with Diana and Camilla have been relentlessly targeted.

32. Hodgson, pp.319–21.

33. 'King Charles: Mr Fix-It for a Broken Britain', Dr David Starkey, published in the *Sunday Times*, 16 December 2007.

34. *www.royal.gov.uk/output/Page5571*. This is the modern equivalent of the morganatic marriage.

35. From April 2005 to April 2006 he carried out 642 official engagements, many of them overseas. *www.royal.gov.uk/output/Page5572.asp*

36. TNA FCO 38/184.

37. The Prince of Wales and the Duchess of Cornwall: *Annual Review*, p.21.

38. Ibid, p.4. The Duchess of Cornwall's convalescence after a major operation led to a reduction in her public engagements for 2007.

39. The Roscoe Lecture, delivered by Prince Charles on receiving an Honorary Fellowship from Liverpool John Moores University, St George's Hall, Liverpool, 23 April 2007.

40. *The National Trust Magazine*, Autumn 2008, pp.21–3.

41. *The Prince of Wales and the Duchess of Cornwall: Annual Review*, p.7. The initial target set was 12.5 per cent, and the target achieved in 2007–8 was 18.4 per cent.

42. Ibid, p.11.

43. 'King Charles: Mr Fix-It for a Broken Britain', Dr David Starkey, published in the *Sunday Times*, 16 December 2007.

44. Ibid, p.26; see also *The Prince's Charities*, 2008.

45. *The Prince of Wales and the Duchess of Cornwall: Annual Review*, pp.17, 26.

46. Speaking at the Swan Theatre in Stratford on Avon on one occasion cited in Hodgson, *Charles*, p.629.

47. *www.princes-foundation.org*

48. *The Prince of Wales and the Duchess of Cornwall: Annual Review*, pp.13.

49. Ibid., p.8.

50. Ibid., p.9.

51 Ibid., p.37.

52. Ibid., p.15.

53. Ibid., pp.22–3.

54. Starkey, *The Sunday Times*, 16 December 2007.

Select Bibliography

Allmand, C., *Henry V,* 1997

Anglo, Sydney, *Spectacle, Pageantry and Early Tudor Policy,* 1969

Arthurson, Ian, *The Perkin Warbeck Conspiracy,* 1994

Barber, Richard, *Edward, The Black Prince,* 1978

Baskerville, S.W., *Walpole in Power, 1720–1742,* 1983

Bayley, J.J., *Margaret of Anjou, Queen of England,* 1948

Baynes, John, *The Jacobite Rising of 1715,* 1970

Bennett, J.W. Wheeler, *King George VI,* 1958

Bennett, Michael, *Richard II and the Revolution of 1399,* 1999

Birch, T., *The Life of Henry, Prince of Wales,* 1760

Black, Jeremy, *Sir Robert Walpole and the Nature of Politics in Early Eighteenth Century Britain,* 1990

Bloch, Michael, *The Reign and Abdication of Edward VIII,* 1990

Bloch, Michael, *Operation Will: The Plot to kidnap the Duke of Windsor, July 1940,* 1984

Bone, A., *The Bolsheviks and the October Revolution,* 1974

Bradford, Sarah, *King George VI,* 1989

Butler, Rohan, *Choiseul: Father and Son, 1719–1754,* 1980

Calder, Angus, *The People's War: Britain 1939–1945,* 1992

Campbell, Judith, *Elizabeth and Philip,* 1972

Carr, A.D., *Medieval Wales,* 1995

Carswell, John, *The South Sea Bubble,* 1993

Chaplais, Pierre, *Piers Gaveston, Edward II's Adoptive Brother,* 1994

Chrimes, S.B. *Henry VII,* 1972

Clarke, John *The Life and Times of George III,* 1972

Colley, Linda, *In Defiance of Oligarchy: The Tory Party 1719–1754,* 1982

Coogan, T.P., and George Morrison, *The Irish Civil War,* 1998

Coulton, C., *Charles I,* 1983

Coward, B., *The Stuart Age,* 1980

Cruikshank, C. G., *Elizabeth's Army,* 1966

Davies, J.C., *The Baronial Opposition to Edward II,* 1918

Davies, R.R., *The Age of Conquest: Wales 1063–1415,* 1992

Davies, R.R., *The Revolt of Owain Glyn Dŵr,* 1995

Derry, J.W., *British Politics in the Age of Fox, Pitt, and Liverpool,* 1990

Dimbleby, Jonathan, *The Prince of Wales, a Biography,* 1994

Donaldson, Frances, *Edward VIII,* 1986

Dunlop, Ian, *Edward VII,* 2004

Earle, Peter, *The Life and Times of James II,* 1972

Edwards, J. Goronwy, *The Principality of Wales, 1267–1967,* 1968

Ellis, Peter B., *Wale, a Nation Again. The Nationalist Struggle for Freedom,* 1968

Elton, G.R., *The Tudor Constitution,* 1982

Elton, G.R., *Thomas Cromwell,* 1991

Ensor, R.C.K., *England 1870–1914,* 1963

Evans, E.J., *Political Parties in Britain, 1783–1867,* 1985

Evans, E.J., *The Forging of the Modern State, 1783–1870,* 1996

Foster, R., *Modern Ireland, 1600–1972,* 1988

Fraser, Antonia, *King James VI of Scotland, I of England,* 1974

Froissart, Jean, The Chronicle of Froissart, tr. Bourchier, 1903

Fulford, Roger, *Royal Dukes; The Father and Uncles of Queen Victoria,* 1933

Garvin, T., *The Evolution of Irish Nationalist Politics,* 1981

Goodman, Anthony, *The Loyal Conspiracy: the Lords Appellant under Richard II,* 1971

Goodman, Anthony, *John of Gaunt: the essence of Princely Power in Fourteenth Century Europe,* 1992

Goodman, Anthony, and James Gillespie, eds., *Richard II: the Art of Kingship,* 1998

Graham, Caroline, *Camilla: Her True Story,* 2003

Griffiths, R.A., *The Reign of King Henry VI,* 1981

Griffiths, R.A., *The Principality of Wales in the Later Middle Ages: South Wales 1277–1538,* 1972

Griffiths, R.A., *King and Country: England and Wales in the Fifteenth Century,* 1991

Haines, R.M., *King Edward II: Edward of Caernarfon, his life, his reign and its aftermath, 1284–1330,* 2003

Haines, R.M., *Archbishop John Stratford; Political Revolutionary and Champion of the Liberties of the English Church, c.1275/80–1348,* 1986

Hardie, Frank, *The Political Influence of the British Monarchy, 1868–1952,* 1970

Hatton, Ragnhild, *George I: Elector and King,* 1978

Haythornethwaite, Philip, The Napoleonic Sourcebook, 1990

Hennessy, James Pope, *Queen Mary,* 1959

Hibbert, Christopher, *George III: A Personal History,* 1998

Hibbert, Christopher, *George IV: Prince of Wales,* 1972

Hibbert, Christopher, *George IV: Regent,* 1973

Hibbert, Christopher, *King Edward VII,* 1976

Hilton, R.H. and T.H. Aston, eds., *The Peasants' Revolt of 1381,* 1984 .

Hinde, Wendy, *George Canning,* 1973

Hodgson, Howard, *Charles: The Man who Will be King,* 2007

Holden, Anthony, *Charles: A Biography,* 1998

Holmes, Geoffrey, *The Making of a Great Power, 1660–1722,* 1993

Holmes, Geoffrey and Daniel Szechi, *The Age of Oligarchy, 1722–1783,* 1993

Hoppen, K.T., *Elections, Politics and Society in Ireland, 1832–1885,* 1984

Hoppen, K.T., *Ireland since 1800: Conflict and Conformity,* 1999

Hutton, R., *The Royalist War Effort, 1642–6,* 1982

Jacob, E.F., *The Fifteenth Century,* 1961

Jenkins, Geraint, *The Foundations of Modern Wales, 1642–1780,* 1987

Jenkins, R., *Asquith,* 1964

Johnstone, Hilda, *Edward of Caernarfon, 1284–1307,* 1946

Jones, J.R., *The Revolution of 1688 in England,* 1972

Jones, M.K., and M.G. Underwood, *The King's Mother: Lady Margaret Beaufort,* 1992

Jowett, Derek, *Britain, 1688–1815,* 1965

Judd, Dennis, *George V,* 1973

Kamen, Henry, *Spain 1469–1714: a Society in Conflict,* 1983

Kenyon, J.P., *The Stuart Constitution,* 1966

Kirby, J.L., *Henry IV of England,* 1970

Lander, J.R., *Conflict and Stability in Fifteenth Century England,* 1969

Lane, Peter, *Prince Charles: A Study in Development,* 1988

Langford, Elizabeth, *Elizabeth R.: A Biography,* 1983

Langford, Paul, *The Eighteenth Century,* 1976

Langford, Paul, *A Polite and Commercial People,* 1989

Lloyd, J.E., *Owen Glendower,* 1931

Loach, Jennifer, *Parliament and the Crown in the Reign of Mary I,* 1986

Loach, Jennifer, *Edward VI,* 1999

Loades, David, *The Cecils,* 2007

Loades, David, *Tudor Government,* 1997

Loades, David, *Henry VIII,* 2007

Loades, David, *Mary Tudor: A Life,* 1989

MacCulloch, Diarmaid, *Thomas Cranmer,* 1996

Maddicott, J.R., *Thomas of Lancaster, 1307–1322,* 1970

Magnus, Philip, *King Edward VII,* 1964

Mattingly, Garrett, *Catherine of Aragon,* 1963

Michael, W., *England under George I,* 1936

Middlemas, Keith *The Life and Times of Edward VII,* 1972

Mitchell, L.G., *Charles James Fox and the Disintegration of the Whig Party, 1782–1794,* 1971

Morgan, K.O., *The Labour Party in Power, 1945–1951,* 1984

Morgan, Piers, *The Insider,* 2005

Morton, Andrew, *Diana: Her True Story,* 1992

Morton, Andrew, *Diana: In Pursuit of Love,* 2004

Mowat, C.L., *Britain Between the Wars,* 1955

Murphy, B., *Bastard Prince: Henry VIII's Lost Son ,* 2001

Musgrove, Clifford, *The Royal Pavilion: An Episode in the Romantic,* 1964

Namier, Sir Lewis, *The Structure of Politics at the Accession of George III,* 1973

Newsome, David, *The History of Wellington College,* 1959

Nicholson, Sir Harold, *George V: His Life and Reign,* 1952

Norwich, John Julius, *Shakespeare's Kings,* 1991, 2001

Ormerod, W.M., *The Reign of Edward III: Crown and Political Society in England 1327–1377,* 1990

Osgerby, Bill, *Youth in Britain since 1945,* 1998

Oxford Dictionary of National Biography
Palmer, Alan *George IV*, 1972
Philip, A.B., *The Welsh Question: Nationalism in Welsh Politics, 1945–1970*, 1971
Philip, M., ed., *The French Revolution and the British People*, 1991
Plumb, J.H., *The First Four Georges*, 1975
Prestwich, Michael, *Plantagenet England, 1127–1360*, 2005
Pugh, T.B., *The Marcher Lordships of South Wales*, 1963
Pugh, T.B., *Henry V and the Southampton Plot of 1415*, 1988
Rawcliffe, Carole, *The Staffords: Earls of Stafford and Dukes of Buckingham*, 1978
Richards, Ivor, and Damien Welfare: *Unfinished Business*, 1999
Rose, Kenneth, *King George V*, 1983
Ross, Charles, *Edward IV*, 1974
Ross, Charles, *Richard III*, 1981
Scarisbrick, J.J., *Henry VIII*, 1968
Shannon, Richard, *Gladstone*, 1999
St Aubyn, Giles, *Edward VII*, 1979
Strickland, Agnes, *Lives of the Queens of England*, 1902
Stevenson, J., *Popular Disturbances in England, 1700–1870*, 1979
Taylor, A.J.P., *The First World War*, 1963
Thielemans, M -R., *Bourgogne et Angleterre: relations politiques, 1435–1467*, 1968
Thomas, W.S.K., *Tudor Wales*, 1982
Thompson, G. Scott, *Lords Lieutenant in the Sixteenth Century*, 1913
Tuck, A., *Richard II & the English Nobility*, 1974
Tucker, N., *North Wales in the Civil War*, 1968
Vale, Malcolm, *Edward III and Chivalry*, 1983
Watson, D.R., *Charles I*, 1972
Williams, Glanmor, *Recovery, Reorientation and Reformation: Wales 1415–1642*, 1987
Williams, Penry, *The Council in the Marches of Wales under Elizabeth I*, 1958
Williams, Penry, *The Tudor Regime*, 1979
Williams, Susan *The People's King*, 2003
Wilson, E.C., *Prince Henry and English Literature*, 1946
Wilson, Trevor, *The Myriad Faces of War*, 1986
Windsor, HRH, Duke of, *A King's Story*, 1951
Windsor, the Duchess of, *The Heart has its Reasons*, 1956
Winter, J.M., *The Great War and the British People*, 1986
Young, N. Denholm, *History & Heraldry*, 1965
Ziegler, Philip, *King Edward VIII*, 2001

Index